POLITICAL SCIENCE RESEARC

Turn the standard research methods teaching model on its head with *Political Science Research in Practice*. Malici and Smith engage students first with pressing political questions and then demonstrate how a researcher has gone about answering them, walking through real political science research that contributors have conducted. Through the exemplary use of survey research, experiments, field research, case studies, content analysis, interviews, document analysis, statistical research, and formal modeling, each chapter introduces students to a method of empirical inquiry through a specific topic that will spark their interest and curiosity. Each chapter shows the process of developing a research question, how and why a particular method was used, and the rewards and challenges discovered along the way. Students can better appreciate why we need a science of politics—why methods matter—with these first-hand, issue-based discussions.

Akan Malici is Associate Professor of Political Science at Furman University where he teaches International Relations and Research Methodology. His scholarly interests are in the areas of foreign policy decision making and peace and conflict studies. His books include *When Leaders Learn and When They Don't, The Search for a Common European Foreign and Security Policy, U.S. Presidents and Foreign Policy Mistakes*, and *Rethinking Foreign Policy Analysis*.

Elizabeth S. Smith is Professor of Political Science at Furman University where she teaches Research Methodology, American Politics, Political Behavior, and Women and Politics. Her scholarly interests are in the areas of political socialization, political psychology, and gender and politics. She has authored articles on the teaching of political science, service learning, social capital formation among young people, and gender and politics. She is the 2007 recipient of the Excellence in Teaching Award from the South Carolina Independent Colleges and Universities.

Acquisitions Editor: Michael Kerns
Senior Development Editors: Nicole Solano and Rebecca Pearce
Editorial Assistant: Darcy Bullock
Production Editor: Emma Håkonsen
Marketing Manager: Christine Swedowsky
Text Design: Keystroke
Copy-editor: Martin Barr
Proofreader: Ruth Coleman
Indexer: Susan Park
Cover Design: Eva Horanszky
Companion Website Designer: Marie Mansfield

POLITICAL SCIENCE RESEARCH IN PRACTICE

Edited by

Akan Malici
and Elizabeth S. Smith

Routledge
Taylor & Francis Group

NEW YORK AND LONDON

First published 2013
by Routledge
711 Third Avenue, New York, NY 10017

Simultaneously published in the UK
by Routledge
2 Park Square, Milton Park, Abingdon, Oxon OX14 4RN

Routledge is an imprint of the Taylor & Francis Group, an informa business

Library of Congress Cataloging in Publication Data
Malici, Akan, 1974–
    Political science research in practice / Akan Malici and Elizabeth S. Smith.
      p. cm.
    1. Political science—Research—Methodology. I. Smith, Elizabeth S.
    (Elizabeth Sue) II. Title.
    JA86.M34 2012
    320.072–dc23   2012000275

ISBN 13: 978-0-415-88772-4 (hbk)
ISBN 13: 978-0-415-88773-1 (pbk)
ISBN 13: 978-0-203-83096-3 (ebk)

Typeset in Garamond
by Keystroke, Station Road, Codsall, Wolverhampton

Contents

Tables and Figures

TABLES

FIGURES

NOTES ON CONTRIBUTORS

Joshua M. Cowen is Assistant Professor of Public Policy at the Martin School of Public Policy and Administration at the University of Kentucky. He is also a senior analyst of a new and official evaluation of the Milwaukee voucher program. He has published papers on charter school sponsorship and compliance models in school voucher randomized trials. At the Martin School, he teaches courses in public policy and program evaluation.

David J. Fleming is Assistant Professor of Political Science at Furman University. He received his Ph.D. from the University of Wisconsin, Madison in 2009. He has published work in the *Journal of School Choice* and is a member of the research team that is evaluating the Milwaukee Parental Choice Program. He teaches classes in American politics, research methods, and public policy.

Sarah Allen Gershon is Assistant Professor of Political Science at Georgia State University. Her research interests include political communication, gender politics, and race and ethnicity. She has published articles in the *Journal of Politics*, *Social Science Quarterly*, *Party Politics*, and the *International Journal of Press/Politics*. She has also contributed chapters to the edited volumes *Latinas/os in the United States: Changing the Face of América* (2008) and *The Promise of Welfare Reform: Rhetoric or Reality?* (2006).

James L. Guth is William R. Kenan, Jr. Professor of Political Science at Furman University. He received his B.S. from the University of Wisconsin and Ph.D. from Harvard University. He is the co-author or co-editor of *The Oxford Handbook of Religion and American Politics* (2009), *The Bully Pulpit* (2002), *Religion and the Culture Wars* (1996), and *The Bible and the Ballot Box* (1991). His work has also appeared in the *American Journal of Political Science*, *Journal of Politics*, *Political Research Quarterly*, *Public Opinion Quarterly*, *European Union Politics*, *Sociological Analysis*, *Journal for the Scientific Study of Religion*, and in many other journals and edited collections.

Kai He is Assistant Professor of Political Science at Utah State University. He is the author of *Institutional Balancing in the Asia Pacific: Economic Interdependence and China's Rise* (2009). He has published articles in the *European Journal of International Relations*, *Security Studies*, *Pacific Review*, *Journal of Contemporary China*, *Asian Security*, *Asian Perspective*, and *International Relations of the Asia Pacific*. He is a recipient of the 2009–10 Princeton–Harvard China and the World Program Postdoctoral Fellowship.

Lyman A. Kellstedt is Emeritus Professor of Political Science at Wheaton College (IL). He is the co-author or co-editor of various books, including *The Oxford Handbook of Religion and American Politics* (2009). In addition, he has written scores of journal articles and book chapters in the field of religion and politics.

Akan Malici is Associate Professor of Political Science at Furman University. He is the author of *When Leaders Learn and When They Don't* (2008) and *The Search for a Common European Foreign and Security Policy* (2008). He is the co-author of *U.S. Presidents and Foreign Policy Mistakes* (2011); the co-editor of *Rethinking Foreign Policy Analysis* (2011). His published articles appear in the *Journal of Conflict Resolution, Journal of Peace Research*, and *Political Psychology*, among others.

Katherine Palmer Kaup is Professor of Political Science and Asian Studies at Furman University. She is author of *Creating the Zhuang: Ethnic Politics in China* (2000), editor of *Understanding Contemporary Asia Pacific* (2007), and has written numerous articles and book chapters on ethnic politics in China. She served as Visiting Scholar at the Yunnan Nationalities Institute and the Guangxi Ethnic Affairs Commission in China and as Senior Adviser on Minority Nationality Affairs for the US Congressional–Executive Commission on China.

Adrian D. Pantoja is Associate Professor of Political Studies and Chicano Studies at Pitzer College, a member of the Claremont Colleges. Professor Pantoja's research revolves around the Latino population, immigration, public opinion, and voter behavior. His research has appeared in journals including *Political Research Quarterly; Political Behavior; Social Science Quarterly; Journal of Ethnic and Migration Studies; International Migration; Journal of Women, Politics & Policy*. He has also written chapters in numerous edited volumes.

Elizabeth S. Smith is Professor of Political Science at Furman University. She received her Ph.D. in American politics with a minor in political psychology from the University of Minnesota. She has taught research methods for over fourteen years. She has published articles and chapters in the *Journal of Political Science Education, Polity, Political Psychology, Handbook for Teaching Social Issues, American Education Research Journal*, and in an edited volume entitled *Competition in Theory and Practice: A Multidisciplinary Approach* (2009).

Kristina Thalhammer is Professor of Political Science at St. Olaf College in Northfield (MN). She is co-author of *Courageous Resistance: The Power of Ordinary People* (2007), a chapter in *Charter Schools, Vouchers, and Public Education* (2001), and articles in *Perspectives on Politics* and *Political Psychology*, among other publications.

C. Danielle Vinson is Professor of Political Science at Furman University. She is the author of *Local Media Coverage of Congress and Its Members* (2003); *Congress and the Media* (2013). She has published articles or chapters in *Political Communication*; *Harvard International Journal of Press/Politics*; *The Oxford Handbook of Religion and American Politics* (2009); and in the edited volumes *Media Power, Media Politics* (2003) and *Blind Spot: When Journalists Don't Get Religion* (2008).

Stephen G. Walker is Emeritus Professor of Political Science at Arizona State University. His publications in edited volumes include chapters in *Role Theory and Foreign Policy Analysis* (1987); *The Psychological Assessment of Political Leaders* (2003); *Beliefs and Leadership in World Politics* (2006); *The Oxford Handbook of the American Presidency* (2009). His research has also appeared in several journals, including *World Politics*, *Journal of Conflict Resolution*, *Journal of Peace Research*, *Political Psychology*, *International Studies Quarterly*.

ACKNOWLEDGMENTS

We want to express our gratitude to Michael Kerns, our editor at Routledge, and Nicole Solano and Rebecca Pearce, our editorial review analysts. All three were most wonderful professionals to work with. Their experience and expertise were invaluable in providing us with important guidance as we developed this book. We also want to thank the many careful reviewers commissioned by Routledge. Their attentive and engaged reading and extensive commentary on each chapter helped us in fundamental ways to create a better book. We want to thank our colleagues and contributors to this book who patiently worked with us to make our vision of a new kind of methodology book a reality. We also want to thank Furman University and the Department of Political Science for the institutional support that we received. We thank our research and editorial assistant Katie Fearington. Last but not least, we want to thank our students. It is from them that we learn to be ever better teachers. This book is dedicated to our students.

Akan Malici, Elizabeth S. Smith
Greenville, South Carolina

PREFACE

Research methodology classes can be very difficult for teachers and students alike. Both of us have taught research methodology to undergraduate students for several years. We believe that we are well aware of the challenges and frustrations that come with teaching this class. We are also well aware of students' frustrations and their hesitations to take this class. An increasing number of political science departments in the United States and around the world, however, require their undergraduate students to take at least one research methodology class before they graduate. We are confident that this is a valuable requirement. Research skills are relevant, useful, and applicable because students will need to utilize them at some point or frequently in almost any career they may choose.

We saw the need for a new book mainly for two reasons: First, research methodology classes tend to be rather abstract. They are not topical and it is difficult to invoke students' interest in them. Students are naturally drawn to the field of political science because they can entertain interesting and engaging discussions about important and current topics such as contested elections, poverty, wars, etc. We agree with the students that political science should be first about the *political* and second about the *science*. All too often, however, we observe in our discipline that the *science* takes prominence over the *politics*. We also believe that typical methodology books, to undergraduate students, appear too divorced from actual politics and even from actual, real-world research. In this book we take a different approach to teaching methodology. We put the *political* first and the *science* second. We believe that any political science class should be guided by important political questions, problems, or phenomena. The question then becomes *how* to study these issues.

This book is designed to expose students to the joy and rewards of research. In particular, we have asked excellent scholars in the field to use one of their published scholarly works to show students how research is done. These scholars explain to students how they got interested in their particular research question, how they decided on what methodology would be most appropriate to answer that question, and what were the lessons they learned from engaging in this research. Students learn about the various methods used in political science by seeing it applied by these scholars. Unlike the typical methods textbook, students get a realistic picture of how the research process really works. They learn that the research process can be messy, frustrating, surprising but, most often, highly rewarding. We feel this approach is more engaging for students and does not set them up for the kind of unrealistic expectations (and, thus, frustrations) created by the standard textbook.

Our second reason for a new book is that we believe that typical research methodology books used at the undergraduate level have become too ambitious.

We find that students get overwhelmed by the comprehensiveness, the extensiveness, and complexity found in these books. If they remain undeterred nevertheless, we find too often that they get lost in the detail provided in typical research methodology books. For instructors it is impossible to cover everything in these books and for students it is difficult to discriminate and separate for each class meeting what they should focus on and what is of secondary relevance at this stage of their methodological training.

Even though in this book we give the *political* in political science more prominence and even though our elaborations on the various research methodologies presented in this book are more succinct, we believe that students learn better everything they need to learn about research methodology because they see how such methods are applied by excellent researchers. They are encouraged to engage actively with the real-world experience of the researcher as he/she explains the true story behind the scholarship. We hope that your experience will confirm this.

Why Do We Need a Science of Politics?

Elizabeth S. Smith and Akan Malici

When the systematic destruction of over six million people during the Holocaust came to full light at the end of World War II, the world was aghast. Many believed that the atrocities revealed something uniquely sinister about the German character. A 1945 story in the *New York Times* read:

> Besides all the routine methods of torturing and killing, chaining, beating, running an electrical machine up and down the spine and hanging by the feet until the victim died of a heart attack were some so hideous that they cannot be indicated, and could have been conceived only by obscenely perverted minds.[1]

In other words, normal, ordinary, people could not have even thought up such atrocities, let alone committed them. No sane person would have followed the orders of Nazi officials and complied with such vulgar commands.

In April of 2004, the abuse and torture of Iraqi prisoners at Abu Ghraib prison by American soldiers was exposed by the popular press. Photographic images were shown on the CBS news program *60 Minutes II* of prisoners stripped naked, forced to simulate homosexual acts, chained to leashes and hooked up to electrodes. Commentators again suggested these acts were not committed by normal people, but were instead the product of just a "few 'bad apples.'"[2] It was just a common *assumption* that ordinary individuals could never be induced to engage in such immoral behavior against their fellow man. These had to be the acts of just a few sinister minds.

The high school geometry teacher of one of us (Elizabeth Smith) once printed the word ASSUME on the board and to our teenage amusement pointed out that when you ASSUME you are making an "ass" of "u" and "me." Quite cleverly, she illustrated why in fact we need science. Our assumptions, our hunches, our general gut-level feelings about the "truths" of the world are often proven wrong once we engage in careful, systematic, and scientific analysis. How can we *know* how, when, and why atrocities like those committed during the Holocaust or at Abu Ghraib occur?

SCIENCE: A WAY TO KNOW

To know, according to *Webster's*, is "to have a clear perception or understanding of; to be sure or well informed about." There are various types of knowledge. Among them are religious knowledge, instinctual knowledge, common sense, scientific knowledge, and so on. Although our book is about scientific knowledge, we do want to point out that scientific knowledge is not necessarily "better" than the other types of knowledge. A mother's intuition of what to do with her unsettled child may trump the conclusions of scientific studies many times, for example. We value scientific knowledge, but we believe it is important to retain an appreciation also for other types of knowledge.

Science is a distinct type of knowledge and it stands apart from any other type of knowledge. The noun "science" originates from the Latin verb "*scire*" and translates into "knowing objectively," more specifically it is a way of knowing that is *systematic, replicable, verifiable*, and *mutable*. In other words, scientific knowledge is based on careful and comprehensive observation of the data (*systematic*), collected and analyzed in such a way that others can reproduce the analysis and verify its veracity (*replicable* and *verifiable*), and develops over time as new data is examined using multiple methodologies (*mutable*).

Take, for example, the atrocities that occurred during the Holocaust and at Abu Ghraib. An easy assumption to make is that only a few select monsters would engage in such behavior. And, yet, we now know, thanks to countless scientific studies of obedience to unjust authority by political psychologists (a cross-disciplinary field made up of political and social psychologists)—most notably begun by the social psychologist Stanley Milgram—that ordinary individuals, when put in certain circumstances, can usually be made to comply with quite unjust and immoral orders to hurt others.[3]

So, how did scientists "prove" that most ordinary individuals could be induced to obey unjust and immoral orders against others? Objective data was needed to prove the point. Milgram set out to deliver this data and his obedience study has been one brick in building a rather solid wall providing such evidence. In his famous study, Milgram recruited ordinary citizens of New Haven, Connecticut under a cover story that he needed them to help him find out the best way to teach people to remember things. Milgram told the participants of his study that when people missed a word-pairing item on a test they were to shock them and increase the shock level with each subsequent error up to the highest level of over 450 volts of electricity. Milgram's experiment, as you might have guessed, was not about memory but was instead designed to see if people would obey the order of the experimenter to shock strangers at dangerously high levels just because they forgot a word-pairing.

The *assumption* or hunch of even the experts, forty psychiatrists polled by Milgram before the study was conducted, was that in fact only a very small minority (less than 1 percent) would be willing to engage in such tormenting of their fellow man. However, the assumptions of the experts were proved wrong—illustrating nicely for us why we should not assume but should instead use the tools of science to help us discover truth. In this study and many other replications of it in a variety of forms, a vast majority of ordinary people actually *were* willing to inflict the most severe physical punishment on another person in obedience to the authority figure (the experimenter). The assumed "truth" that only monsters could have performed such atrocities as were committed during the Holocaust was debunked by such scientific evidence to the contrary.

Similarly, related research on immoral behavior by Stanford psychologist, Philip Zimbardo, shows that indeed ordinary individuals under certain circumstances can very quickly turn into torturers of the kind seen at the Abu Ghraib prison in Iraq. In the 1970s—long before the events of Abu Ghraib, in a famous prison study experiment, Zimbardo recruited regular college students (screened in advance to ensure they had no psychological problems) to participate in a prison simulation on the Stanford campus. Students were randomly assigned to play the role of prison guard or prisoner. Though the study was scheduled to last two weeks, it had to be called off after just a few days as the "guards" quickly began to abuse the prisoners in many ways very similar to the abuse that occurred at Abu Ghraib. We will return to this example at the end of this book.

For now, we want to ask: Did these researchers indeed find out the absolute "truth" about this aspect of human nature? Scientists would caution that scientific findings do not indicate absolute certainty if that is what we mean by "truths." Instead, scientists tell us that any scientific knowledge is in fact tentative and mutable. Scientists have ensured themselves job security in the fact that it is an enterprise based on continual investigation of new data in new ways. As the evidence accumulates, we certainly feel more confident about our conclusions but any good scientist knows that their conclusions could one day be disproven by the accumulation of contrary scientific evidence. That is why most of us find science so fun! We are constantly exploring our surroundings, making careful observations and testing and retesting our hunches in a search for knowledge and understanding of the complex and interesting world in which we live.

THE SCIENTIFIC STUDY OF POLITICS: THE BIRTH OF THE DISCIPLINE OF POLITICAL SCIENCE

It is easy to think of false truths in the natural world that have been disproven by systematic, cumulative, scientific evidence: the false truth that the world was flat; the false truth that draining someone's blood (a practice done by early doctors known as "bloodletting") would cure someone of disease; the false truth that the sun revolved around the earth; the false truth that a heavy object travels faster through space than a lighter one (Elizabeth still finds that one hard to let go of). As with the misunderstandings of malevolent behavior of the kind seen during the Holocaust or at Abu Ghraib, the world of politics has been plagued by false truths.

False truths exist everywhere, including the political world, and for this reason it was suggested that a science of politics be created. In fact, in 1903, the **American Political Science Association** (APSA) was formally created in an attempt to create an objective, systematic, scientific study of claims made about the political world. The address by the first president of the APSA, Frank J. Goodnow, to the Associations' members emphasized that "scientific knowledge provided a check on the tendencies of political theory 'to soar in the empyrean realms of speculation'."[4]

Prior to the creation of this association, the study of politics was often **normative**, meaning it was concerned more often with theorizing about how things *ought* to be rather than on understanding how things actually *are*. Students of politics began to understand that one important way to credibly make claims about how things ought to be would be to have a better understanding of how they actually are (a **positivist** approach). The discipline gradually evolved over time—at first, being concerned with merely documenting the institutions and rules of the political game then developing, particularly with the advance of more precise scientific methods and tools (like survey research, statistical analysis aided by computers, etc. around the 1950s—a period known as the **Behavioral Revolution in Political Science** when generalities in political behavior were sought through the use of empirical data) into a more precise, empirical, and explanatory science.

Political science as a field is divided into four major subfields: **American Politics**, **Comparative Politics**, **International Relations**, and *political theory*. Unlike the first three subfields, political theory does not depend on *empiricism* (the observation of the data) but instead relies on logical, discursive consideration of ideas without systematically examining their validity. Because the process of political theory research is fundamentally different from the empirical subfields of American politics, comparative politics, and international relations, we will not discuss it in this textbook. However, the fact that we will not discuss political theory in this textbook should not be taken as an indication of its lack of importance. The thoughts and theories set forth by political theorists have been extremely important to the study of politics and to the creation of our political institutions. In addition, the ideas of political theorists are often the basis for the ideas being tested in systematic, scientific ways by the other subfields which do rely on empirical data.

Let's consider a few of the many examples of the ways scientific knowledge accumulated by political scientists has disproven our assumptions regarding what is true in politics in each of these three subfields: American politics, comparative politics, and international relations.

THE IMPORTANCE OF SCIENCE: DEBUNKING FALSE TRUTH IN AMERICAN POLITICS

The subfield of **American Politics** is concerned with the study of political institutions and behavior in the American political system. Scientific study of American politics has helped debunk some common assumptions made by both the people and the press regarding how things really work in the American political system. For example, consider the problem of women's underrepresentation in elected office in the United States. Despite the fact that women make up over 50 percent of the U.S. population, in our entire nation's history, of the 12,000 or so members of Congress who have ever served, only 2 percent of them have been female.[5] It has long been an assumption that one significant reason that women are underrepresented in politics is because voters are biased against females and unwilling to vote for them. Public opinion polling tells us that this is what most voters think. As Lynne Ford, a political scientist who studies women and politics points out, one poll found that "two-thirds of voters believed that women have a tougher time winning elections than men do."[6] Another study found that potential female candidates also believe that there is a sex bias by voters against female political candidates.[7] A significant number of scientific studies by political scientists, however, have disproven this assumption. In fact, all other things being equal (like professional background, financial resources, and political context), female candidates fare as well, and in certain situations, fare even better than their male counterparts.[8]

False assumptions can have important, real-life consequences. In this particular case, scholarly research shows that these false assumptions in fact perpetuate the problem of women's underrepresentation as qualified women decide not to run believing that voters will treat them in an unfair and biased way. Political scientists interested in women's underrepresentation have a responsibility to share the truth as we know false truths affect our behavior and decisions, most especially in this case, the choices made by qualified, potential female candidates.

Oftentimes, the false assumptions we make about the political world are the result of untested claims or false assumptions made by the media. For example, in 2004, almost uniformly, media commentators reported that the 2004 presidential election was decided on the basis of moral values issues. MSNBC analyst (and, once presidential contender himself) Pat Buchanan reported on the program *Scarborough Country* that "it wasn't the economy or the war in Iraq or even the war on terror. Exit polls tell us moral values were most important in choosing a president."[9] Similarly, CNN anchorwoman Paula Zahn reported that "it appears that moral issues trumped just about every other issue on the map here."[10] It was suggested by commentators that the Democratic Party was unable to defeat the Republicans in the presidential election because they were the party deficient in attending to the great moral issues of the day.

Careful, scientific analysis by political scientists has shown that these assertions, however, were untrue. In fact, Langer and Cohen show that the assertions made by the media commentators are based on the misreading of a flawed measuring instrument—namely, an overly vague exit poll question.[11] Just as a natural scientist depends on an accurate measuring instrument, let's say, for example, a thermometer to measure the temperature of the air and if that instrument is broken it will lead to incorrect conclusions, political scientists' findings are only as good as the measuring instruments they use. In this case, voters were asked in the 2004 National Election Poll (NEP) exit survey to choose among a list of issues that affected their presidential vote choice. The items from which they could choose were: moral values, economy/jobs, terrorism, Iraq, health care, taxes, and education. As Langer and Cohen point out, the moral values choice, as opposed to the other items, was really a catch-all, "ill-defined grab bag" that meant vastly different things to different respondents. Langer and Cohen show, using more sophisticated statistical analysis (see Chapter 6 in this volume for a discussion of this method) which allowed them to control for other important variables that affect vote choice like party identification, race, religion, etc., that the issues of terrorism, the economy, and Iraq were in fact more important in affecting voters' presidential choice than were moral issues. Thus, careful, systematic, scientific analysis disproves the commonly held assumption by the media that moral values determined the 2004 presidential election result.

THE IMPORTANCE OF SCIENCE: DEBUNKING FALSE TRUTH IN COMPARATIVE POLITICS

Let's consider some examples of the importance of science in addressing false assumptions in the subfield of political science known as **Comparative Politics**.

While the subfield of **American Politics** is concerned with studying the institutions and behavior of the American political system, comparative politics is the study of the differences and similarities in institutions and processes of politics across political entities, often involving comparisons of different nation-states. Political scientists in this subfield use what is called the **comparative method** to understand and explain the political world (see the discussion in Chapter 3). The comparative method may involve one of two approaches: (1) comparing nations (or any other political entities of interest) that are similar in all respects except for one to see the cause/effect of that one difference (called the **method of difference**); or (2) comparing nations (or any other political entities of interest) that are different in all ways except for one to understand the cause–effect of that similarity (called the **method of similarity**).

One question that has been of interest to political scientists since the dawning of the field is the question: "Why do some [new] democratic governments succeed and others fail?"[12] One commonly held assumption or theory held by scholars was that economic prosperity was an essential (if not the most important) component to democratic success. Many scholars have asserted that economic development and modernization are fundamental to the creation and maintenance of a successful democracy.[13] In a fascinating comparative analysis, however, Robert Putnam finds very interesting evidence showing that economic prosperity and development may not be the determining factor it was once thought to be in shaping effective democracies. Putnam uses the **method of similarity**, comparing twenty different regional governments in Italy who, though very different on a variety of variables especially in the Northern versus the Southern regions, were all similar in one important respect—they were all created in a top-down way with similar structures and rules by the central government in 1948 under a new Italian constitution. Putnam and his colleagues, using numerous scientific methodologies including personal interviews with political elites, find that contrary to the popular belief that economic development predicts democratic success it is instead a long history of civicness in a region, including civic engagement and social capital, defined as "trust, norms, and networks" (167), that is most important in predicting democratic institutional success.[14] The methods Putnam uses are discussed in this book, including field research (Chapter 4), multiple nation-wide surveys (Chapter 7), analysis of statistical data (Chapter 6), and even an experiment (see Chapter 10).

Putnam's work received a lot of attention and praise precisely because its innovative, systematic, and scientific approach to an issue long felt settled helped upend traditional scholarly thinking on the question of what makes for effective democratic institutions. Thus, scientific knowledge not only provides clarity for false popular and media assumptions but also for false scholarly assumptions.

THE IMPORTANCE OF SCIENCE: DEBUNKING FALSE TRUTH IN INTERNATIONAL RELATIONS

Scientific knowledge about the political world is important not only to overcome faulty assumptions made by the public, the media, and scholars but also to overcome faulty assumptions made by politicians. Let's take an example in the subfield of political science known as **international relations** to see how this has worked. International relations is the study of the relationships between or among the various states and other political entities of the world such as governmental or non-governmental international organizations. Most, but not all, international relations theory is what scholars call **positivist**—in that it relies on the scientific method and empirical data to help explain and understand the relationships among political entities. Let's consider one assumption made by politicians regarding how nations interact with each other which international relations scholars have since proven wrong by using scientific analysis, or a positivist approach.

When thinking about the security of one's nation, politicians have often concluded that building up arms, establishing military alliances and defense systems should make a nation safer. On the face of it, this belief appears logical as more weapons and a stronger military with more alliances provide protection against aggression by one's enemies. As a defensive security strategy, the thinking goes, a buildup of arms and the creation of alliances should not worry other nations unless they already have the intention of acting aggressively toward us. Consider this exchange by Senator Tom Connally and Secretary of State Dean Acheson regarding the ratification of NATO,[15] which was an attempt to bolster the defenses of cooperating nations against aggression, particularly by the Soviet Union. This exchange shows the logic of politicians regarding how military buildup will be interpreted by other nations:

> **Secretary Acheson**: [The treaty] is aimed solely at armed aggression.
> **Senator Connally**: In other words, unless a nation . . . contemplates, mediates, or makes plans looking toward aggression or armed attack on another nation, it has no cause to fear this treaty.

These politicians believed that only a nefarious nation would be concerned with another country's purely defensive actions. As they go on to discuss in this exchange, just as only a person likely to commit crimes needs to worry about stricter crime laws, only a nation with evil intent needs to worry about another nation's buildup of military arms and defenses.

A leading scholar in the field of international relations by the name of Robert Jervis,[16] however, uses a scientific methodology known as **formal modeling** to disprove this theory (see Chapter 11 in this volume). Formal modeling is a method whereby a mathematical and logical model coupled with examination of real-world politics is used to examine relationships and predict and test interactions among entities. Using this technique, Jervis develops what is known as the *theory of the security dilemma*. The theory starts with the assumption of anarchy. Anarchy, when used by international relations theorists, does not mean "chaos." Rather it refers to the absence of hierarchy in the international system: above states, there is no authority such as an overarching governing body (a world government) that can enforce how nation-states interact with one another. A domestic system, by contrast, is organized hierarchically: there is an authority (the court system) that is able to enforce how citizens of this state interact with each other.

Jervis shows that in fact in an anarchic international system one nation's defensive move to build up arms and form alliances will likely be interpreted by other nations not as defensive but as aggressive, thus leading that nation to build up its military defenses and arms eventually leading to an even more precarious situation for all. In other words, as one country attempts to be more secure they are actually instigating a series of responses from others which in the long run makes them less secure than they were to begin with. Because nation-states cannot assume that the intentions of a nation are merely defensive, they must react with more weapons and defenses themselves. Nation-states become less willing to work with one another as the fear and mistrust grows in response to the buildup. Thus, the threat of aggressive interactions between the two sides increases rather than decreases as intended. Misunderstanding of the security dilemma, Jervis states, can have important political consequences as politicians fail to consider other means (such as diplomacy) which might actually be more likely to result in enhanced security for a nation than would a buildup of arms and defenses. Scholarly research on the security dilemma has been used to inform politicians in their considerations of the best security strategies.

THE NAÏVE SCIENTIST AND BEYOND

You may have heard the term "naïve scientist" before. Political scientists use it sometimes, but it originates from our cognate discipline psychology and there is a fascinating insight behind it if you think about it. Before any of us receive any methodological and scientific training, we are all naïve scientists. As laypeople we are "scientists" because we perform exactly the same tasks as trained scientists do: we collect data (through observation), we observe correlations between different observations, we make generalizations from these observations, and we also formulate causal hypotheses and theories to predict events. Finally, we test these theories against new observations. Yet we are naïve, because as human beings, we are biased in many ways and we are not following a rigorous and systematic logic (method) when going through these steps. The very simple goal of this book is to help us become less naïve and more method-ological—as every day citizens and as political scientists.

Being methodological in answering our questions is important. Consider the following questions: Does democratization lead to peaceful foreign rela-tions? Do diverse cultures necessarily clash with each other? Does religion impact politics? If so, in what ways? Do "values" have an impact on politics? Do women have equal chances in elections? These are all interesting and indeed very important research questions. The popular media and journalistic accounts of domestic and international accounts have led to many "false truths" in answering these and other important questions. However, both citizens and political scientists have an interest in acquiring "truth statements" about such questions. Political scientists especially have a responsibility to provide such knowledge as they are to communicate their results not only to a community of scholars but also to all people. The competence in research methodology justifies the making of statements that help constitute general or particular bodies of knowledge justifiably described as "truthful" or "scientific."

In this textbook, you will be introduced to the scientific study of politics and how it is conducted through a conversation with scholars in the field. These scholars will expose you to the various methodologies by discussing precisely how they themselves went about engaging in the research process. Each chapter's author(s) will use one of their own published studies to show you an example of one of the variety of methodologies available to us to answer impor-tant political questions. These methodologies include case studies (Chapter 3), field research (Chapter 4), interviews (Chapter 5), statistical analysis (Chapter 6), survey research (Chapter 7), secondary data analysis (Chapter 8), content analysis (Chapter 9), experiments (Chapter 10) and formal modeling (Chapter 11). These methodologies range from the more **qualitative** (non-numerical, usually done with a smaller sample of data and often more hypothesis-generating than hypothesis-testing methods such as **case studies** (Chapter 3)) to the more **quantitative** (numerical and usually involving a larger sample of data such as *statistical research* (Chapter 10)).

You will hear firsthand from the political scientists who conducted this research. You will discover why they got interested in their particular research question, what challenges they faced in answering it, what methodologies they found were most appropriate to answer their question, and what "truths" they were able to discover. You will see how being a scientist is much like being a detective. Solving a problem or political mystery requires information-gathering and analysis in a systematic and thorough way. You will see that scholars are motivated by an unanswered question or a tension they feel regarding what is assumed to be true and what they have observed to be true. And, you will hopefully learn not just about the methodologies available to you but also about the fun you can have applying these methodologies to the search for truth about politics.

Exercises and Discussion Questions:

1. Do you think that *religious knowledge* and **scientific knowledge** are reconcilable?
2. Identify and describe a situation in which you were a "*naïve scientist.*"
3. Identify a claim about the political world made by the media (for example, Congress is more partisan than ever). Then, find scholarly research in political science that addresses that claim. Is the claim true according to this research? Does the scientific data support the media claim? What *methodology* does the scholarly research use to evaluate this claim *scientifically*?

Recommended Resources:

American Political Science Association (www.apsanet.org): This website will provide you with information about the primary professional association for political scientists. You can find out about the history of the field, can access links to journal articles and read about the important activities in which political scientists are engaged.

New York Times (www.nytimes.com): Check out one of the most comprehensive media outlets for coverage of both domestic and international politics.

Politico (www.politico.com): For some of the most current discussion of American politics by journalists, check out this political website.

Gallup (www.gallup.com): A reputable polling organization using scientific sampling methods to assess public opinion on the most pressing political issues of the day.

Survey Documentation and Analysis: (www.sda.berkeley.edu): This website provides you with access to some of the best academic surveys in political science including the General Social Survey and the National Election Study. The website allows you to select survey questions of interest to you and do basic statistical analyses with them.

Notes

1 Denny Feb. 17, 4.
2 Zimbardo 2007: 324–325.
3 Milgram 1974.
4 Gunnell 2006, 483.
5 Center for American Women and Politics 2010 (at: www.cawp.rutgers.edu).
6 Ford 2011, 140.
7 Lawless and Fox 2005.
8 Seltzer et al. 1997.

9 MediaMatters.org 2004.
10 Ibid. 4; see also Langer and Cohen 2005, for more examples.
11 Langer and Cohen 2005.
12 Putnam 1993, 3.
13 See, for example, Dahl 1971; Lipset 1960.
14 Putnam 1993.
15 As cited by Robert Jervis 1978: 181.
16 Jervis 1978.

CONTENTS

How Do We Get a Science of Politics?

Akan Malici and Elizabeth S. Smith

One of the most prominent theories in political science is the Democratic Peace Theory. It is a theory developed by political scientists and employed by policymakers. Many would say this is how it should be—that there is a bridge between academics and policymakers and that both work together towards good policy. Unfortunately, this is not always the case. As a matter of fact, it is the case much too rarely. But the Democratic Peace Theory is a good example where political science research impacted policy. The development and application of this theory also illustrates the symbiotic relationship between scholars of politics at universities on the one hand and politicians in government on the other. In recent years we have seen the theory applied in countries like Iraq, Afghanistan, Pakistan, and others.

The answer to the question of how one gets a science of politics is by adopting a language of science and by proceeding scientifically in one's inquiry of politics. In this chapter we begin by providing a basic language of science as we trace step by step the journey of the Democratic Peace Theory from its inception to its influence in the highest offices of policymaking in Washington, DC. In doing so we shall highlight those terms that will be important for you while reading and studying this book.

GETTING CURIOUS

The origins of the Democratic Peace Theory are very interesting. They date back more than two hundred years. It all started with the observations of the German philosopher Immanuel Kant in his hometown of Konigsberg which was then the capital of Prussia. Kant was very concerned about all the conflict he observed all around the world. Natural for a philosopher, he thought a lot about this issue and he wrote down his thoughts in a little book that was first published in 1795. The title of the book was *Perpetual Peace*.

The phenomenon that Kant set out to study was world peace and he asked a fundamental **research question**. A research question is a statement that identifies the phenomenon we want to study. It generally is motivated by our curiosity about something that we consider important but that has not been asked, addressed or answered yet—at least not satisfactorily. Kant's research question was: How could the world attain peace? Even more ambitious, as the title of his book suggests, he asked how the world could attain perpetual peace, meaning peace that would last into eternity. Kant's question was indeed a big question. But his answer is relatively simple. Here it is:

> [The] republican constitution . . . provided for this desirable result, namely perpetual peace, and the reason for this is as follows: If (as must inevitably be the case, given this form of constitution) the consent of the citizenry is required in order to determine whether or not there will be a war, it is natural that they consider all its calamities before committing themselves to so risky a game. (Among these are doing the fighting themselves, paying the costs of war from their own resources, having to repair at great sacrifice the war's devastation, and finally, the ultimate evil that would make peace itself better, never being able – because of new and constant wars – to expunge the burden of debt.) By contrast, under a nonrepublican constitution, whose subjects are not citizens, the easiest thing in the world is to declare war. Here the ruler is not a fellow citizen, but the nation's owner, and war does not affect his table, his hunt, his pleasure, his court festivals, and so on. Thus, he can decide to go to war for the most meaningless of reasons, as if it were a kind of pleasure party, and he can blithely leave its justification (which decency requires) to his diplomatic corps, who are always prepared for such exercises.[1]

In short, Kant is saying that if a country is a republic, then it will be very hesitant to go to war. Notice that *republic* is a Latin term (*res-publica*) and translates literally into "the affairs of the public." Semantically it is very similar to the term *democracy* which has Greek roots (*demos kratein*) and translates literally into "the rule of the people." Thus, in more familiar language we may say that Kant advanced the **proposition** that democracies are unlikely to go to war. A proposition is an expression of a judgment or a declaration about the relationship of at least two **concepts**. The concepts in this proposition are *democracy* and *war*. **Concepts** are the words we choose to describe the phenomena we are interested in.

Concepts must be **conceptualized**, which simply means that they must be defined. In other words: What is a war? What is a democracy? Let's focus on the latter concept—democracy. Some adopt a narrow definition emphasizing the competition of at least two parties and free elections. Others add on and say that for a country to qualify as a democracy it must also have and guarantee fundamental freedoms such as the freedom of speech, the freedom of religion, and a free media. It will be obvious to you that if researchers adopt differing **conceptualizations** for their concepts, then they are likely to use different indicators (or precise measures) of their concepts. The process of denoting the indicators of a concept is known as **operationalization** of that concept. The strength of the relationship between a concept and its indicator is known as the *epistemic correlation*. So, for example, an IQ test is often used as an indicator of the concept intelligence, although some would make the argument that it is a poor indicator of that concept (they would be arguing that the epistemic correlation between the indicator and the concept is weak). If operationalizations differ among scholars, then the research findings are likely to be different. As a result the *comparability* of their research is jettisoned—yet, comparability should be a central goal of any research community.

An important next step in the research process is to ask: Is the proposition true? So, in this example, is the proposition that democracies are less likely to go to war true? By definition, **propositions** must be either true or false. Immanuel Kant was a philosopher and his proposition appeared plausible, but at his time there was no **empirical evidence** to support it. Empirical evidence is proof that a proposition is true. In the social sciences we often like to have **data** as proof. Data is nothing more than systematically collected and objective observations about the phenomenon we are studying. It can come in two forms: quantitative or qualitative (numerical or textual). If we have data confirming a proposition, then we gain more confidence in it. The proposition then also becomes more relevant for it may carry implications on our actions and doings. For example, if Kant's proposition is indeed true, then one important implication would be that the establishment of democratic governments should be actively promoted as a way to minimize conflict and promote peace.

WORKING TOWARD AN ANSWER

It was not until about 150 years later, in the 1950s and 1960s that political scientists embarked upon delivering empirical evidence for Immanuel Kant's proposition. These researchers proceeded step by step and very systematically.

Let us go through and explain each step. The researchers began by articulating two specific research questions that are derived from Kant's proposition, but they are a little more specific. Their **research questions** were twofold: (1) Are democracies more peaceful in general? (2) Are democracies more peaceful only toward other democracies?

Here we reach a good opportunity to elaborate a little more on what a good or appropriate **research question** should look like. First, a research question should be a **positive question**. This does not mean that it should be a 'good' question. It means that the question should be about phenomena in the existing world. The opposite of a positive question is a **normative question**. Normative questions are about how things ought to be in an imagined world. An example of a normative question would be: How should a country be governed? A good way to think about positive questions versus normative questions is that the first address a 'What *is*?' question whereas the latter address a 'What *ought* (to be)?' question. This does not mean that positive questions cannot have normative implications. In fact, many would say they should. We will return to this issue at the end of this chapter and also at the end of this book.

Second, **research questions** should not be about single factual issues, such as the question, "How high or low is the voter turnout in national elections in country X?" There is not much to be researched here—the answer can be looked up very quickly. Perhaps more importantly though, there is nothing puzzling behind this question. Instead, research questions should be about relationships or associations between at least two issues. An example would be, "Do negative campaign ads lead to a depression in voter turnouts?" The two issues here are (a) the nature of campaign ads and (b) the voter turnout. One way of thinking about this second point is that research questions should be less "*What?*" questions, and more "*Why?*" questions. In the present example, we are seeking an answer to *why* there may be low participation in national elections.

The third, fourth, and fifth point for a good research question can quickly be stated together. The third point is that research questions should be concrete; that is, their scope should be clearly defined. Our example of the nature of campaign ads could perhaps be revised to read "Do negative campaign ads *on television* lead to a depression in voter turnout?" This formulation makes it clearer what the researchers are about to investigate—the question is concerned specifically with television ads. Third, data should be available towards answering the posed research question. Indeed, voter participation in national elections are often available online and negative campaign ads on television can also easily be quantified (counted) by a research team. Fourth, research questions should be subjected to the "*So what?*" test. The "So what?" test ensures that the answers we will gain from engaging in these questions should be relevant and have implications that go beyond the bounds of a particular research project.

After stating their research questions, the researchers often formulate **hypotheses** to guide their research. Hypotheses are very similar to propositions and oftentimes a hypothesis can be derived from either a proposition or a research question. Hypotheses are expected, but not yet confirmed relationships between two or more variables. A good hypothesis should meet several criteria. First, like a research question, it should be a *positive statement*, that is, it should be an informed guess about an expected relationship in the existing world. Second, a good hypothesis should be a *general statement*. This means it should not just address a single event, such as the cause(s) of a *particular* election with a low voter turnout, but it should address the cause(s) for low voter turnout, *generally*. Third, it should be a *plausible statement*. This means there should be some good reason why we believe that a proposed relationship is true (this is why we refer to a hypothesis as an 'educated guess'). Fourth, again like a research question, it should be a *testable statement*. This means, data should be available so we can assess whether the hypothesis can be confirmed or must be disconfirmed.

The formal hypotheses corresponded to the research questions above. The hypotheses were:

- *If a regime is a democracy, it will engage in peaceful crisis behavior.* This hypothesis was called the monadic version. It is called monadic because it asserts that a democracy will engage in peaceful crisis behavior (not resort to force) regardless of whether the other regime is a democracy or not.

- *If two democratic regimes encounter each other in a crisis, they will resolve it peacefully.* This was the dyadic version. It is called dyadic because it asserts that a settlement will be the outcome only if both contending sides are democracies. In other words, it takes two democracies to make peace.

The **unit of analysis** in these hypotheses is countries. A unit of analysis is simply the object or the entity under study. In our example, our study is concerned with states and their behavior (towards other states) in crises situations. In other studies, such as the voting behavior of individuals in national elections, the unit of analysis would be, as just suggested, individuals. If the study would examine the voting behavior of religious denominations, the unit of analysis would be (religious) groups.

By formulating hypotheses, the researchers express the purported cause and effect in scientific terms. Across all sciences the presumed cause is referred to as the **independent variable** (often referred to as **IV**) and the presumed effect is referred to as **dependent variable** (often referred to as **DV**). The independent variable was type of regime and the dependent variable was crisis behavior for the monadic hypothesis and crisis outcome for the dyadic hypothesis. We refer to independent and dependent variables as *variables* because they can vary, that is because they can take on different variations or *values*. In fact, any variable must be able to assume at least two distinct values. Otherwise, by definition, it is not a variable. The independent variable can take on the values democratic or non-democratic. The dependent variable can take on the values peaceful or conflictual conflict behavior (in the monadic version) and settlement or war (in the dyadic version).

A third type of variable is an **antecedent variable**. An antecedent variable occurs in time prior to an independent variable and may act as a catalyst for the independent variable. What could be an antecedent variable in our case? Or, let's ask more specifically: What could be an antecedent variable to democracy? Scholars of democratization have identified a host of factors. Among them are: Social and political pluralism, high levels of literacy and education, traditions of toleration and compromise, economic development and social modernization. A market economy is considered one of the most prominent factors in generating a democratic regime in a country. So we could say that a market economy or, more specifically, a liberal and open economy is an **antecedent variable** (or a **precondition**) to democracy.

Researchers embarked upon **quantitative research** to test the above hypotheses and provide answers for their research questions. **Quantitative research** is basically **statistical** or numerical research and it works by assigning numbers to the terms we are studying. In our case of the Democratic Peace Proposition, when the independent variable took the value 'democratic', it got a "1" for example, and when it took the value "non-democratic" it got a "2." The researchers also assigned numbers for the values of the dependent variable. When it assumed the value peaceful crisis behavior or settlement it got a "3" and when it took the value "conflictual crisis behavior" or "war" it got a "4." Afterwards, with the aid of computers, the researchers determined whether the "1s" tended to match up with the "3s."

Please notice that we very much simplified the actual process the quantitative researchers were engaged in. However, in essence quantitative research is about establishing relationships or **correlations** between two or more variables. In our specific case they attempted to determine whether there was a correlation between the type of regime (**IV**) on the one hand and crisis behavior or crisis outcome on the other hand (**DV**). Another word for correlation is **law** and we distinguish between **absolute law** (sometimes also referred to as *deterministic law*) and **probabilistic law**. An absolute law states: "Whenever we observe x, we will observe y" or "If x, then always y." A probabilistic law states: "Whenever we observe x, we will observe y, with the probability of z."

FINDING THE ANSWER

The results of this quantitative research suggested that while democracies did engage in war with non-democracies, they resolved any crises they had with each other peacefully. In other words, the researchers did not find much support for the monadic version of the hypothesis, but they found strong support for the dyadic version of the hypothesis. In fact, the strong support for the dyadic version has been described to approach the ideal of an **absolute law** or a perfect **correlation**. In other words: Democracies never go to war with each other. This is a strong conclusion and we shall return and discuss it critically. First, however, we need to address a few more things about the research process.

Quantitative researchers addressed the *whether* question, that is *whether* democracies are more peaceful generally or whether they are peaceful more particularly among themselves. What was missing was an answer to the *why* question—the **causal mechanism**. A causal mechanism is not about *that* we observe a certain relationship (this is what laws are about); it is about *why* we observe this relationship, that is the *reason* behind it. In other words, it is the explanation for *why* something happens. In our case: Why are democracies not fighting each other? Answering this question became the task for **qualitative research**. In simple terms, qualitative research is non-numerical, in-depth research or data collection limited to a few cases. There are many types of qualitative research. Among them are, for example: Observation, field research, interviews, document analysis, case studies, and others. Some of the most prominent qualitative methods in political science will be discussed in subsequent chapters of this book.

The distinction between *whether*-questions and *why*-questions illustrates nicely that **quantitative** and **qualitative** research methods can complement each other. It may surprise you to hear that political scientists often argue over which method is the better one. **Quantitative** researchers sometimes claim that statistical research is more objective. **Qualitative** researchers argue that their research is more context-sensitive and empathetic. Indeed, both methods have advantages. **Quantitative methods** are well suited to test **hypotheses** and deliver correlational conclusions about purported causes and effects. **Qualitative methods**, on the other hand, are well suited to investigate the underlying causal mechanisms of established relationships. They should be cast not as competitors, but as collaborators towards addressing the same research questions.

Let us now return to our discussion of the Democratic Peace Theory and the efforts of qualitative researchers. This group of scholars studied in great depth the cases where two democracies were in a crisis with each other, but where they ultimately settled it peacefully. They found that in these crises there were often inclinations for war, sometimes very strong inclinations. But, fortunately, the situation did not come to it. They identified two causal mechanisms to explain this outcome. One mechanism was labeled the "cultural argument" and the other mechanism was labeled the "structural argument." Let us look at each causal mechanism in more detail.

According to the "cultural" argument, a democratic political culture is distinct from other types of political cultures such as authoritarianism. It is said that democratic rules and regulations create a culture that socializes the members of the polity into norms of mutual tolerance, collaboration, compromise, and encourages peaceful means of internal conflict resolution. It is also said that this culture comes to apply not only within a democracy, but also across national boundaries toward other democracies. Here we encounter yet another type of **variable** in addition to the ones we discussed already, namely an **intervening variable**. An intervening variable is an intermediate factor between two other variables (IV and DV) in a causal chain—it is caused by the independent variable and it causes the dependent variable.

It will be evident to you what the **intervening variable** in the present case is. It is the culture of conflict resolution as we just described it. This culture is caused by the democratic governance of the state and it causes democratic states to approach each other in like manner—in an effort to mediate the crisis and any disagreement rather than to prevail over the other through the use of force.

The "structural" argument is different, but also somewhat related. According to the structural argument it is the internal makeup (the structures) of democracies that are responsible for the observed peace among democracies. The architecture of democracies is fundamentally different from non-democracies. The main characteristic of a democracy is that it is constituted through a system of checks and balances. Who or what are the "checkers" and "balancers"? Some of them are quite obvious. For example, the three independent branches of the United States government, namely the Executive, the Judiciary, and the Legislative, act as checks and balances on each other. But there are also other checkers and balancers such as the media and the people, for example. In short, in a democracy, no single leader, group, or institution can simply declare war. It requires a broad consensus, and this consensus is hard to come by because war is something that is costly in many ways. The checkers and balancers act as brakes on further escalation and allow more time for peaceful conflict resolution. In an authoritarian state, by contrast, if the dictator wants to go to war, there is not too much that can stop him. There are no checkers and balancers that could put on the brakes on an escalation course and avert war.

QUESTIONING THE ANSWER

Above we stated that researchers found that democracies indeed do not fight each other and some went even so far as to claim that this finding is approximating an **absolute law** or a perfect **correlation**. This is indeed a very strong conclusion. However, just because there *seems* to be good evidence for such a conclusion, does not mean that we should readily accept it. When engaging with theories, propositions, hypotheses, data analysis, and conclusions that follow from such it is very important to remain critical and not to accept them too readily. Let us problematize at least two aspects of the Democratic Peace Theory.

The first aspect we shall problematize is the purported **causality** in the Democratic Peace Theory. In order to establish causality three criteria must be met. First, the assumed independent variable and the dependent variable must correlate. Second, the independent variable must precede the dependent variable in time. These two criteria are generally relatively easy to establish. Also in the present case we can easily see how they are met. The third criterion is that the relationship between the independent variable and the dependent variable must not be **spurious**. A relationship is spurious if the assumed independent variable and the dependent variable are in fact not causally related, if there is, in fact, a third (hidden) **extraneous variable** causing the correlation between them. An **extraneous variable** (sometimes also referred to as a *confounding variable*) is a factor that could have created an "accidental" or "noncausal" relationship between the independent and dependent variables. The third criterion for causality is generally the most difficult one to establish.

As critical students of politics we should ask: Could the strong relationship between the variable regime and the variable crisis behavior/crisis outcome be **spurious**? In other words, we must ask: Is there a variable that causes both democracy and peaceful crisis behavior or resolution? You will remember that earlier we said that a liberal and open market economy is an antecedent variable to democracy. However, it could also be a confounding variable. How so? The answer is simple: Open market economies often lead to subsequent democratization processes in a country. At the same time, however, it may be well known to you that countries with open market economies tend to engage in commerce and trade with each other and that they, therefore have normal (not conflictual) relationships with each other. Thus, in this case, while there might be a relation between democracies and peace, they may not be causally related to each other. Instead, they may both be caused by a third factor—open market economies.

The second aspect we shall problematize is about the operationalization of the Democratic Peace Theory's **concepts**. We already mentioned above that the definition of **concepts** such as "democracy" and "war" is very important. In simple terms, what counts as a war? Or in more blunt terms, how many people have to die for a conflict to be counted as a war? If 100 people die, does this qualify as a war? The answer is 'no'. It will be seen as unfortunate, but it will not be seen as a war. Researchers agreed that a war is a situation in which there are at least 1,000 battle deaths. There is nothing special about this number— it has just become the convention. However, settling on this operationalization allows for the exclusion of some troublesome cases. For example, although proponents of the Democratic Peace Theory consider Finland a democracy, the country's alliance with Nazi Germany in World War II is dismissed because there were fewer than 1,000 Finnish casualties. Thus, the critics contend that democratic peace theorists tinker with the operationalization of concepts to dismiss important cases that the theory fails to account for.

Thus, we must ask: Could it be that the conclusion of the Democratic Peace Theory as approximating an absolute law is overstated? Does the theory "work" because it is "set up" to work? We do not want to suggest that the Democratic Peace Theory is wrong. Rather, we want to suggest that we, whether we are students of politics or not, must always remain critical toward theories and any research findings and conclusions they generate. This will allow us to work towards knowledge that we can have more confidence in. This is very important because research should have practical *implications* and *policy relevance*. In other words, the knowledge that we are gaining from our research should benefit us in the real world.

THE IMPLICATIONS AND POLICY RELEVANCE

If it is indeed true that democracies do not fight each other, then the **normative implication** is to work towards democratizations in countries that are lacking this system. Indeed, the Democratic Peace Theory has been applied in the real world. More specifically, it served as a very important guide for the making of foreign policy for various U.S. Presidents. In contemporary times it was used perhaps most explicitly during the administration of President Bill Clinton, but also during the administrations of following Presidents George W. Bush and Barack Obama. You may know that each administration develops at least one National Security Strategy. Usually this is a document of about thirty to fifty pages and it summarizes the main goal of the administration as well as the strategies by which these goals should be attained. The National Security Strategy of the Clinton Administration was titled *A National Security Strategy of Engagement and Enlargement*.

You might ask "engagement and enlargement of what?" The answer is engagement of the United States in the world to enlarge the zone of democracies. In simple language, the task for the U.S. was to encourage and support the inception, building, and furthering of democracies. This can happen through various means such as financial and economic aid, trade agreements, support of democratic grassroots movements in the target country, (military) intervention, and through many other ways. Whatever means are chosen towards the enlargement of the zone of democracies, the endeavor is often very costly. Yet, the makers of U.S. foreign policy have been willing to take on the cost exactly because they believe that the Democratic Peace Theory is true. In the Preface to *A National Security Strategy of Engagement and Enlargement*,

President Bill Clinton wrote "The community of democratic nations is grow-ing, enhancing the prospects for political stability [and] peaceful conflict resolution . . ." On the second page, the document argues "we know that the larger the pool of democracies, the better off we, and the entire community of nations will be." And on the fifth page it expressed a "firm commitment [of the United States] to expanding the global realm of democracy." In fact, leaders in Washington have taken action. The document points out that the United States

> has supported South Africa's . . . transformation, provided aid to a new democratic Russia and other new independent states as well as Central and Eastern European nations, assisted Cambodia, and worked with our Western Hemisphere neighbors restoring the democratically elected government in Haiti and hosting the Summit of the Americas, which reaffirmed and strengthened our mutual commitment to democracy.

These are examples from the 1990s. More recent examples of U.S. engagement towards building or furthering democracies are to be found in Afghanistan, Iraq, and Pakistan. It is the explicit goal of the U.S. to further the establishment of democracies and to strengthen those that have been estab-lished already. Of course, it remains to be seen just how successful these efforts will be and whether the U.S. is going about them in the right way. But this is another discussion.

Exercises and Discussion Questions:

1. Why, do you think, *comparability* of research findings is important?
2. Provide examples for **absolute laws** and **probabilistic laws**. These do not have to be political examples. Subsequently, formulate the corresponding *theories*.
3. Do you believe the Democratic Peace Theory is valid/true? In what other ways than the ones discussed above, could the Democratic Peace Theory be *criticized*?
4. If researchers found that negative campaign ads lead to lower voter turnouts in national elections, what would the *implications* be?
5. Do you believe that politicians can *learn* from political scientists?
6. What is the possible ramification if war were operationalized as a situation where there are not 1,000 battle deaths, but 100?

Recommended Resources:

Elman, Miriam, ed. 1997. *Paths to Peace: Is Democracy the Answer?* Cambridge, MA: MIT Press.

Kant, Immanuel. 1975. *To Perpetual Peace: A Philosophical Sketch.* Translated by Ted Humphrey. Indianapolis: Hacket.

Ray, James Lee. 1998. *Democracy and International Conflict: An Evaluation of the Democratic Peace Proposition.* Columbia: University of South Carolina Press.

Note

1 Kant 1975: 113.

CONTENTS

Case Study and the Comparative Method

Why Do States Join Institutions?

Kai He

▐ **GETTING CURIOUS: THE INSTITUTIONALIZATION OF WORLD POLITICS AFTER THE COLD WAR**

The end of the cold war signified the structural transformation of world politics from bipolarity to unipolarity. International relations scholars heatedly debated what the world would look like in the post-cold war era. *Realists* foresaw more conflicts in international relations, arguing for "back to the future"[1] and the "clash of civilizations" visions of the twenty-first century.[2] *Liberals*, however, cheered for the possible "end of history" after the cold war.[3] The reality of world politics, however, shows that neither of these two schools of thought is right. Unlike realists' predictions, world politics is relatively peaceful despite some regional hot spots. Contrary to liberals' optimism, democracy has not widely prevailed in the world and is still far from transforming world politics. Realists and Liberals are the most well-established scholars in International Relations theory, yet both camps are seemingly getting the world wrong. Why?

Before trying to answer this question, we need to empirically examine some new and unique international phenomena in the post-cold war era. Yes, we certainly experienced some relative peace in world politics since we have not observed another World War in three decades although there are some regional conflicts, such as in the Middle East. In Europe, the Kosovo and Bosnia wars are basically ethnic conflicts in nature but with external interventions. One interesting empirical observation in the post-cold war world is what has been termed "Asian exceptionalism."[4] There is no military conflict among nations in Asia after the cold war even though there are territorial disputes as well as some unfinished warfare between states.

More interestingly, Asian security in the context of China's rise after the cold war is characterized by the proliferation and dynamics of multilateral institutions in the region, such as the enlargement of the Association of Southeast Asian Nations (ASEAN), the inception of the ASEAN Regional Forum (ARF), and the institutionalization of ASEAN Plus Three—China, Japan, and the Republic of Korea (APT). Although it is premature to argue that these multilateral institutions have led to a perpetual peace in the region, they have at least "institutionalized" security dialogues in the Asia-Pacific. Multilateral institutions have become an alternative for states to seek security under anarchy and are new arenas of strategic interactions between China and other Asian-Pacific countries after the cold war. Therefore, my research question is: Why is there institutionalization of security in the Asia-Pacific? In other words, why do states actively participate in multilateral institutions since the end of the cold war?

The institutionalization of world politics is by no means unique in the Asia-Pacific. The normative and legalistic function of the United Nations in world politics was prominent in the post-cold war era. The economic and political integration of the European Union is also astonishing for international relations students. My curiosity about the institutionalization of security in the Asia-Pacific is based on the broad background of dramatic changes in international politics after the cold war. Although the institutionalization of world politics does not fundamentally transform international relations among nations, it deserves serious theoretical and empirical investigation. My research focus on the Asia-Pacific, hopefully, can deepen our understanding of the institutionalization of international politics in the post-cold war world.

THE RESEARCH STRATEGY: WHAT IS A COMPARATIVE CASE STUDY?

After formulating the **research question**, the next task is to think about how to conduct your research, i.e., what kind of research methods to employ in order to investigate your research question. Recalling my research interest, "Why states actively participate in multilateral institutions after the cold war," we find that the unit of analysis in my question is the state and the time frame of my study is the post-cold war era. Although there are many states or countries in the Asia-Pacific, it is still too limited to conduct a large-N quantitative analysis. Here, N refers to the number of cases and Large-N means large numbers of cases. There are only about 20 countries in the Asia-Pacific region. However, the sample size of 20 observations is too small to make accurate estimates. All other things being equal, larger samples are better than smaller samples because larger samples tend to minimize the probability of errors, maximize the accuracy of population estimates, and increase the generalizability of the results. According to some statisticians, only a sample size of 200 cases, i.e., N>200, can make a fair estimate.[5] Therefore, I decided to employ case study and comparative methods in this research.

A **case** refers to a "phenomenon for which we report and interpret only a single measure on any pertinent variable."[6] In plain language, a case means an event or an observation which can help researchers investigate their research questions. A **case study**, therefore, refers to the investigation of an event that scholars select for analysis. If I only focus on one case, my analysis is called a *single-case study*. In this research project, for example, if I only examine why the United States participated in multilateral institutions in the Asia-Pacific, then I am conducting a single-case study. However, even if my findings from the United States case study may be very interesting, a single case study of the United States cannot adequately answer the research question I proposed, which focuses more on a general pattern of state behavior in the Asia-Pacific after the cold war. Therefore, I need to investigate more than one case for my research. By comparing more states, my research can be more generalizable. Therefore, I used a *comparative case study* method to conduct the investigation. It should be noted that the comparative case study is one of the important research methods that political scientists usually employ in their empirical investigations. Here, I used this method to study a research question I am interested in in terms of international relations. Comparative politics scholars also like to employ this method to conduct comparative investigations. For example, Barrington Moore conducted a comparative study of modernization in Britain, France, the United States, China, Japan, and India in his famous book—a *Social Origins of Dictatorship and Democracy: Lord and Peasant in the Making of the Modern World*. However, it is worth noting that it will be a mistake to think comparative case study method is exclusively reserved for topics in comparative politics.

Selecting cases to study was my next task and it is a very important one. Case selection should not be based on convenience but on scientific criteria. There are basically two types of case selection approaches, John Stuart Mill's **method of agreement** and **method of difference**.[7] Mill's **method of agreement** has two requirements. First that there is "agreement" on the value of the dependent variable, that is, in all cases under investigation we have the same outcome on the right side of the equation. Second, on the left side of the equation, the side of possible independent variables, the cases must be dissimilar, but in one regard. Therefore, the method of agreement is also called "the least similar" case comparison.[8] The logic here is straightforward: If we can identify one variable on the left side of the equation that is similar or the same, while all other variables on this side are dissimilar, then we are in a position to draw a causal inference about this particular variable.

An example will make all this abstract language clearer. Figure 3.1 shows two cases which have the same outcome Y. Comparing Case 1 and Case 2, we can see that the only common independent variable across the two cases is A. Therefore, we can draw the inference that A causes Y.

Mill's second method of comparative inquiry is the **method of difference**. Also this method has two requirements. First, the outcome in the investigated cases must be different. Second, on the left side of the equation, all possible **independent variables** should be similar with only one variable as an exception. This exceptional variable, therefore, can be inferred as the causal variable leading to the different outcomes for the two cases. The method of difference is also called the "most similar" case comparison because the selected cases should ideally be identical in all respects except for the value of only one independent variable. For example, Figure 3.2 shows two cases which have the different outcomes, Y and –Y. Comparing these two cases, we see that these two cases are identical for all but one variable, which takes the value of A (present) in case 1 and –A (absent) in case 2. Therefore, we can make an inference by saying that A causes Y, while –A causes –Y.

In my research, the empirical observation is that almost all states actively participated in multilateral institutions in the Asia-Pacific after the cold war. My observations have the same value for the dependent variable and my research goal is to investigate the convergent behavior of different states toward participation in multilateral institutions. Therefore, I decided to choose Mill's method of agreement for my research. I selected four cases, the foreign policies of the United States, China, Japan, and ASEAN toward multilateral institutions, to conduct my comparative case studies.

	Independent variables	**Dependent variable**
Case 1	A B C D E F	Y
Case 2	A G H I J K	Y

Figure 3.1 Mill's method of agreement

	Independent variables	**Dependent variable**
Case 1	A B C D E F	Y
Case 2	–A B C D E F	–Y

Figure 3.2 Mill's method of difference

Why did I choose these four cases? First, the U.S., China, Japan, and ASEAN are four major actors in Asian security after the cold war. The U.S. is a global hegemon trying to sustain its primacy in the region through both bilateral alliances and multilateral institutions. China is a rising power with the potential to become a regional hegemon. China's participation and policy changes towards multilateral institutions are remarkable. As an economic superpower, Japan faces two strategic dilemmas in forming its own regional policy: China's challenge and America's constraint. As a group of middle and small countries, ASEAN has played an unprecedented role in institutionalizing post-cold war Asian security through initiating and driving regional organizations like the ASEAN Regional Forum (ARF) and the ASEAN Plus Three (APT). Therefore, these four cases address key empirical and theoretical issues of interest; they also represent the foreign policies of four different types of powers (rising, global, regional, and small/middle) towards institutions in general.

Second, these four cases lend themselves very well to Mill's "method of agreement" or the "least similar" case comparison. As mentioned above, China, the U.S., Japan, and ASEAN represent four different types of powers with different national interests. Their policymaking is influenced by many variables, such as regime type, leaders' personality, bureaucratic structure, as well as social factors that differ significantly across these three cases. However, the policy outcomes of these four cases are similar—all of these actors in the region chose to join multilateral institutions or conduct institutional balancing after the cold war—although the levels of their involvement in different institutions may differ to some degree. The question is why such different countries chose a similar policy after the cold war. To explain this outcome, I need to identify the similar independent variables across these four different cases and construct a causal explanation in my analysis.

ISSUES WITH THIS RESEARCH STRATEGY: RIVAL EXPLANATIONS

A research design based on Mill's method of agreement or method of difference will face the equifinality problem. **Equifinality** means that the same outcome can be explained by different pathways or combinations of variables.[9] For example, comparing cases through the method of agreement, we identify that A is the common variable in two different cases which lead to the same outcome Y (see Figure 3.1). Our inference, therefore, is that A causes Y. However, A may be only a necessary variable in causing the outcome Y. There may be other variables, such as Z, that can also cause Y but we omit it in our analysis. In other words, if both A and Z can cause Y, then there are at least two causal paths to the same outcome Y. Our comparative case study based on the method of agreement will face challenges and criticisms from rival explanations. For example, childhood depression (Y) can be caused by different early experiences in life, such as parental divorce and physical abuse. Here, both parental divorce (X) and physical abuse (Z) are necessary variables in causing the same outcome of childhood depression (Y).

In order to solve the equifinality problem, I employed the process-tracing technique and added within-case comparisons to my research.[10] **Process-tracing** is a method of within-case analysis. It focuses on specifying *causal mechanisms* between independent variables and dependent variables and it strengthens the inference of my analysis through examining chains of evidence from hypothesized cause to observed effect. By examining historical archives, government documents, interview transcripts, and other sources related to foreign policy making by ASEAN, China, Japan, and the U.S. after the cold war, my analysis identified the causal mechanisms and traced the processes linking the independent variables with the dependent variable.

I also conducted within-case comparisons, respectively, to examine the foreign policy decision making by these four major powers' towards three major multilateral institutions, the Asia-Pacific Economic Cooperation (APEC), ARF, and APT/EAS (East Asia Summit), across different time periods. For example, I explored China's changing policies toward APEC, ARF, and APT/EAS. China's attitudes toward these three institutions changed dramatically from resistant to pro-active. Through with-in case comparisons, I can examine why China changed its policies toward multilateral institutions over time after the cold war and how the changing values of **independent variables** lead to the variation of the **dependent variable**. Within-case comparisons can strengthen the validity of my inferences based on cross-case comparisons in this research. Validity is a technical term to describe the correspondence between a measure and the concept it is supposed to measure. Here, validity refers to the accuracy and soundness of my argument.

There are two major advantages of the comparative case study method. First, my case study directly answers the research question I intend to investigate. By examining the United States, China, Japan, and ASEAN's foreign policies toward multilateral institutions, I can obtain a clear picture of why these states actively participated in multilateral institutions after the cold war. The internal validity of my research is strong because of my detailed research on each case. **Internal validity** means that I have strong evidence to show that the independent variables caused the variation of the dependent variable in my research.

Second, through comparing different countries' foreign policies toward multilateral institutions, I can identify new causal mechanisms and generate new theories in the study of state behavior in multilateral institutions. Generally, detailed case studies are very conducive for scholars to discover new variables and work towards novel explanations for their research questions. For example, in his seminal work *Making Democracy Work: Civic Traditions in Modern Italy*, Robert Putnam and his colleagues conducted an in-depth comparative case study since 1970 on the performance of twenty regional Italian governments, which were similar institutions but differed in their social, economic, and cultural context. He suggested that "social capital"—the horizontal bonds in the society— is the key for the success of democracies. Without the detailed case study in Italy, Putnam might not be able to discover the importance of "social capital"—a novel variable—in the study of democracy.

The comparative case study has also two disadvantages. First, the case study method faces a weak external validity problem. **External validity** refers to whether we can generalize our findings to other cases. For example, my research findings are based on my analyses of major powers' behavior toward multilateral institutions in the Asia-Pacific. One legitimate concern is whether my findings in the Asia-Pacific can be applied to other regions, such as Europe. In other words, can I use my argument for the Asia-Pacific to explain why European countries were enthusiastic about the European Union? The answer is, unfortunately, "not sure." What I can do in my present research is to make my hypothesis as generalizable as possible and test my hypothesis as rigorously as possible. Further research is needed to confirm or refute my argument in other cases beyond the Asia-Pacific.

Another common criticism of case study methods is the **selection bias** problem. Unlike quantitative scholars, researchers of case study methods do not randomly select cases. Instead, cases are selected purposefully for investigation. "Selection bias," therefore, normally occurs when the researcher selects cases that represent a truncated sample of the relevant universe of cases along the values for the dependent variable.[11] In other words, case study scholars are criticized for only selecting the cases that can support their arguments in their research.

Whether researchers can or should select their cases based on the value of dependent variables is an ongoing debate. Ideally, researchers can **control** or manipulate the values of independent variables and examine how the changing values of independent variables are causally related to the changing values of dependent variables. However, most research designs (except the experimental design method) do not have the luxury of a controlled environment. For example, with my research my empirical observation is that all the great powers in the Asia-Pacific actively participated in multilateral institutions. In terms of the value of the dependent variable, almost all cases in my study are the same, i.e., the countries under investigation participated in multilateral institutions, although their degrees of enthusiasm of states toward various institutions are different across the cases. Therefore, it is important to remember that case selection is one of the major issues faced by case study scholars. A good case study scholar needs to prepare for the criticism of **selection bias** and try their best to mitigate the problem.

My comparative case study based on the method of agreement is a clear target of such "selection bias" criticism. To deal with this problem, I need to find a case with variation on the dependent variable. Fortunately, the United

States case in my study has such variation on the dependent variable because the United States was not a member of APT and EAS, which China, Japan, and ASEAN states collectively formed after the 1998 Asian economic crisis. Therefore, I need to examine why the United States actively participated in other regional organizations, such as APEC and ARF, but not the APT/EAS. The United States case, to a certain extent, can help me mitigate the "selection bias" criticism.

THE LITERATURE REVIEW: THREE SCHOOLS OF THOUGHT IN INTERNATIONAL RELATIONS

After deciding on the research question and research strategy, my next task was to conduct a **literature review**. A literature review is different from an annotated bibliography although the latter is the first step to accomplish the former. While scholars normally report what a book or a journal article is about and how this material is related to their research in an annotated bibliography, a literature review requires researchers to critically and systematically analyze relevant materials. A literature review does not mean to focus on one book or one journal article; it needs to be organized by theoretical themes around the research question.

The literature review is important for any research, because it is a necessary step for scholars to know how their research questions have been previously addressed by other scholars. We do not want to simply repeat what others have argued in our research area, and the goal of research is to offer some new contributions to the existing scholarship. Therefore, I need to critically review relevant literature on my research question before formulating my own hypotheses.

My research question was: Why did major powers in the Asia-Pacific actively participate in multilateral institutions after the cold war? The books and journal articles that I reviewed had to have a focus on state motivations and behavior toward multilateral institutions. I needed to critically evaluate the existing arguments which have directly or indirectly answered my question. If there is a book on the European Union that provides an explanation of why states actively engaged in multilateral institutions, I needed to evaluate this argument to see how it can or cannot adequately provide an answer to my question. The most important thing for a literature review is to identify the weaknesses of the existing arguments so that one's own research can make a potential contribution to existing scholarship. If I couldn't find weaknesses in the already existing arguments, too bad! I would have had to give up my research project because there was no academic value for me to continue my research—it would not make a contribution.

Fortunately, I did find "problems" in existing arguments through my literature review. I organized my literature review by categorizing the existing arguments based on three schools of thought in international relations (IR) theory, i.e., neorealism, neoliberalism, and constructivism. As I mentioned earlier, a literature review should be organized around one's research question. I need to evaluate how these three schools of thought have answered my question and what weaknesses they have.

For neorealists, institutions are **epiphenomenal** or unimportant in world politics. However, if institutions do not matter, why did states devote resources and energy to them after the cold war? In the Asian case, neorealists argue that regional security mainly depends on the power configuration in the larger regional and global system and alliance arrangements between great powers. It was true in the cold war. However, the end of the cold war not only challenged neorealist premises in world politics, but also questioned the reliability of neorealism in Asian security studies. The relatively stable, post-cold war era in Asia refutes neorealist pessimistic predictions about Asian security after the cold war. In addition, the development of multilateralism in Asian security during the post-cold war era becomes the weakest link for the realist position. The response from realists is to downplay the significance of multilateral institutions, such as ASEAN and ARF, and later the APT dialogues.

It is worth noting that some modern realists offer the "voice opportunity" or "binding" hypothesis, in an effort to rescue realism from the institutionalists.[12] For them, institutions could be used by weak but important states to increase their "voices" in the decision-making process through binding stronger states in the institutions. In Asia, it seems understandable why ASEAN, a group of small and middle powers, chose multilateral institutions as their balancing tool to deal with challenges from great powers in the post-cold war era. However, neither the voice of opportunity nor the binding or double-binding arguments explain why regional great powers—the U.S., China, and Japan—participate rather than oppose these "disadvantaged" institutional arrangements led by the weaker states. In other words, the revised realist theories may explain why weaker states choose institutions as a binding strategy, but they fail to account for why powerful states also agree to bind themselves within institutions.

Neoliberal Institutionalism shares many key assumptions with neorealism, such as the anarchic system and the self-help nature of states.[13] However, challenging the pessimistic view of neorealism regarding international cooperation, neoliberal institutionalism offers a brighter picture by underscoring the importance of interdependence and introducing the role of institutions in mitigating the security dilemma and enhancing cooperation among states.[14] Neoliberals suggest a "functional theory of institutions," which argues that institutions could "provide information, reduce transaction costs, make commitments more credible, establish focal points of coordination, and in general facilitate the operation of reciprocity."[15]

Neoliberal institutionalism challenges the major arguments of neorealism in Asian security studies. Neoliberals benefited mainly from the increasing number of multilateral institutions in the region, such as ASEAN, ARF, and APT. However, the Asian economic crisis of 1997 revealed the weakness of neoliberal institutionalism. It is true that institutions can facilitate inter-state cooperation, but neoliberal institutionalism fails to answer a more critical question: when and under what conditions can institutions change states' behavior from pursuing relative gains to absolute gains?[16] Facing an economic shock, the three major regional multilateral institutions, ASEAN, ARF, and APEC, failed to function and coordinate any effective regional actions to cope with the crisis. Instead, the ASEAN states blamed each other and long-time harmonious intra-regional relations were seriously damaged. To what extent institutions can weather storms like the economic crisis remains an unanswered question for neoliberals.

Constructivism as a social theory of international politics focuses on the role of ideas, norms, knowledge, and identity in constituting state behaviors. To constructivists, ideational rather than material factors are "what make the world hang together."[17] While ideational factors refer to ideas, norms, and identity, material ones normally mean military capabilities and economic strengths. They believe that "the course of international relations is an interactive process in which the ideas of and communications among *agents* (or actors: individuals, groups, and social structures, including states) serve to create *structures* (treaties, laws, international organizations, and other aspects of international system), which, in turn influence the ideas and communications of the agents."[18] The major premise of constructivism in Asian security focuses on the development of ASEAN in Southeast Asia. Constructivists emphasize that ASEAN is moving towards a "security community" with its member states ruling out the use of force against each other and committing to settle their disputes in peaceful ways. Further, a "security community" is defined as a social construct or structure achieved from norm-setting and identity-building processes of socialization and interactions.[19] In particular, the ASEAN norms of non-interference, non-use of force, and peaceful settlement of disputes are seen as important institutional mechanisms for overcoming the security dilemma and constructing a "collective identity" among states.[20]

However, how to apply constructivism to a broader Asia-Pacific region is still problematic. Rather than sharing a common identity, the U.S., China, Japan, and Southeast Asian states are divided by cultural, religious, social, and linguistic differences. Although some scholars use identity-based constructivism to account for why the U.S. did not form an "Asian NATO,"[21] it is still unclear why the U.S. even participated in the ARF, a multilateral institution led by the ASEAN states, which have different identities from the U.S.

To sum up, neorealism underestimates the utility of international institutions. Neoliberalism overestimates the importance of institutions. Identity-based constructivism facilitates our understanding of multilateral institutions but has limited explanatory power in the Asia-Pacific. After critically reviewing the existing arguments, my next task is to develop my own hypotheses. A **hypothesis** is also referred to as an "educated guess" (see also Chapter 2). It is a statement proposing a relationship between two or more variables. In other words, it is your proposed answer to the question you raise in the research.

There are mainly two ways to develop a **hypothesis**. One is to introduce a novel explanation significantly different from the existing arguments. Sometimes, scholars borrow theoretical insights from neighboring disciplines, such as psychology and sociology, and apply them to political science questions. For example, some scholars employ prospect theory, a psychological theory, to explain risky behavior in international relations.[22] Another approach to generate hypotheses is to synthesize existing arguments. Synthesizing does not mean to include all possible variables of the existing arguments and suggest that all of them matter. The purpose of synthesizing is to introduce new insights based on the reviewed literature and to identify innovative connections among existing variables.

Although the novel explanation approach may lead to a theoretical breakthrough, the synthesizing approach can also make great contributions to the scholarship. I employed the synthesizing approach to develop my hypotheses for this research. Built on balance-of-power theory (neorealism) and neoliberal "interdependence" argument , I suggested an institutional balancing argument which postulates that (1) high economic interdependence makes states choose a new realist balancing strategy—institutional balancing—rather than traditional military alliances to cope with threats or pressures from the system; (2) the distribution of capabilities in the regional system indicates how states conduct institutional balancing, either inclusively or exclusively. While inclusive institutional balancing means to include the target state into the institution and rely on institutions to constrain its behavior, exclusive institutional balancing refers to strategies to intentionally exclude the target states from the institution and use collective actions within the institution to pressure the outside target state.

The two independent variables in my hypotheses are polarity (the distribution of capabilities) in the regional system and economic interdependence among states. Polarity can be measured as unipolarity (only one superpower in the system), bipolarity (two superpowers in the system) and multipolarity (more than three similar great powers in the system). Economic interdependence has two values: high and low. While polarity is a realist variable, economic interdependence is a variable emphasized by liberals. I argue that the interplay of polarity in the regional system and economic interdependence among states shapes states' foreign policy choices between power balancing and institutional balancing. Through incorporating a neoliberal variable, economic interdependence, into a realism framework, I suggest that the strategic purpose for states to engage in multilateral institutions in the Asia-Pacific is not to cooperate, but to compete through new means. In other words, institutions have become a new diplomatic tool for states to compete with one another and pursue security under anarchy in the context of high economic interdependence after the cold war.

DOING THE STUDY: COLLECTING THE DATA AND DOING THE ANALYSIS

In order to test the validity of my hypotheses, I needed to collect data and conduct analysis. Collecting relevant data is the first step of any analysis. Differing from quantitative analysis, a case study does not need to quantify variables and rely on statistics to find a relationship between variables. Instead, a researcher needs to evaluate relevant materials and find evidence to test his/her hypothesis. There are two types of materials or data that a researcher needs to look for. The first type of data are materials a researcher can use to measure **independent** and **dependent variables**. After formulating hypotheses, a researcher needs to consider how to measure these variables. The second type of materials is about collecting events. Since my study is about international affairs, materials I need to collect are international events, i.e., what happened before, during, and after one country made a decision to participate in an international institution. How these events in the research take place and how a series of events connect to each other are critical for the later analysis of the causal narrative or story that connect the variables.

For my research, I have to collect materials to measure my independent variables and dependent variables. My two **independent variables** are economic interdependence and power distributions in the regional system after the cold war and my dependent variable is state behavior toward three major institutions, APEC, ARF, and APT/EAS. For economic interdependence, I need to collect data and materials on trade, investment, and other economic indicators that can help me measure the economic relationship among states in the Asia-Pacific. In order to qualitatively measure the degree of interdependence (high or low), some descriptive statistics are needed here. International organizations, such as the World Trade Organization, the United Nations, the World Bank, and the International Monetary Fund, have the statistical data I need. For example, one indicator of economic interdependence is one country's trade proportion in their gross domestic product (GDP). The higher the trade proportion, the higher the degree of economic interdependence. In addition, I was able to look for such data and materials in the official statistics published by individual states.

For the power distributions in the regional system, I need to collect some military-related data and materials to measure military capabilities in the region. Defense spending and military budgets are useful data sources for my research. Generally speaking, rich (more powerful) countries have more money to spend on military. Therefore, military budget and defense spending are good indicators of a country's military strength and power. In addition, leaders' statements, public speeches, and official documents are also important to measure the perceptions of leaders regarding the power distribution in the region. Library research and document analysis (see Chapter 6 in this book) are the major channels for me to obtain data for my research.

As for the **dependent variable**, I need to collect historical documents and official materials to trace each individual state's decision-making process toward multilateral institutions. For example, some governments, like Japan, publish annual diplomatic yearbooks or white papers, through which we can study the motives and considerations behind some important diplomatic decisions. Foreign policy leaders' biographies as well as news reports are good sources for collecting these materials. If time and financial circumstances permit, traveling to do personal interviews with government officials should also be considered. Unfortunately, I did not have the luxury to conduct personal interviews for this research.

Another type of material I needed to collect is event data. I needed to know how states make their decisions to participate in these institutions as well as how they negotiated before and after joining these institutions. As mentioned above, detailed information about these events is important for my later analysis. Again, I needed to rely on library research and document analysis to get secondary sources on these events, because I did not participate in these events nor conduct first-hand interviews with participants of these events. Secondary sources are also called second-hand materials, which are mainly from other scholars' research. My personal experience is that a chronology or a timeline of events is helpful for me to grasp the development of the events for the cases in my research. For example, when I conducted research on the U.S. decision to join the ARF, I made a timeline of diplomatic events between US–ASEAN and US–China before and after U.S. membership in the ARF. The timeline not only helped me connect related events together, but also facilitated evaluating the impacts of U.S. membership in the ARF.

After collecting useful materials and data, I needed to do my analysis. Conducting the analysis was the most time-consuming task in the research project. What I needed to do is to read, think, and write. In the process of analysis, a researcher needs to think about the research question and hypotheses all the time. The purpose of analysis is to test the validity of the hypotheses. If successful, a researcher can find evidence to support the hypotheses. If not, a researcher may need to discard or develop new hypotheses for future research. My analysis supported my hypotheses in this research and I concluded that despite different strategic interests, the United States, Japan, the ASEAN states, and China have conducted different forms of institutional balancing through multilateral institutions after the cold war because of deepening economic interdependence and multipolarized power distribution in the Asia-Pacific.

Lessons to Be Learned

What did I learn from this research experience? The most important thing I learned is that research is difficult and needs real commitment. Second, it is crucial to start with a good research question. A good question is not pure imagination. Yes, imagination is important for good research. But a good question is mainly rooted in your interests, your hard study and critical thinking. Interest is the best teacher for learning. Selecting a topic you are really interested in is the first step for any good research. However, interest alone is not enough. You need to read relevant literature to see how other scholars have conducted research on the topic you intend to investigate. It is a time-consuming process since hundreds or even thousands of scholars may have done the research you are interested in. You need to not only summarize what they have done, but also evaluate what they did not do well and what you can contribute. Diligence and critical thinking are two necessary skills to accomplish this work.

In this research, case selection is one of the major difficulties I have to overcome. I chose ASEAN—an organization of Southeast Asian countries—as one of my case studies. There are ten countries in ASEAN. How to find the convergent point among ten ASEAN countries in their foreign policies is one of the toughest tasks for my research. Before conducting the case study, I was not sure whether I could find evidence to support my hypotheses. What I did was to examine not only ASEAN documents on foreign policy but also ten individual countries' foreign policy literature. Again, it is not an easy and fun job to do. But, remember, research is important, exciting, and a highly rewarding enterprise because you may contribute to people's understanding of political life.

Interested to Know More about the Study Discussed in this Chapter?

Consult the following publication:

He, Kai. 2009. *Institutional Balancing in the Asia Pacific: Economic Interdependence and China's Rise*. London and New York: Routledge.

Exercises and Discussion Questions:

1. What are the *advantages* for selecting comparative case study methods?
2. What are the *weaknesses* of the case study method?
3. How can a case study researcher *collect data* or materials for his or her research?
4. What are the two *case selection methods*? Try to use the two case selection methods to investigate the following research question: "Why did the United States invade Iraq in 2003?" Hint: the United States was involved in two wars with Iraq after the cold war.

Recommended Resources:

American Political Science Association's (APSA) Qualitative and Multi-method Research Section/ Consortium on Qualitative Research Methods (CQRM) (www.maxwell.syr.edu/moynihan_cqrm.aspx)

George, Alexander and Andrew Bennett. 2005. *Case Studies and Theory Development in Social Sciences.* Cambridge, MA: MIT Press.

Notes

1 Mearsheimer (1990) predicted in his article that after the Cold War, Europe would again experience fierce great power competition fuelled by the power and fear of a rising Germany (back to the future).

2 Huntington 1993.

3 Fukuyama (1992) argued that the Western liberal democracy was the end point of mankind's ideological evolution and the final form of human government after the Cold War.

4 "Asian Exceptionalism" is based on the "Asian values" debate in the 1990s in which Asian pundits, officials, and scholars argued for unique cultural and political practices in Asia. Western scholars criticized that the "Asian values" argument was aimed to justify authoritarian regimes in Asia. Here, I used the term to refer to a unique international policy practice in Asia through multilateral institutions after the Cold War.

5 Comfrey and Lee 1992: 217.

6 Eckstein 1975.

7 Mill 1862.

8 George and Bennett 2005.

9 Bennett 2004.

10 George and Bennett 2005.

11 Bennett 2004; Collier and Mahoney 1996; King et al. 1994.

12 Grieco 2002.

13 The anarchic system means that there is no overarching authority to protect states in world politics. Therefore, states need to protect themselves.

14 "Security dilemma" is a key concept to understand how in an anarchic international system security-seeking states still end up in competition and war. It refers to the situation that "many of the means by which a state tries to increase its security decrease the security of others" (Jervis 1978: 169).

15 Keohane and Martin 1995.

16 The notion of relative gains vs. absolute gains is rooted in the great debate between neorealism and neoliberalism in the 1980s and the early 1990s. While neoliberals suggest that a state will consider what it can get from cooperation (absolute gains), neorealists argue that a state will be more concerned about how much it can get compared to others (relative gains). The concern about relative gains, according to neorealists, is one of the major obstacles for cooperation in international politics. For the "relative gains vs. absolute gains" debate, see Baldwin 1993.

17 Ruggie 1998.

18 Rourke and Boyer 2010: G2.
19 Adler and Barnett 1998.
20 Acharya 2001.
21 Hemmer and Katzenstein 2002.
22 McDermott 2001.

CHAPTER 4

Field Research

Zhuang Ethnic Identity and the Chinese State

Katherine Palmer Kaup

GETTING CURIOUS: WHO ARE THE ZHUANG? ARE THEY A CHALLENGE TO CHINESE COMMUNIST PARTY RULE?

The year I began planning my first field study in China, well over a million people died in bloody ethnic violence across the globe. The 1990s were particularly wracked with ethnic warfare, as the Soviet Union fractured along ethnic lines, Yugoslavia saw widespread ethnic genocide, millions fled their homes in Rwanda to escape slaughter by machete, and ethnic violence continued to rage across parts of the Middle East.

Ethnic protests occurred across China as well, though few, if any, substantive studies of ethnic politics in China had been written since the 1970s. With the collapse of the Soviet Union, Western journalists and human rights groups began to report on increased ethnic tensions in China's northwest province of Xinjiang, as the Chinese Communist Party (CCP) tried to keep the Muslim minorities there from demanding independence like their counterparts had in bordering Kyrgyzstan, Kazahkstan, Uzbekistan, and Tajikistan.

I had always been fascinated by the CCP's propaganda machine, and its efforts to foster national loyalties while downplaying ethnic differences. I wanted to understand why ethnic violence had erupted in Xinjiang and why the government was cracking down so harshly on religious groups in the region. The topic seemed imminently important, not just from an intellectual perspective, but because real people were involved in the conflict and desperately needed a solution.

A number of very real obstacles to conducting such research immediately became apparent, however, as I started exploring various research topics and strategies; not the least of which was the Chinese government's near absolute refusal to allow outside researchers into the region. Many Chinese researchers had been arrested for studying less controversial topics, and I was worried about my own physical safety. The question was important and someone needed to reveal the details of what was happening in Xinjiang: I just wasn't willing to take the risks required. Even putting aside the physical dangers, I would have had to master at least one of the languages spoken in the region. It had taken me five years, including a solid year of full-time immersion study in Taiwan, to be able to use Mandarin Chinese well, and I did not relish the prospect of starting a new language before I could even delve into the topic.

When language challenges, political sensitivities, and restrictions on access barred my studying the Uighur group in Xinijiang, my adviser suggested "How about the Zhuang?" I remember thinking "the *who?*" All I knew about the Zhuang, in large part because that was all that had been published about them at the time, was that they were China's largest minority group, had been given one of five provincial-level autonomous governments, and were no different from the Han majority. Though there were only a handful of references in English to the Zhuang, a number of questions immediately became apparent: Why did the Chinese government claim that they were a unique nationality with a unique and rich cultural history if Western scholars contended that they were no different from the Han? If they *were* really no different from the Han, why were they given the right to self-government, particularly over such a large territory as Guangxi Province? How had official recognition and self-government affected their ethnic identity, and, in turn, their interactions with the state? And, finally, if they were different, how, and why have outside scholars had such a mistaken understanding of them? Though I would need to read everything I could get my hands on about the Zhuang in English and Chinese, given the conflicting information available, I was clearly going to need to go to Zhuang areas to understand the situation for myself. I needed to develop a strategy for fieldwork in Zhuang territory.

THE RESEARCH STRATEGY: WHAT IS FIELDWORK?

So what exactly is **fieldwork**, and why use it? What makes fieldwork unique is that it involves on-site and in-depth gathering of information from human subjects in their everyday settings, where their place in the surroundings informs the study just as much as the fieldworker's questions.[1] In other words, the researcher needs to use fieldwork when written archival materials, surveys, phone interviews or interviews outside of the area alone won't provide the answers needed. In contrast to *experimental studies* that involve controlled or semi-controlled experiments, fieldwork entails studying human subjects in their natural environment, ideally without influencing their responses during the fieldwork process. Fieldwork is required to gain an understanding of the complex interplay of social interactions, geography, resource management, and other factors that may influence how the people being studied are impacted, and in turn impact, these diverse factors. Fieldwork can produce nuanced findings on sensitive topics generally not available through **quantitative methods** that rely on quantifiable datasets or surveys. Properly conducted fieldwork avoids the hazard of forcing preconceived notions on subjects through survey questionnaires. What is observed in the field is often quite different from what respondents self-report in surveys or interviews. I heard, for example, time and again from Zhuang that a common language is what unifies and in part defines the Zhuang. I also regularly heard from Zhuang scholars that the Zhuang are a unified group with common traits and that Zhuang in Guangxi and Yunnan work together to promote Zhuang cultural development. Had I relied solely on surveys or even on extended interviews, the story would have ended there. Only through extended observations in the field did I discover that Zhuang actually often have trouble communicating with one another across their smaller "branch" divisions (best conceived of as sub-ethnic categories) and that clear divisions exist across provincial boundaries, thanks to strong regional sentiment that often overpowers ethnic sentiment. These divisions were so apparent that I concluded they prevent the Zhuang from effectively mobilizing to strengthen their collective bargaining position vis-à-vis the state. This idea became a key element in my final thesis. Not only were many Zhuang unaware of these issues (particularly given how few of them travel across provincial boundaries) but others had political motivations for downplaying internal divisions among the Zhuang and would not have shared that information through surveys or interviews alone.

"Field research" can incorporate an array of methods, including **surveys, interviews, direct observation, participant observation**, and collection of written materials for **content, textual,** or **discourse analysis**. Surveys ask respondents questions that can be quantified and tabulated. While some surveys might be administered through mailings or over the phone, in developing countries with poor infrastructure, the surveys often have to be administered in person, in the field. Written material can be analyzed in a variety of ways, including looking for how often and in what ways particular topics are covered in the media, government documents, or other outlets: a process known as **content analysis**. Close analysis of text (**textual analysis**) and the discourse used in speeches or published materials (**discourse analysis**) can reveal changes in attitudes or may provide clues as to why a particular policy evolved at a particular time or why a particular event unfolded as it did. Many written materials can only be found in the field, and after reading through them carefully, the scholar may decide to tweak the original research design or pursue new questions that arise from findings revealed by written sources. Participant observation is a technique in which the researcher observes subjects for extended (though unspecified) periods of time through participating in some role in the community. A scholar studying non-profit organizations' leadership might, for example, contact a battered women's shelter, explain the project to the director, and volunteer to work at the shelter while she observes the organizers' work firsthand. Through prolonged observations, the scholar may discover issues, interpersonal dynamics, and challenges that those involved may not even recognize.

Direct observation may also be employed. Direct observation generally does not require extended time in the field and the researcher has a specific phenomenon he or she hopes to observe directly. Direct observation is designed to test hypotheses whereas participant observation often does not begin with a hypothesis (though sometimes it does) but rather lets new research questions emerge from what is observed in the field. Both participant observation and direct observation may be overt (with the subjects understanding they are the object of study) or covert (with the subjects unaware they are being studied). When I started my fieldwork, I presented myself as a visiting scholar studying Zhuang culture. In addition to those I interviewed formally, I also encountered and made friends with a wide array of people during my seven months in China. In observing their interactions and discussing issues with them in a wide variety of informal and social settings, I discovered new questions that needed to be explored in order to answer my initial research questions.

I wanted to figure out if the Zhuang really were different from the Han Chinese, or if they at least *believed* they were different. I was hoping to see whether Zhuang interpreted government policies, or their own political needs, differently than non-Zhuang do. Do they, or do they not, pose unique political challenges for the Chinese government? The Chinese government carefully censors published work on such topics, however. I needed to ask people specifically about these issues personally to avoid government distortions. I immediately faced a common problem in fieldwork, however: my very presence could easily distort my findings because once people knew I was researching the Zhuang, they were more likely to think and talk about Zhuang issues with me than they might be otherwise. Those with vested interests in demonstrating how important the Zhuang are (Zhuang scholars, ethnic affairs officials, tourist industry professionals, etc.) were likely to seek me out and might distort my understanding of how Zhuang generally view identity issues. I needed to observe dynamics within villages and cities to see if ethnic issues seemed relevant to citizens when they were not being asked to reflect on them through leading interview questions.

Fieldwork often falls into two broad categories: studies that seek to *generate new theories* from empirical findings and those seeking to *test existing theories* and hypothesis through *verification* in the field. Mine fell somewhere in between. I left for China with two completely contradictory explanations of who the Zhuang were, one supplied by Western scholars who doubted whether they really constitute a unique ethnic group at all, and one supplied by Chinese sources that stressed their long and rich history as a unique people. I wanted to test both theories, and in the process discovered new theories for explaining how government policy helped shape a new corps of Zhuang activists who adopted the government definition of their ethnicity.

There are a number of key issues that any field researcher faces as she develops her research strategy. Two of the most important decisions are site selection and deciding on a specific strategy for gathering information. Like all scholars, when I was selecting my site/s, I had to consider a number of factors. Depending on the research question and the *variables* being explored, the researcher may need to consider demographics, socioeconomic makeup in the region, geography, transportation access, or the political history of the locality.

Careful site selection is extremely important and if not properly done, can alter findings dramatically. To examine the impact of village elections on democratization in China, for example, a scholar obviously needs to go to the countryside. But should the site be in a prosperous region that has had conflict-free elections for decades, or in a remote village in a poverty-affected county that has only more recently introduced elections? Do existing studies suggest that elections are most influenced by levels of education and wealth in a specific area? If so, the scholar may choose a single site with a prosperous, well-educated population to test whether the prevailing theory holds true in China. Or perhaps the scholar will opt to conduct interviews in two different sites, one quite prosperous and one very poor. Researchers need to think carefully about what other factors might influence or alter findings—does the distance of the site, rich or poor, from the nation's capital matter, for example? How about if one of the sites had a negative experience with elections when they were first introduced and the others' experiences have consistently been positive? There's lots to think about! The scholar needs to be as well read and informed about the region as possible to make a good selection.

Some field studies focus on a single site, explaining patterns of behavior by providing rich details about the numerous factors that contribute to that behavior.[2] I could have studied only one rural county in Guangxi, for example, and noted how Zhuang rarely appealed to specifically Zhuang needs when seeking government subsidies or preferential policies. That would have been an interesting observation in itself, and I could have perhaps even argued that similar patterns were likely to be found in other rural areas across Guangxi, noting that further field studies would need to verify that hypothesis. I opted to study several sites, however, to identify variations in Zhuang consciousness influenced by urban–rural divides, educational divides, and provincial divides. In so doing, I discovered that rural Zhuang typically are less conscious than urban Zhuang of how their ethnicity influences their political needs. Many researchers opt for a *comparative study* looking at several sites to find differences among them by either selecting *most similar sites* or *most different sites* and *controlling* for *variables*. In the most similar site comparative method, scholars identify a variable (level of development, for example) that they think may influence behavior. They then choose two sites that are as closely similar as possible in all ways *except* for level of development. This then allows them to argue that level of development is the cause for any differences they discover in behavior. In the most different sites approach, in contrast, the scholar looks for sites that are extremely different *except* for their levels of development.

These comparative approaches can be useful for teasing out the relative importance of a particular variable in influencing behavior, but can be limiting in focusing in on only a few variables and therefore missing nuances that could emerge through a more open-ended design. Selecting multiple sites does not necessarily require comparison across them, but could rather help explain a single case or question, in what one scholar calls a *one-case multi-field-site approach.*[3] This was the method I used. In order to address my single question of whether Zhuang identity influences policy and political behavior, I selected a number of separate sites in order to see how these questions played out in different provinces, rural and urban areas, and in areas with different levels of economic development. Selecting more than one field site, though time-consuming and sometimes expensive, can help minimize the risk that interview respondents at one site might not prove helpful or that what one hopes to observe at a particular site in the end is not present.

In addition to selecting the site/s well, scholars also need to enter the field with a strategy for gathering their information. Thorough *preparation* before entering the field is crucial: Scholars read as widely as possible both theoretical studies that might relate to their research question and empirical studies of the locality where they will be based. Researchers will likely use a full toolkit of strategies, including interviews, observation, and gathering of written documents. Those using interviews have to think carefully about the best **interview design**. There are a number of different types of interviews that can be used. Structured and semi-structured interviews both raise a series of specific interview questions, usually in a relatively quiet place that has been reserved to conduct the interviews.

In a **structured interview**, the interviewer raises a specific set of pre-formulated questions, often in a specific order that are usually **closed-ended** questions, or questions that can be answered briefly with a specific answer. For example, "Did your mother ever spank you when you were growing up?" A semi-structured interview allows the interviewer to raise more open-ended questions that allow the respondents more room to respond as they would like, and allow the interviewer to ask follow-up questions that arise from the respondent's comments. "What kind of relationship did you have with your parents growing up?" would be an open-ended question.

While the interviewer usually schedules structured or semi-structured interviews, **unstructured** interviews occur more surreptitiously. The researcher may literally bump into someone on the street and strike up a casual conversation. The researcher can then try to gear the conversation towards questions the interviewer finds interesting. Some of my best findings came from unstructured interviews. While attending a traditional outdoor Zhuang festival in one village, I happened to stand next to a woman dressed in a Zhuang ethnic outfit and overheard her talking with her friend. When I asked her what language she was speaking, she replied "Nong." "Aren't the Nong a branch of the Zhuang?" I followed up. "No," she replied, "the Nong are Nong and the Zhuang are Zhuang." This brief encounter was important because the Chinese government officially classifies several small groups as "branches" of the Zhuang, though these citizens sometimes do not accept the Zhuang classification and remain loyal to their smaller ethnic affiliation. Once noting this in an unstructured interview, I found evidence of it in follow-up interviews across Zhuang territory.

In the course of interviews and observations, new research questions may emerge or theories that previously seemed irrelevant may prove crucial in explaining the question. The first few days or weeks in the field may be highly exploratory, and depend on open-ended questioning and observation, as well as assessing what *access* the scholar can garner to explore the question further. Constantly refining both the research question itself and the research design, often leads to more exciting and significant conclusions than could be anticipated at the beginning of a project.

ISSUES WITH THIS RESEARCH STRATEGY

Fieldwork is often not only beneficial, but absolutely *essential,* when the issue being studied requires subtleties in interpretation or when dealing with a politically sensitive topic that leads to biased or censored reporting and analysis. Surveys often miss nuances needed to understand complex issues such as identity and motivations for collective mobilization. Moreover, though surveys are increasingly used in China, they cannot be conducted from the United States. Survey techniques can be quite different in China, and rely on scholars conducting surveys in the field.[4] For example, many rural respondents in China have never taken a survey, are distrustful of them, and unwilling to put their answers in writing. Many also have trouble interpreting the surveys due to low levels of education. There are a host of other challenges, including insuring that the person or household given the survey actually takes the survey rather than a proxy. Many of these issues can be addressed by experienced surveyors conducting the surveys in person in the field.

Though a key benefit of fieldwork is that the scholar can interpret nuances in interviewees' responses, this can also be one of the main challenges or methodological risks of conducting fieldwork. How can the scholar ensure that his or her interpretation is valid, particularly when there are no "objective" or quantifiable means to measure the findings? Scholars must provide robust support for their analyses and consider a wide variety of factors when interpreting their findings. Two scholars conducting fieldwork at the same site, even interviewing the same subjects, may reach two very different conclusions. Though there are clearly discrepancies among quantitative studies as well, two scholars using the same dataset and same statistical model arguably have a greater likelihood of reaching the same conclusions than do two field researchers.

Fieldwork is often the only method of studying the complexity of relationships within a particular site, but it can be difficult to determine how well findings can be *generalized*. I may have found high levels of Zhuang activism among urban Zhuang elite, for example, but was that true just in Yunnan? Were similar trends apparent in Guangxi? What about in the nation's capital? By comparing more and more sites, it may be possible to become more precise in identifying key variables that influence patterns of behavior (i.e. Zhuang in the cities that are not in an autonomous region may ironically be more active), but it is impossible to study an infinite number of sites. There is an ongoing debate among scholars over whether it is best to use a large number of cases for greater breadth or a smaller number of cases to achieve more depth.

On a very practical level, one of the primary costs of opting to conduct field research is, well, costs. Financial costs of conducting fieldwork can be particularly high if you need to travel long distances to your site, or if you need to be in the field for extended periods of time. Fieldwork in China obviously requires an international flight, hotels, and local transportation. In addition, visas are expensive, and there are a host of required, but often unanticipated costs, including gifts for hosts, meals for interviewees, translation services, etc.

Though fieldwork can provide rich and nuanced findings, the method itself can sometimes distort findings if the researcher is not alert to several potential problems. Field researchers must be on the constant lookout for how their own presence and role in the research process might impact their findings and must work to avoid *observational bias*. I was trying to determine whether ethnicity played an important role in how people labeled "Zhuang" understood themselves, their place in society, and their political decision-making. Wouldn't the very presence of a foreign scholar studying the Zhuang lead people to discuss their ethnicity and reflect on it in ways they might not ordinarily? This was particularly problematic for me as the regions where I worked had not seen a foreigner in decades, so I attracted a great deal of attention.

Findings can also be distorted by overreliance on particularly helpful sources, whether those be written sources or a few key contacts who lead the researcher to explore questions in a particular direction. For example, Zhuang who cared most about ethnic issues would be most likely to spend time discussing them with me, and their views might be overrepresented in the conclusions I drew. The field researcher must also be careful not to impose theoretical tools and categories inappropriate for the unique context of the field. My first few weeks in the field, for example, I asked several interviewees if Zhuang had any particular political interests different from Han Chinese. Very few understood the concept of "interests" much less how these interests might be uniquely Zhuang. If I had employed a rigid set of closed-ended questions in structured interviews, I would have erroneously concluded that Zhuang "interests" are not the least important. Instead, I had to use a number of different questions to get at the concept, and avoided using **structured** interview questions that would give respondents only limited options for responding. Though Zhuang peasants didn't understand the concept of "interests," they clearly had a number of issues that were important to them and which were impacted by their ethnicity.

There are no hard and fast rules or easy fixes for ensuring the researcher's role in the gathering of material does not influence or distort findings, but being constantly aware of this possibility is important as you shape your research design and carry out the project.

THE LITERATURE REVIEW

When I first decided to research the Zhuang, I literally knew only that they were the largest minority group in all of China and that the central government had awarded them a provincial-level autonomous government of their own. I knew that many other minorities, particularly the Uighurs and the Tibetans, had had violent run-ins with central authorities, and that there was an active separatist movement among many Tibetans and Uighurs. But what about the Zhuang? Who were they? Why did the central government grant them their own autonomous government? Did they ever challenge the government? If so, on what grounds, and if not, why not? Had other scholars already written on this topic? I needed to shape my initial interest into a valid research question, and could only do that by first learning more about the topic and what other scholars were saying: a "literature review" in many ways is just a term to describe this process.

It was quite apparent as soon as I began my literature review that my study would be filling a gap in the literature since no Western scholar had ever published on the Zhuang. But, frankly, so what? Why should anyone care about the Zhuang necessarily? I had to show why the Zhuang themselves were important and figure out how to link a study of the Zhuang to broader political science questions. My literature review was four pronged. First, I tried to unearth English-language materials on the Zhuang, Guangxi, and the creation of the Guangxi Zhuang Autonomous Region in 1958. Next, I read English-language studies on minority policy in China, and how other Chinese groups interacted with the Chinese state, looking for clues that might explain the Zhuang. I discovered new anthropological field studies on several of China's fifty-five minorities, but none that addressed how state policy and ethnic identity interacted.[5] I was getting closer to seeing how a study of the Zhuang could contribute to the political science literature, though I still had no answers to my initial questions.

I also read English-language theories on how ethnic groups develop and what motivates ethnic groups to mobilize politically, sometimes even violently. Here I saw four primary schools of thought used to explain ethnic identity and mobilization, known as the primordialist, subjectivist, instrumentalist, and structuralist interpretations. Briefly stated, the primordialists contend that there are specific "givens" such as a common origin or common cultural practices that define ethnic boundaries. The subjectivists note that it is not so much the actual commonalities that bind people into groups, but rather the people's subjective commitment to them. In other words, people may share a common origin, but if they are not subjectively aware of this common origin, it matters little. Instrumentalists argue that primordial ties and subjective sentiment are important, but that the strength of primordial sentiments and subjective loyalties varies among individuals, places, and time and can be manipulated by individuals. Ethnic elites or government officials can rally citizens to action by convincing them that they share ethnic ties and thus specific rights. Finally, structuralists agree with instrumentalists that primordial sentiments are malleable, but structuralists believe larger societal changes influence changes in ethnic attitudes rather than individuals' activism.

When I left for my fieldwork, I was familiar with these four main approaches to explaining ethnic identity, but did not know which would help explain the Zhuang case best. It was not until *after* I finished my fieldwork that I realized a major flaw in each of these primary approaches. None of the approaches recognized that the relative importance of each explanatory model varies over time. When the Communist Party first seized power in 1949, primordial divisions among the people living in Guangxi and Yunnan limited the development of a greater Zhuang consciousness. Through careful instrumentalist strategies, the government consciously campaigned to strengthen greater Zhuang identity in order to convince all of the groups that they were being represented by one of their own under the government's Regional Autonomy policy. Structural changes in the People's Republic of China from 1950–2000, including economic and political developments, led the government to lose interest in the Zhuang just as the Zhuang's subjectivist loyalties strengthened, leading the newly created Zhuang elite to feel abandoned by the Chinese state in the 1990s.

My initial literature review also entailed exploring Chinese language sources on the Zhuang, though very few were available in the United States. Chinese-language materials are much easier to search for and obtain now than when I began working on the Zhuang. In the 1990s, there were no full-text databases available in Chinese, no easy Googling options in Chinese, and even library catalogs were only beginning to be digitized. I relied largely on the Chinese-language *Encyclopedia of the Zhuang* until I arrived on site to complete a review of the Chinese language literature on Zhuang ethnicity and minority policy.

DOING THE STUDY: COLLECTING THE DATA AND DOING THE ANALYSIS

Completing the literature review was just one of many steps needed to get to the field. Students conducting research involving human subjects, including interview subjects, will need to apply for approval from their school's **Institutional Review Board** (see also Chapters 10 and 12). Among other tasks, Institutional Review Boards assure that all research is conducted ethically, and with as little risk to the subjects as possible. I also had to obtain Chinese government permits for conducting research in China. Depending on their research topic, some China scholars opt not to apply for official research approval. Though some of my shorter trips to China to visit established contacts have proven quite informative for various research projects, I would not venture a full-scale research project requiring extensive interviewing, time in the field, or interactions with strangers without official approval. Official approval and the required hosting organization provide the scholar and those whom she contacts, a degree of protection against government sanctions.

Perhaps I should start with the conclusions I drew from my fieldwork, and then work backward to show how I arrived at them. By the end of my seven months in China, I had rejected both prevailing understandings in the West of the Zhuang as no different from the Han and Chinese official depictions of the Zhuang as a unified people with a long history. The truth was somewhere in the middle, and had been radically shaped by the interplay of government policy and ethnic identities over the last seventy years. On the eve of the Communist takeover in 1949, areas today labeled "Zhuang" were inhabited by diverse peoples who referred to themselves by a variety of names, spoke different languages, and had different cultural practices. They were clearly different from the Han, but shared no sense of common identity.

Before fully understanding how complex ethnic relations were in the southwest and before even seizing power, the CCP announced its regional autonomy policy, promising all minorities the right to govern themselves. Over 400 groups demanded autonomy once the CCP took power. In an effort to integrate these diverse peoples into a unified state and to make good on its autonomy promises in a manageable manner, the Chinese Communist Party grouped several smaller groups into a single Zhuang category and awarded them the provincial-sized Guangxi Zhuang Autonomous Region. Once having done so, the government had to convince these people that they belonged to a single group and were being represented by "one of their own" as promised. The government launched an intense propaganda campaign to build Zhuang ethnic consciousness and pride and stamp out alternative histories of Zhuang subgroups. Zhuang now largely conceive of themselves as such, though their political mobilization is limited by internal divisions including sub-ethnic, urban–rural, educational, and regional divides. That's a long way to come from knowing almost nothing about the group the day I arrived on site!

I arrived in Yunnan Province in January 1995, with an open-ended, exploratory research design. I knew I would have to be flexible, because I had no idea what access I might be granted (or denied!) or exactly what I might discover, given the dearth of written material available. I was able to obtain approval to conduct research in Yunnan before leaving the United States thanks to the University of Virginia's institutional exchange program with the Yunnan Nationalities Institute (YNI), but I needed Guangxi government approval to begin fieldwork in Guangxi. The process was delayed for nearly four months because the government considers minority issues politically sensitive and because my field site was in counties closed to foreigners, bordering the still militarized Chinese–Vietnamese border. This delay, so aggravating at the time, ended up aiding my research immensely because it gave me time I had initially not intended to use in Yunnan and its capital city of Kunming. I ended up discovering key differences between Zhuang identities in Yunnan and Guangxi.

At YNI, my research approach was primarily participant observation. My role was Visiting Scholar at the Institute's Ethnic Research Center, and through this avenue I met with both ethnically Zhuang scholars and those studying the Zhuang. I became friends with several Zhuang, some of whom had moved to the city from the countryside recently and others who had been in the capital for several decades, government officials, waitresses, teachers, students, and musicians. In addition to observing their interactions and listening for any reference to specifically Zhuang issues (what those might be I wasn't quite sure, but I was listening for them!), I also used a completely unstructured interview approach. At several meals, for example, my contacts mentioned different officials' ethnic backgrounds. I would then pay particular attention to the conversation, gauging others' reactions and comments, and then pipe in with some of my own questions if the conversation lagged. I was interested in whether Zhuang felt they needed to be represented by one of their own in government offices, so I might ask "Oh? Director Peng is a Yao nationality? I thought he was from a Zhuang county?" The response often proved quite informative, and provided a completely different set of responses than I might have obtained through a more structured interview. Some I observed gave angry explanations on how the official had risen to power because Zhuang "didn't assert their rights" while others gave different explanations on the officials' rise (education, personal connections, a particular set of events, etc) that I would not have thought to include in a survey or closed-ended interview questions. It can be challenging when using participant observation to get an *unbiased sampling* of subjects, but I tried to meet with people from a wide variety of backgrounds, educational levels, ages, and occupations.

I took copious **fieldnotes**, also known as an *observational log*, during my time in the field, never knowing exactly what might be important at some later point as patterns began to emerge and my thesis took shape. It was important to note as much as possible about my subjects (gender, age, occupation, place of birth and residence, educational levels, etc) as well as to note the context in which the observation or interview occurred. I would then record what I heard or saw, followed by a brief analysis of the observation or interview. In Kunming, I noticed two common responses to my questions about "who are the Zhuang? How are the Zhuang any different from other groups?" Most urbanites who were not Zhuang first repeated the official government line that the "Zhuang are the largest minority group in China" but then told me that the Zhuang weren't really much different from the Han at all and weren't at all worth researching. A bit frightening to hear, as I sat over 6,000 miles from home with a great deal of energy and finances already invested in doing just that!

Almost all Zhuang living in Kunming, however, had much clearer answers to my questions and emphasized both that the Zhuang were culturally different from the Han, and internally unified. A number of Zhuang scholars told me that Zhuang culture was best preserved in the Wenshan Zhuang-Miao Autonomous Prefecture in eastern Yunnan. "If you want to understand the real Zhuang, you should study them in Yunnan, not in Guangxi where they've abandoned their true ethnic culture," I was told. I didn't quite know what to make of these various comments early in the research process, but as my work progressed, I recognized a key divide between ethnic identity in Yunnan and Guangxi, a divide that proved politically relevant as it limited Zhuangs' ability to cooperate.

Committed to capitalizing on new opportunities, I took up a Zhuang photographer's offer to accompany him to rural Wenshan for three weeks on a photo shoot. One of the most important unexpected findings there was the important role that *zhixi* or "branch" divisions play in self-identification among those officially designated Zhuang. Though officially classified as "Zhuang" (with the label clearly stamped on their official identification cards), most people in Wenshan affiliated more closely with three smaller groupings, the Sha, Nong, or Tu. Interestingly, Zhuang scholars in Kunming, including the one accompanying me in Wenshan, emphasized that all these branches can understand each other and think of themselves as Zhuang first and members of a *zhixi* only secondarily. But when we encountered members of different *zhixi*, my colleague actually often had to switch to Mandarin Chinese to communicate. Some peasants clearly identified *only* with their branch affiliation and did not conceive of themselves as Zhuang at all. Had I not been on the ground to observe these interactions, I would have been misled even by interviewing those in Kunming.

My time in Wenshan also revealed that Zhuang living in the countryside retained several "objective markers" of ethnicity (unique clothing, preservation of traditional cultural festivals, monolingual use of the Zhuang language) though their level of Zhuang consciousness seemed to lag behind Zhuang scholars in Kunming. I tried to get at this question through both observations and a variety of interview formats. I used both semi-structured and unstructured interviews. I conducted some of these interviews in *individual settings* and others in *group settings*. There are pros and cons to both approaches. In group settings, respondents often jointly came up with ideas they may not have had on their own. Though this was at times useful, particularly if I was trying to obtain factual information that may have required collective memory, it proved problematic when I was trying to decide if individuals held certain nuanced views on their ethnicity. Another factor I had to consider was how individuals might be reluctant to share controversial views in a group setting on issues as politically sensitive as challenging state discourse on minorities.

Throughout my fieldwork I sought opportunities to *cross-verify* my findings. Because one source indicated something, did not necessarily make it so. My colleagues' insistence that Zhuang all speak the same language is a perfect example. Sometimes this cross-verification can come from written sources, further interviews, or personal observations. I read media reports on the early decision to recognize the Zhuang, as well as the minutes of several meetings debating the decision, and followed these with interviews of several scholars actually involved in the fieldwork and classification campaign in the 1950s. Only by approaching the issues from a variety of angles and sources, could I discover important differences and consistencies that helped explain the puzzle of why the Zhuang were recognized when they clearly were not making the demand themselves or in a unified voice.

I also used written materials throughout my fieldwork, constantly searching for new data and views that would inform my study. I used content analysis and discourse analysis to see how government propaganda had changed over time and how that might explain shifts in ethnic consciousness apparent during my interviews. I also looked for statistical reports on socioeconomic indicators in different areas, and was able to demonstrate pronounced differences in Zhuang areas and Han-dominated areas. I found unpublished drafts of local histories and diaries from Zhuang areas.

Lessons to Be Learned

First, perhaps most importantly of all, I have learned through doing fieldwork the importance of remaining flexible and being willing to adapt my research design to fit new discoveries, opportunities, and obstacles. Relatedly, I've learned not to panic when things don't work out exactly as planned. Taking copious notes allowed me to make sense of what I had learned as I added new information that enabled me to interpret my initial unexplained, confusing, or contradictory discoveries. I've learned the importance of reading as widely as possible before starting my fieldwork for possible research models, but have gained confidence in starting my fieldwork without a fully fleshed out set of specific questions or a detailed schedule of interviews and appointments. Fieldwork is as much a craft as a science, and I found that I learned and got better as I gained some experience.

I also learned how important it is to choose a topic that can feasibly be researched in the time available, with the access available, and at the particular fieldsite. I started off wanting to research Xinjiang, but realized that the political risks, restrictions on access, and language barriers were going to bar me from answering the questions I wanted to address. During the course of my fieldwork in Guangxi, I discovered a number of additional questions that could have been integrated into my book (including cross-border relations among ethnically similar groups in Vietnam, Laos, and Thailand, for example) but would have slowed the completion of my project. There's always time for a follow-up fieldtrip, and it's not necessary to have all of the answers before offering valuable insights.

I also learned to weigh whether the question I was researching merited the risks and time required to complete the project. Any researcher needs to consider this question, whether it be for a single reflection piece for class, an honors research project, or a full book-length study. But this question perhaps becomes even more urgent when considering both large financial costs of travel and field expenses as well as the political risks I subjected myself to and those I studied.

Though fieldwork can be challenging, frightening, and emotionally draining, there is little more rewarding.

Interested to Know More about the Study Discussed in this Chapter?

Consult the research publication:

Kaup, Katherine Palmer. 2000. *Creating the Zhuang: Ethnic Politics in China.* Boulder, CO: Lynne Rienner.

Exercises and Discussion Questions:

1. What are some important guidelines for selecting your *fieldsite*? What guidelines are available for determining how many sites to use?
2. How did the scholar in this chapter remain flexible and willing to redesign *field strategies* without losing a solid theoretical framework?
3. Are there *methods* that could have been used instead of fieldwork or to *supplement* the fieldwork for this study?
4. What might be some ways to prevent *observational bias* in this study? Can observational bias ever be completely eliminated? If not, is fieldwork still a useful political science research method?

Recommended Resources:

Congressional–Executive Commission on China (www.cecc.gov): See particularly the Virtual Academy resources and the 2005 Annual Report Special Focus on China's Minorities and Government Implementation of the Regional Ethnic Autonomy Law (www.cecc.gov/pages/annualRpt/annual Rpt05/2005_3a_minorities.php).

Notes

1 Read 2010.
2 Hinton 1984.
3 Heimer 2006.
4 Manion 2010.
5 Gladney 1991; Harrell 1995.

CHAPTER 5

Interviews

What Are the Pathways to Human Rights Activism?

Kristina Thalhammer

▌ GETTING CURIOUS: WHO STANDS UP TO DICTATORS?

In the 1970s and early 1980s, military regimes in some Latin American states systematically tortured and murdered thousands of people and seemed to be getting away with it. How could this be happening in my lifetime? Didn't the world's response to the Holocaust teach states not to do this? Who could stop this abuse?

The military junta that controlled Argentina from 1976 to 1983 authorized the kidnapping of tens of thousands of ordinary people, including students, who were taken from their homes, schools, and workplaces and never heard from again. Those suspected of disloyalty were denied their rights to legal processes and never had a chance to prove their innocence. Held in hundreds of clandestine prisons (we later learned), the unofficial prisoners included pregnant women, whose newborns were sometimes placed in the homes of their captors and raised by the very people who had killed their mothers. Nearly all prisoners were brutally tortured then executed. Some were drugged and thrown into the Atlantic Ocean or Rio de la Plata from helicopters; their bodies washed ashore in neighboring countries or were never found. Virtually everyone in Argentina was afraid to criticize the regime, lest they be next to disappear. Yet, in this context emerged human rights activists, who demonstrated against these abuses in broad daylight, right in the heart of Buenos Aires.

Demanding fair treatment for those "disappeared," demonstrators drew domestic and international attention to the abuses and helped apply pressure on the military junta that eventually led to a dramatic decline in the number of disappearances. Some scholars credit them both with having brought about the international pressure that ended the brutality and with keeping open a small but highly visible public space within Argentina that became crucial in ending the disappearances, helping the country return to democracy, and in the past few years finally bringing perpetrators to justice.

The nature of the disappearances, the fact that the abuses went on for years and the generally passive response of most Argentineans to state agents seizing innocent people and refusing to reveal their fates, reminded me of my own family's history and the unanswered questions it inspired. My mother was a child in Germany when Hitler came to power. Her family survived the period of Nazi repression by behaving as most other Christian families did: Not speaking out against the regime, even as Jewish, Roma, and other purported "state enemies" were rounded up and sent to death camps. While my grandparents took risks to help one victim, they did not risk taking a public stance against the Nazi policies. Knowing that critics of the Nazis could also be apprehended, should they have done more? Would I have acted any differently? Argentine resisters did not back down in the face of grave risk. How were such people different from the rest of us? This final question became the core of my research agenda.

Despite grave risks, the Argentine resisters documented and publicized the abuses, filed *writs of habeas corpus*, and urged international figures (ranging from the Pope to rock stars) and even schoolchildren to pressure the Argentine ruling junta into stopping the disappearances and bringing justice to those assumed to be held in clandestine prisons. The most famous of the Argentine human rights groups was the Madres (Mothers) de Plaza de Mayo. This group of middle-aged women, wearing distinctive white headscarves, gained international visibility by holding weekly public marches in Buenos Aires' most popular square, right across from the presidential palace. These women, whose adolescent and young adult children had disappeared, first met as they visited government offices looking for their loved ones. After months of fruitless probing, some united and decided to demonstrate, trying to draw attention to the disappearances. Others joined them as they came to march every Thursday near the presidential palace. They first asked, and then demanded that those who disappeared be proven to be alive. The Madres continued their protests throughout the worst periods of repression, even as they received death threats, were attacked by police, and after a number of the group's founders also disappeared, were tortured, and killed. Despite violent tactics used against them, the Madres and members of other Argentine human rights groups never resorted to violence. They faced the well-armed and demonstrably ruthless regime, armed only with raw courage and one another's presence.

How could anyone face such brutality and keep coming back? I first attributed this bravery to "maternal love." Perhaps women can't help but risk everything to protect their children. An early account of the Madres[1] asserted this gender-based explanation as well. But if that was the case, why hadn't *all* the mothers of those taken prisoner joined the protesters? Seven other human rights groups also worked within that repressive context, trying to stop the regime from terrorizing its own population. Those groups included men and women, including many *not* related to the missing. My early, simple hypothesis that protestors were women made fearless by maternal instinct or family bonds explained neither why only some affected mothers joined the human rights movement nor why some who had not lost loved ones risked everything to fight the abuses. Members of all the human rights groups were targeted by the regime. Why did they risk action while so many others remained silent?

Eventually the military lost control of the country, brought down by its own incompetence and powerful protests. Hundreds of thousands of citizens joined the Madres in the streets, demanding a return to democracy and accountable government. Following the regime's fall and the democratic election of President Raul Alfonsin in 1983, the democratic government (pressured by the human rights groups and the general public) took the unprecedented steps of trying the military leaders and creating an official truth commission to document abuses that occurred under the regime. The military's silence limited investigations and the fate of most disappeared remained a mystery. Presidential decrees soon freed the convicted junta members, and limited further prosecution and civil suits against alleged perpetrators. With the abuses unresolved, the eight groups remained intact, continuing to use domestic and international courts and to pressure each new presidential administration for information about still-missing loved ones and for policies that would bring punishment for their torturers and murderers.

Scholarly research examined the impact of Argentina's human rights movement and the strategies they employed,[2] but none answered the question of why activists had done what they did, despite the fear-evoking context. I wondered whether they differed from their more passive countrymen and women in ways similar to those that distinguished brave altruists and resisters in Nazi occupied Europe[3] and I resolved to investigate this puzzle myself. Nearly ten years after the regime collapsed, I headed to Argentina to conduct interviews to answer my research question: How did Argentine activists differ from nonactivists in their psychological traits, prior experiences, physical resources, and characteristics, or their relationships with others?

THE RESEARCH STRATEGY: USING INTERVIEWS TO SOLVE THE PUZZLE

Interviewing is an important method for gathering information in a systematic way. When we can identify a particular group and want to know things about how they think, feel, or interpret events, typically there is no better way to gain that information than to ask them. That does not mean that asking people questions will necessarily yield all the information we seek, that it will always be accurate or that people even will be willing to answer the questions we would like to ask them. For example, people answering questions years after they made decisions may no longer remember certain things or may not wish to share information that is unflattering. How an interviewer finds and gains subjects' cooperation, the nature and order of questions, and how one records answers and makes sense of them all have important effects on the knowledge that can be gained.

Depending on the question you are trying to answer, the number of interviews you need to conduct and the way that you locate your subjects can also vary dramatically, ranging from interviewing all those involved (if you are studying a fairly small group of people) to a **sample** selected to represent the larger whole. By either randomly sampling enough people or selecting a representative sample, we may be able to generalize findings and make claims about the overall population. Sampling is generally far more efficient and cost effective than trying to gather responses from an entire population. In some contexts, particularly where levels of trust are not high or where the topic being researched is highly sensitive, picking a sample at random is unlikely to work. Employing other techniques such as the **snowball technique** (asking those interviewed to suggest names of potential interview subjects with particular characteristics, viewpoints, or opinions) can help one gain access to the right people to solve a research puzzle.

It is critical to develop rapport with the interview subject, treat them with respect and protect them and the information they share. This requires a great deal of preparation and awareness of the context. For researchers working outside our native culture, it may require years of language training and consultation with experts on and within the cultural venue. For example, even though I could create and ask interview questions myself,[4] I consulted with a number of Argentine natives, especially a Buenos Aires psychologist who worked with those traumatized by regime violence, and made changes according to their suggestions. I had native speakers translate the questions from English to Spanish and back again, to make sure that the intended meaning remained intact. I also hired a local historian in Argentina to accompany me on some interviews. I also recorded all interviews and replayed confusing passages to her for clarification. Using the recordings I could double check my notes. I then *coded* the responses to particular questions (changed into numeric values e.g. yes for question 12 = 1; no = 2) for databases that I created and then analyzed. The recordings also allowed me to select which portions to **transcribe** (transform from an oral version into typed format) and use as illustrative examples.

No archive or database of interviews with Argentine human rights advocates existed at the time I began my research, although several books had extensive quotations from members of the Madres. Even if there had been interviews with members of all eight organizations, my research question required that I go beyond solely interviewing activists and summarizing their responses. To learn how they differed on particular dimensions from those who did not engage in human rights activism during this period, I needed to ask the same questions of people in both categories (i.e. the activists and nonactivists). Further, to give enough attention to the impact that might come from having a family member seized by the military, I wanted to break apart each of these two categories. By creating four types (see Table 5.1), I could compare those whose families had been directly affected by regime violence and those whose families were relatively unscathed as well as those who had taken public action with those who had not. To make the comparisons I needed, then, I decided to interview those who fit into the following types: Group 1: Those with relatives affected by the violence who took action against the regime (whom I came to call *Advocates* such as the Madres), Group 2: Those with relatives affected by the violence who did not take action (*Beholders*), Group 3: Those with families not directly affected by regime violence who did resist the regime (*Altruists*), and Group 4: Those whose families were not affected by regime violence who did *not* resist the regime (*Bystanders*).

Groups 2 and 4 would serve as comparable groups for Groups 1 and 3 respectively. I could also compare all members of Groups 1 and 3 (all the Courageous Resisters) with all members of Groups 2 and 4 (the Nonresisters). I sought similar numbers of subjects with fairly comparable demographic characteristics for each of the four groups and asked them the same questions.

TABLE 5.1 Categorization of respondents on two dimensions

		Affected by regime violence	
		Yes	No
Active in human rights movement during peak of repression	Yes (Courageous Resisters)	Advocates (N=27)	Altruists (N=23)
	No (Nonresisters)	Beholders (N=11)	Bystanders (N=17)

Note: N= Number of subjects interviewed in each category

Differences in the proportions of the group members answering in particular ways signaled how the groups were similar and how they differed from one another. I used a simple statistical analysis (called chi-square) to test whether the differences in the proportions responding to particular questions were significantly different from what one would expect.

In other words, my strategy required me to identify a comparable group that would differ primarily in the **dependent variable** I was trying to study: the level of nonviolent political activism in this repressive context. Interview questions (including both structured and semi-structured) would help me to gather information about **independent variables** I hypothesized might explain activism. Simple statistical tests of significance indicated which factors differentiated the four types from one another (especially from their respective comparison groups) or distinguished Courageous Resisters from Nonresisters.

ISSUES WITH THIS RESEARCH STRATEGY: PROBLEMS WITH RECALL

One disadvantage of interviewing people about events that have already taken place is that it is difficult to gauge the impact that subsequent life experiences have had on the memories of their past experiences. I tried to address this problem by using largely open-ended questions that guided my subjects through childhood, young adulthood and their lives right before and after the coup. I hoped that remembering details of their lives at various times before the repression would help them more accurately remember what they had really thought and felt about events as they unfolded. This holistic approach to interviewing subjects also allowed me to gain a deeper understanding of many of the factors that came into play in the lives of the Argentines as they were deciding whether to courageously resist the evil around them. I heard unforgettable stories of people who sacrificed their own safety and family unity, including one woman who shielded her children from the danger her activism would entail by sending them to live with relatives while she fought for human rights for all. Another woman revealed that she still hoped for the return of her only son, a nuclear physicist, whom she believed might still be held somewhere, secretly creating nuclear arms for his captors fifteen years after his disappearance.

Despite my best efforts to help people recall their experiences accurately, I sometimes detected problems during the interviews. For those who were part of the human rights organizations, particularly some members of the Madres of the Plaza, it was clear that they had told the story of themselves and their organization many times before. Though they had distinct stories about their lives before the coup, a number of them used virtually identical wording to talk about "their" experiences in the early days of the organization. They seemed to share a "script" that included similar words and sequences of activities, always delivered in the first person plural—whether they had actually been at an event or not! For example, several women reported a narrative very much like the following: "Then we went to stand in front of the president's house. We didn't know then that he knew what was happening. We thought if we could draw his attention to the fact that our children were missing, he would help us." When pressed on whether each had personally been there for these very early impromptu public demonstrations, most admitted that they had joined months later, when the Mothers were already walking around the obelisk at the center of the square and no longer believed that the president was naively unaware of what was happening. These women were not deliberately trying to mislead me. Having told the story of the organization so often, they had formed a collective narrative that dominated their memories and only with prodding could they again individualize their stories to tell about what each of them specifically had experienced, thought, and done. Even when these women did talk about their own experiences, I wondered how much their stories were altered by having shared the common story and experience of being a member of the close-knit core of one branch of the Mothers of the Plaza.

Despite these shortcomings, there is no better way to learn about how ordinary people decide to become courageous resisters than by asking them about themselves and comparing their responses to others who did not take action. Comparing responses of resisters to those of nonresisters and comparing the four groups (using tests of statistical significance) led to interesting results.

THE LITERATURE REVIEW

In order to contextualize my own research efforts and to identify where I could make a contribution, I conducted a **literature review**. Research trying to explain inhumane treatment expanded dramatically after World War II, as scholars sought to understand how unprecedented levels of human suffering were perpetrated. Some research looked at the psychology of leaders and followers, some at the structures of situations in which individuals played particular roles or felt themselves subject to others' orders, seemingly absolving them of responsibility. Yet I found that even in studies that demonstrated appallingly high levels of cooperation with unjust authorities by seemingly average civilians, significant numbers of individuals defied orders to harm others.[5] Because these courageous resisters were not the focus of these experiments and studies, however, their behavior was not well explained in those studies. In addition to trying to explain why perpetrators of human rights abuses are able to do the unthinkable, some researchers, particularly Staub and Goldhagen, emphasized the important role that passive bystanders play in encouraging oppression and even repression.[6]

The twentieth and twenty-first centuries are full of other examples of resistance to even the most violent acts of state and societal repression, some of which have succeeded in saving lives, changing policies, and even driving bloody dictatorships from power. Unfortunately, scholars considering these movements rarely look at individual actors and how they became mobile or continued activism despite high risks.[7] In fact, very little research had been done on why individuals refuse to go along with authorities when they demand compliance with unjust demands such as torture and extralegal executions. Experiments on pro-social behavior and altruism seem very distant from the life-endangering context of Argentina under the military regime. Other than biographies of famous activists and some systematic studies of those who became active in the US civil rights movement, I could find little research that tried to explain why people engaged in high-risk, other-oriented public action. Very few researchers shed light on real-life episodes of other-oriented, high-risk action, or suggested characteristics that might distinguish courageous resisters from nonresisters. Scholars who wrote about the period of Argentine repression similarly failed to address why some people mobilized while others did not, although some research did shed light on human rights groups' histories, strategies, goals, or impact.[8]

To transform my initial suspicions into refined hypotheses about what might affect individuals' behavior in the Argentine context, I read research on socioeconomic and political mobilization and civic voluntarism, as well as social science and psychology literature. I focused on action in fear-evoking contexts and altruistic behaviors. I was especially intrigued by psychological experiments that explored factors influencing altruistic behaviors.[9] **Experimental settings** cannot recreate a context of real and ongoing danger comparable to life under authoritarianism, however. Only two studies of altruism I came across compared altruists, who had faced real peril, to bystanders who remained inactive in that context. Decades after the Holocaust, Samuel and Pearl Oliner conducted interviews with almost 700 people who had lived in Nazi-controlled Europe, most of whom had rescued Jews.[10] While the rescuers' actions were private rather than public, their activities were other-oriented and very high risk, paralleling the Argentine resistance in key ways. The other study, by Kristen Renwick Monroe, also looked at action during the Holocaust, but compared the life histories of ten European rescuers with those of passive bystanders and others.[11] I speculated that the factors distinguishing rescuers from non-rescuers in that dangerous setting might also explain action and inaction in Argentina.

My review of research yielded 65 possible factors that might influence resistance or acquiescence to the regime's policies. I reduced these into a handful of categories and a few hypotheses. I hypothesized that human rights activists might differ from nonactivists in some or all of the following ways. Hypothesis 1: Activists had different external factors (e.g. safer venues or greater access to resources) than did nonactivists. Hypothesis 2: Activists had past experiences and socialization (resulting in internalized values or lessons learned throughout their lifetimes) that were different from those of their inactive counterparts. Hypothesis 3: How activists saw themselves and others (i.e. they extended their sense of caring and responsibility for others' well-being quite broadly) differed from their inactive counterparts. Hypothesis 4: Activists whose families had been subjected to regime violence via a disappearance, arrest, or death (e.g. the Madres) differed both from other activists who had not suffered such losses and from others who had suffered similar losses but had not taken action in terms of the dimensions listed in the previous hypotheses.

DOING THE STUDY: COLLECTING THE DATA AND DOING THE ANALYSIS

The first issues I want to talk about here are about finding interview subjects, gaining access and some surprises. By the time I was able to interview subjects in Argentina in 1992 and 1993, the military was no longer running the government, but the pain of the last military regime was still raw. Less than a decade had passed and despite the trial of the junta leaders, none of the perpetrators were in jail. The few victims who had survived secret detention centers and the many grieving family members of the thousands still unaccounted for encountered known and suspected perpetrators on the street, in restaurants and other venues. The publication of the Truth Commission's official report, *Nunca Mas* (Never Again), documented nearly 9,000 episodes of disappearance and torture, but left the ultimate fate of most of the disappeared a mystery. In this context, taking out ads or contacting a random sample of Argentines to ask about what they knew about human rights abuses and how they acted at the time would have been both insensitive and doomed to failure.

I had little trouble finding subjects who had been active in human rights organizations at the time of the repression. Because all eight of the human rights organizations still existed, I contacted each, first by sending an *advance letter* on official university stationery, accompanied by a *letter of introduction* from a scholar who had published research on the regime. I followed up on this letter when I arrived in Buenos Aires, calling each organization to make an appointment with a member. I then presented the letters again in person and asked for the individual and organization's help in spreading the word about my quest to find interview subjects. I explained that I was a scholar, interested in doing interviews to compare the varied life experiences and attitudes of those who had been living in Argentina during the period of military rule. I asked their help in spreading the word among current and previous members that I would like to interview those willing to talk about their experiences and gave them information about how to contact me while I was in Argentina. I also promised to protect the *anonymity* of those I would interview and explained that I could not offer payment for participation. In certain contexts it is crucial for the safety of those interviewed not to reveal their names or other identifying characteristics lest publishing their responses might target them for negative consequences. In Argentina, where military regimes had governed the country more often than democratic ones throughout the twentieth century, the risk of a return to a repressive state was a possibility, so the *Committee on Human Subjects in Research* (academics at my University who review research plans to protect the safety of those participating) had required me to gain written permission and promise those I interviewed that I would use only pseudonyms.

Once in Argentina, I asked almost everyone I met for help in spreading the word to others I might be able to interview. Sometimes I was able to make an announcement about my project at a meeting or activity where current or former human rights group members were present. Sometimes I was given names and phone numbers of people who might be willing to participate. Being able to say that a friend or colleague recommended them to me made those I called far more receptive to listening to my pitch and to participate. Although not all accepted my invitation, many agreed to meet with me. When we met, I gave them the introductory letter with my contact information, let them know they could skip questions or end the interview at any time and had them sign a release form, allowing me to summarize their responses statistically or to quote them without using their name. (This policy of quoting but not identifying the source is called being "*on the record, but without attribution*" as opposed to someone saying something "*off the record*," which means it is not to be quoted at all). For some, this seemed to reassure them and likely led them to speak more candidly. Others wanted their names and the names of their missing loved ones to be recorded. Because victims had disappeared into a killing machine that claimed to have no record of them, while the few released prisoners reported being dehumanized by being referred to solely by number or epitaph, those telling their stories often were eager to name names and to go on the record.

Occasionally, I was invited to the homes of the activists, a powerful experience that sometimes extended interviews for hours as the interview subjects pulled out documents, photos and scrapbooks to illustrate the answers they were offering to my questions about their own and Argentina's history. These unexpected revelations taught me a great deal about the context, society and culture in which resisters and nonresisters lived and greatly informed my research. Some met me for interviews in the offices of the human rights organizations, others in public coffee shops, where I was reminded how vital it is to take notes. Recorders can miss dialogue when background noise overwhelms recorded voices and changing batteries should not interrupt a deeply personal exchange.

I ended each interview by asking the interviewees if they knew others who might speak with me. I would usually mention that I was particularly interested in talking with those who were like them in many ways but had decided not to be active during this period. These individuals (Groups 2 and 4) were the most difficult to locate—particularly those who had lost loved ones to the regime and never learned their fates. Those who had participated in groups actively working against the regime were typically proud of their activism or at least used to talking about it, even if they were still suffering from loss and uncertainty. Those who had not been active in the human rights struggles were typically less practiced at talking about this painful period and likely sensitive about revisiting this time and answering questions about their lack of activism. Those in this category who agreed to be interviewed were without exception referred by friends or relatives, who made the connection between us. No one called me and volunteered to be interviewed, but some of those I interviewed called and gave contact information of a friend willing to speak with me.

Using this snowball method of finding subjects to interview, I was able to find people with comparable demographic and socioeconomic characteristics. Making initial contact with many subjects through their trusted friends and associates also yielded far better results than if I had called people randomly and tried to ask questions about this sensitive period. The drawback of this approach is that it could not necessarily yield a representative or random sample of the population, so I could not with confidence generalize my findings. Yet, the interviews did suggest patterns that both challenged existing theories and generated new theories about sources of activism.

I interviewed people active during the repression from all eight human rights organizations; these individuals were an *elite group* in that they had information that was not known by most others. Elite interviews helped paint a more complete picture of what the organizations did during the repressive period, and how those leading the human rights groups interpreted what they were doing. Interviewing elites and supplementing the interviews with other documents allowed me to draw a more complete picture of how group activism began and evolved.

Elite interviews need not involve a representative or random sample. You identify a target group of people who you believe collectively can illuminate various facets of the research question you are trying to solve. Because of the nature of the information we seek, elite interviews do not require a meeting with every insider. When additional interviews expand our knowledge of key events or information we should keep doing them. When no new perspectives or information is revealed, it's time to stop. An elite interview strategy alone could not answer the question of what made the resisters different, however. I don't think the activists themselves knew exactly what made them different from the friends, neighbors, and family members who chose not to act. Only by finding comparable people in all four groups and systematically comparing their answers to questions about experiences and attitudes throughout their lifetimes could I single out what was distinctive about the lives of the courageous resisters.

Let me now talk about designing the interview questions, conducting them and analyzing the findings. Even more than recording what the human rights groups did, I wanted to see whether those who took action differed in their individual resources, contexts, values, and personality traits and their own experiences with state terror.

I chose not to design a quick survey that could be administered rapidly to many subjects by a crew of interviewers. Without funding at a level that supported work like the Oliners, I knew that I would not be able to hire and train a team of interviewers. I had to consider what kind of interviews I could conduct on my limited budget. As Beth Leech (2002) explains, distinct types of interviews can serve different purposes. **Unstructured interviews** (in which you ask a few, broad open-ended questions about a subject) are like free-wheeling conversations. These can yield an insider's perspective and are sometimes useful when you don't know a lot about a subject. Elite interviews often take this form. An unstructured interview can provide fresh ideas and insights, but is likely to wander in unexpected ways and typically won't yield reliable data that can be compared across interviews. **Structured interviews** (those with **closed-ended responses**, such as "yes or no" or "which of the following . . .") work better when we know a lot about a topic and want reliable data that can be easily compared using statistical methods. If you don't know a lot about the subject you are investigating, however, you might accidentally construct a closed-ended question in a way that leaves out a key response option or doesn't accurately capture what you think it does, so it would not yield a valid measure of the factor you are trying to explore. **Semi-structured interviews** (i.e. asking consistent open-ended questions in the same order), however, "can provide detail, depth, and an insider's perspective, while at the same time allowing hypothesis testing and the quantitative analysis of interview responses."[12]

My interview questions combined the structured and semi-structured interview techniques. The closed-ended questions or looking for particular phrases in some open-ended questions allowed me to collect some data comparable to that in the Oliners' study, and allowed for those I interviewed to fill gaps in my knowledge about how Argentines responded, thought, felt and acted under the repression. This combination was important for several other reasons as well. First, I wanted people to remember their context and thoughts in the time before they chose whether to resist the regime rather than how they currently feel and think. I was trying to learn what these individuals thought, felt, and did before and after they responded to regime violence. Both the wording of questions and the passage of time can create a great challenge to **validity** (i.e. accurately measuring what we're trying to assess). Life experiences can reshape the ways we remember having felt or acted. Memory is more likely to be accurate when it is placed within a broader context of recalling other events from a particular period. For this reason, the sequence of questions was especially important. I first asked about non-threatening early periods in their lives. For example, I presented questions about the makeup of their households as children and as young adults and the interactions of the members of their households and other role models before the violence. This helped me learn something about who they were before the repression began and what their early socialization, resources, and relationships were like. It also should have made their responses somewhat more accurate, because they were placing their responses in a specific context rather than relying on a habitual way of talking about an era or looking solely through the lens of their current experiences. Because the questions about their early lives were typically not painful or threatening, they also helped build **rapport** between us. This trusting relationship became important as we continued on to questions that tapped into potentially more painful memories.

The mixed nature of questions was also helpful when the closed-ended questions I asked appeared to miss the mark. For example, one of the closed-ended questions I used attempted to replicate the Oliners' key *scale* (a series of questions whose answers collectively can be interpreted as a measure) of the personality trait of extensivity, but was adapted to the Argentine context. One of the Oliners' key findings was that rescuers differed from non-rescuers in their degree of extensivity. Rescuers were extensive in that they were significantly more likely to see members of all kinds of social and political groups in their society as "like me" than were their inactive counterparts. Further, rescuers felt a sense of responsibility and care for more of their society than did nonrescuers. My adapted version of the Oliners' questions about extensivity worked well for many subjects. They thoughtfully described their view of the social and political groups in Argentina by choosing from the options I proffered. But the same closed-ended questions turned out to be highly problematic for others. When asked to consider various groups within the society (e.g. members of the military, of particular political parties and social classes) and rank them from "very much like me" to "nothing like me," a significant number refused to answer these questions as I had constructed them. In fact, those who refused to answer the questions rejected the idea of treating any of the groups as monolithic and often lectured me on how within any group one can find good people and bad people.

At the time this frustrated me. Why wouldn't they just answer the questions as I asked them and move on to the next? I diligently jotted down their critiques, just as I wrote down the answers to the other questions I had asked. Half of the Advocates (Group 1) I interviewed refused to answer the questions as asked (see Table 5.2). Over three fourths of Altruists, Beholders and Bystanders (Groups 2, 3, and 4) answered these questions without critique. Further examination showed a dimension I had not run across in anyone else's research: More of the Advocates, who generally had not been as politically active before they lost family members to the regime, tended not to see groups as monolithic or insurmountable units. At least half saw the organizations and political parties as comprised of individuals, some of whom potentially might

TABLE 5.2 Responses to attempts to have respondents categorize members of groups as "Like Me" or "Not Like Me"

X^2(p<.01)*	Advocates (%)	Altruists (%)	Beholders (%)	Bystanders (%)	Total (%)
Objected to or refused to answer question	11	3	2	2	18
Answered the question without critique	11	14	7	15	47
Total	22 (100)	17 (100)	9 (100)	17 (100)	65 (100)

Note: *Chi-square (X^2) is a test statistic that summarizes the difference between the observed and the expected frequencies in a bivariate table; p<.01 means that you would expect the occurred values to occur less than one time out of 100, so the differences are statistically significant.

be sympathetic to requests for helping regime victims. Most surprising to me were Madres, who knew their children had been kidnapped by the military, but refused to categorize members of the military as "not like me." They argued that members of even the groups that had caused them the most heartbreak deserved to be treated as differentiated individuals. Only after doing this analysis did I appreciate that the refusal to accept the question categorizing their countrymen was actually more revealing than if they had just complied with my original request. Perhaps this perspective might be a distinguishing characteristic of other courageous resisters. This was a good reminder to me that qualitative interviews can be *theory generating*. Instead of helping to test a hypotheses, some findings inspire questions and suggest the need for further research, such as whether perceiving opposing organizations as monolithic discourages certain potential activists from believing a positive outcome is possible or seeing individuals within opposing groups encourages greater optimism that change is possible.

Now, let me turn to the findings and the contribution of my work. The Oliners found that altruists differed from passive bystanders not in their access to wealth, space, or other resources. Instead they found that they tended to have a more "extensive" way of seeing the world. Their ethos of care and responsibility extended to a far larger sector of society than their more passive counterparts. In a similar but much smaller study, Kristen Renwick Monroe concluded that rescuers of Jews were distinct in seeing themselves as one with victims they assisted. This all-encompassing view of humanity began at a very early age and continued throughout the altruists' lifetimes, distinguishing them from others, including heroes and philanthropists.

My research echoed some of the Oliners' findings. Like European rescuers, Argentinean courageous resisters were not distinguishable from bystanders in terms of their demographic characteristics, physical resources, and most social-ization or social learning experiences. This finding also differs from literature on more mundane (not high-risk) political mobilization, which suggests that some resources and demographic factors significantly differ between activists and nonactivists. My key findings differ from other research in not finding patterns that generally distinguish those who take action from those who don't. Unlike the findings of both the Oliners' and Monroe, Argentines who acted on behalf of others did not demonstrate significantly different levels of exten-sivity as measured with the Oliners' scale or in content analysis of their language use. As noted earlier, however, it was hard to make this comparison statistically, because about half the Advocates rejected the very idea of categorizing any group in the society as "not like me" and refused to answer the question. The high rate of refusal *did* distinguish the Advocates from all the other groups and suggests they had a distinctive way of looking at the world relative to the others, including other courageous resisters.

When I did find significant differences between one type of resister and its comparable group, the same relationship rarely held for the other resisters relative to their comparable group. Rather, the two groups often showed oppo-site patterns. This is not a dimension that I found in other research on altruism or political mobilization. Perhaps because the definition of altruism implies a distinction between the victims and the person assisting them (but doesn't specify whether it excludes efforts like those of the Madres who were intending to help missing loved ones), the impact of personal loss as a motivator or dis-incentive to action had not been incorporated in the works on altruism. I found that in general, previous research on political mobilization or altruistic behavior didn't transfer well to real high-risk settings, in part because the impact of regime repression was so severe and because it produced such dissimilar responses.

The blow of losing a family member did not immobilize all Argentines. It tended to paralyze those who were fairly well informed about the regime's brutality, had more experience both with politics and with fear-evoking events, and were more aware of the risks likely to result from public activism. These Beholders encountered repression armed with a combination of knowledge and experience, but the disappearance of a loved one apparently made them reluctant to endure (or subject their families to) more punishment by becoming resisters. In contrast, Advocates also lost family members, but they tended to know less about the level of repression, had less political experience and bore fewer scars from previous fear-evoking encounters with the state. They tended to respond to their loved ones' disappearances with less fear and filled with optimism that they could find and help them (including hope of finding help within organi-zations others saw as monolithic). Naively going forward, they started searching for one person and wound up starting a movement that sought justice for 30,000.

The naïve Advocates' path to activism contrasts with that of the Altruists, who tended to be experienced political actors. The Altruists typically had survived previous fear-evoking experiences and seemed to be tougher for it.

They often described their resistance as a continuation of previous efforts and went into action against the regime with their eyes wide open to what was happening. Aware of the dangers of activism, they felt they could strategically position themselves and their families to survive dangers even as they remained active. These characteristics distinguished them not only from the Advocates, but from the Bystanders, who were slightly less knowledgeable, experienced or used to high risk settings.

The impact of recent regime violence against one's family clearly affected individuals' perceptions and responses to the regime. It also interacted with their previous experiences with risk and politics in distinct ways (see Table 5.3). Advocates, who were more likely to be female, depended on narrow circles of friends and electronic media (manipulated by the regime) and were political neophytes. They likely never would have become political activists if not for the loss of a loved one. Altruists were more buffered from the direct effects of regime violence when they decided to continue their activism. They were more likely to be male, well-connected, well-educated, and were used to juggling multiple responsibilities; their political participation was a continuation of public activism begun before the repression. (Nearly all (97 percent) of Altruists described themselves as politically active before the coup, compared with only 30 percent of Advocates; this is significantly different from the scores of Bystanders (47 percent) and Beholders (64 percent)).

A key finding of my research is that the likeliness of people taking action against regime violence relates both to their previous experiences, perspectives, and levels of information and to their relation to the current victims. The interaction between these factors plays out in different ways. While some of those previously active were frightened into silence by close contact with regime violence, others were inspired to undertake activism for the first time because of that violence. Among those not directly affected by current regime violence,

TABLE 5.3 Recalled experiences before 1976 coup that evoked fear

X^2 (p<.05)*	Advocates (%)	Altruists (%)	Beholders (%)	Bystanders (%)	Total (%)
Recalled specific episode that frightened them	10 (45.5)	20 (87)	6 (67)	11 (65)	47 (66)
No recollection of fearful episode	12 (54.5)	3 (13)	3 (33)	6 (35)	24 (34)
Total	22 (100)	23 (100)	9 (100)	17 (100)	71 (100)

Note: *Chi-square (X^2) is a test statistic that summarizes the difference between the observed and the expected frequencies in a bivariate table; p<.05 means you would expect the occurred values to occur less than five times out of 100, so the differences are statistically significant.

some chose to resist the regime in part because they knew the risks, had survived danger before, and were confident that they could handle the new context as they continued their political activism. Those not affected by the regime, who had not been inoculated against fear in this way often chose the more risk-averse pathway of remaining passive bystanders.

Lessons to Be Learned

Using interviews can help us understand more about the backgrounds, resources, and perceptions of the people who behave both in exemplary and more mundane ways. In my research I learned to construct questions carefully and be open to critiques by those being interviewed. Closed-ended questions can speed up the pace of interviews, allowing you to conduct more in a shorter amount of time and with fewer resources. They can also be easier to code and analyze. However, such questions do not always capture what your subjects are really thinking. Semi-structured interviews allow those being interviewed to express themselves more freely and often help add a much deeper level of context and understanding to what you are trying to study. They may, however, be more difficult to compare, require more time to code or defy quantitative summaries all together (it took me months to code and transcribe key portions of the interviews I had done). Semi-structured interviews can also be difficult to control in terms of time (one of mine stretched to more than twelve hours over several days).

Second, it is not always possible to get a random or representative sample of those you would like to interview. Even if random or representative sampling won't work in a particular context, be as systematic as possible in finding subjects, but be prepared to modify your approach if the context demands. In some cases, especially when trying to speak with experts or a particularly wary population, you may wish to try using the snowball technique to find potential subjects and win their confidence. Be aware, however, that when you abandon sampling techniques, you also compromise your ability to generalize your findings. Depending on your research question, however, elite interviews may yield the answers you seek, with no need for comparison.

Third, present those you are hoping to interview with as much information about you, your study and how you will use the material you gain from your interview, then live up to the agreements you make with the people you interview. Being honest with potential subjects by telling them about yourself and your project (in general terms), is not only an ethical approach to interaction, but a practical one. People deserve to know who is interviewing them and what is likely to happen to the information they are sharing as they decide whether or not to participate. They are also more likely to trust you and be willing to cooperate if you are honest. By stating that I wanted to compare varied life experiences and attitudes of those who lived in Argentina during the period of military rule, I was being truthful, but also deliberately vague. I gave potential subjects an idea of the kind of questions I would be asking, but didn't reveal too much of what I was seeking to understand. I didn't want anyone tailoring their responses to prove (or disprove) my hypotheses.

Fourth, put the needs of your potential subjects first and find ways to let them remain in control during the interview; allow them to refuse to answer questions or modify or critique questions if they insist. Sometimes people's unwillingness to answer a particular question may mean that you have a confusing or ambiguous question; listening to their critiques of the question might tell you a significant amount about the way they understand the world and their position within it.

My research helped me discover that direct experience with fear and loss can manifest itself both in mobilizing and immobilizing potential courageous resisters. It also brought me into close contact with people who were still suffering from deep losses and led me to question the ethical trade-off of interviewing in such a context. In order to increase our understanding of what happened and share an important example of successful resistance with a broader audience, we need to conduct research. But is it fair to those we interview to ask them to remember periods that may be painful for them to make this happen?

This study raised other questions about those who fight for justice despite high risks. It inspired me to seek out other colleagues, who also do research on successful resistance to injustice. I gathered with a number of them at a professional conference. After comparing similarities and differences in our work on whistleblowers, anti-genocide efforts, and an episode of successful resistance within Nazi Germany, we decided to collaborate to create a more complex analysis of cases from around the world. Working on that book both answered and raised questions about courageous resisters to injustice.

Interested to Know More about the Study Discussed in this Chapter?

Consult the publication:

Thalhammer, Kristina. 2001. "I'll Take the High Road: Pathways to Human Rights Activism in Authoritarian Argentina." *Political Psychology* 22(3): 493–520.

Or look for the Argentine case study in Chapter 5 of a work on courageous resistance:

Thalhammer, Kristina, Paula O'Loughlin, Sam McFarland, Myron Glazer, Penina Glazer, and Sharon Shepela. 2007. *Courageous Resistance: The Power of Ordinary People.* New York: Palgrave Macmillan.

Exercises and Discussion Questions:

1. What kinds of research questions do you think can best be answered by using the interview method?

2. What questions do you have that you would like to explore through interviews? Would you use **closed-ended** or **open-ended** questions? What questions lend themselves to **in-depth interviews**? When might a closed-ended survey be the more appropriate methodology?

3. What are some of the *challenges to validity* that can arise in studying events that happened some time ago? What techniques might increase the validity of responses?

4. How much information should a researcher give about the study they are doing? Is it ever *ethical* to mislead interview subjects about your research? Is it *ethical* to revisit painful periods in someone's history for the sake of a study?

5. How can someone, who has not lived in a repressive setting, study courageous resistance or other exemplary behavior, without appearing to criticize the people who quite rationally chose the safer route, such as not challenging a brutal regime?

Recommended Resources:

The December 2002 issue of *PS: Political Science and Politics* 35(4) has informative articles on interviewing methods in political science by: Joel Aberback, Jeffrey Berry, Kenneth Goldstein, Polina Kozyreva, Beth L. Leech, Sharon Werning Rivera, Bert Rockman, Eduard Sarovskii, and Laura Woliver.

For more information on the recent successes of the Argentine human rights activists in their struggle for justice see: Sikkink, Kathryn. 2008. "From Pariah State to Human Rights Protagonist: Argentina and the Struggle for International Human Rights." *Latin American Politics and Society* 50(1): 1–29.

Notes

1 Jean Bethke Elshtain's "Antigone's Daughters."
2 e.g. Brysk 1994; Fisher 1989; Keck and Sikkink 1998; Jelin 1985.
3 As had been investigated by Oliner and Oliner 1988.
4 I used and adapted some psychological scales from related previous research such as Oliner and Oliner 1988 and created some new questions.
5 e.g. Zimbardo 1971; Milgram 1974; Kelman and Hamilton 1989.
6 Staub 1989; Goldhagen 1996.
7 e.g. Keck and Sikkink 1998; Ackerman and Duvall 2000.
8 e.g. Brysk 1990, 1994; Feijoo 1989; Fisher 1989; Guest 1990; Mignone 1991; Simpson & Bennett 1985.
9 e.g. Batson 1973; Latane and Darley 1970.
10 Oliner and Oliner 1988.
11 Monroe 1996.
12 Leech 2002: 665.

Statistical Research

To Naturalize or Not to Naturalize?

Adrian D. Pantoja and Sarah Allen Gershon

▌ GETTING CURIOUS: "HISPANICS OVERTAKE BLACKS AS NATION'S LARGEST MINORITY"—SO WHAT?

In early 2000, the United States Census Bureau officially declared Latinos as the nation's largest minority group, a status held by African Americans for over 200 years. Political pundits and scholars began speculating on how Latino demographic ascendance would transform the political landscape. Specifically, would this mean the end of Republican Party dominance in states with large Latino populations like California and Texas? Would the Republican Party no longer control the presidency if it could no longer win California, Texas, and other key electoral states with large numbers of Latino voters? Would Latinos remain loyal to the Democratic Party? Would the Republican Party soften its stances on immigration, bilingual education, and other policy issues in order to attract Latino voters? What exactly are the issues important to Latinos? Were George W. Bush's efforts to court the Latino vote through symbolic gestures, like speaking Spanish, making a difference? It seemed that for much of the decade, and beyond, the growth and size of the Latino population was very much on the minds of Americans.

All of the questions posed above are not only important to scholars of Latino politics, but also to political parties and candidates seeking to win political offices in areas with large Latino populations. However, to us, these questions were based on a flawed assumption—demographic strength equals political power. Latinos may have "overtaken" African Americans demographically, but politically there remained a significant gap between them. For example, a common measure of minority political empowerment is to count the number of elective seats minorities hold nationally or in specific offices like Mayors.[1] The data show that in 2000 there were 9,001 black elected officials compared with 5,019 Latino elected officials.[2] In 2010, the National Conference of Black Mayors listed 650 African American mayors, while the National Association of Latino Elected Officials listed only 271 Latino mayors that year. Of course, in 2008, Barack Obama, an African American, was elected U.S. President. For decades, scholars of Latino politics have written about why Latino political power has barely kept pace with their demographic size. One of the primary findings from this research is that non-citizenship is a significant factor impeding Latino political empowerment.[3] The 2000 US Census reports that out of 23 million adult Latinos, only 13.2 million, or 57 percent, are US citizens. Thus, close to half of the voting-age Latino population remains outside of electoral politics because they are non-citizens. Having a large non-citizen population in itself is not significant if naturalization is undertaken rather quickly. Yet, Latino naturalization rates significantly lag behind other immigrant groups. Why? Why do some Latino immigrants undertake naturalization fairly quickly (most are eligible after five years of being a lawful permanent resident) while others delay that decision for decades?

Writing a research paper on why Latinos do or do not pursue naturalization came out of a series of discussions on this subject in a graduate seminar on Latino politics between Professor Pantoja and his then graduate student Sarah Allen Gershon (now a professor at Georgia State University). Professor Pantoja had assigned a series of articles on naturalization; most of which emphasized the importance of length of residency and socio-demographic characteristics. Both of us hypothesized that other factors were important such as having an interest in politics and attitudes about the value of voting. These political orientations are found to shape political participation among citizens. Therefore, we surmised that similar orientations would shape the naturalization decision among non-citizens. However, this was just a **hypothesis** (an educated guess), and it remained to be seen whether there was data available that could help us test that hypothesis.

Since the question of why Latinos pursue or forgo the naturalization process is both theoretically and politically important, we decided to collaborate on a research project in an effort to answer this question. The **research question** is the question a researcher seeks to answer in their academic writings through the gathering of evidence or data. Almost every political science journal article, book chapter, or book is written to answer a question or series of questions. Typically a single question is sufficient in order to make a research project manageable. In our article, we were broadly concerned with the following question: what are the factors that promote or impede the pursuit of natu-ralization among Latino immigrants?

As noted earlier, political scientists like to answer questions that are both *theoretically* and *politically important*. We believed our question met these criteria. The political importance of the question is obvious, given that the size of the Latino electorate could double if its non-citizen population became U.S. citizens. Having a sizable electorate will not only increase Latinos' political clout but will also shape the American political landscape. Hence, the findings from our project have the potential to inform policymakers and activists seeking to increase Latino political power. Theoretical importance simply means academically important. In other words, do academics in your field, find your question interesting? More importantly, will your answer to this question add to the existing *academic literature* on this subject? If the answer is yes to both, then you are well on your way to writing a theoretically impor-tant paper.

Coming up with a good research question is both fun and challenging, and it has been the case for both of us, that some of the best ideas (research questions) can come over a cup of coffee at Starbucks or round of beers at a pub. The times and places for ideas are never ending. Of course, the challenge is making sure you are asking a question that has not already been asked; finding an answer that has not been developed by others; or using a **method**, **measurement**, or **data** that has not been tried before. In short, the whole pur-pose of research is to come up with something new. There is nothing innovative about research that simply re-states what someone else has said or found. We believe it is far more creative, rewarding and fun to develop original research. And yes, we believe research is fun, otherwise, we would not be doing it!

THE RESEARCH STRATEGY: WHAT IS STATISTICAL ANALYSIS?

Political scientists like other social scientists have a number of methodological tools that allow them to test whether a particular hypothesis is true or false. Throughout this book, each author is highlighting the advantages and dis-advantages of the method they use. Both of us are trained in a variety of methods, yet our method of choice (due largely to our interest in mass political behavior) is statistical analysis. **Statistical analysis** is often used when working with large numbers of observations, allowing researchers to analyze data in a systematic and convenient way. For example, if we examine the likelihood of a single individual immigrant to naturalize, then statistical analysis would not be necessary (or effective), however, with a large scale survey (such as the one used here), statistical analysis can help researchers make sense of hundreds of observations. **Surveys**, asking many **closed-ended questions** to large numbers of people (see Chapter 9) allow researchers to take those responses and quantify them (essentially assigning numerical values to responses).

Statistics allow us to make sense of responses on large surveys like the one used in our paper. There are two broad categories of statistics: **descriptive statistics** and *inferential statistics*.[4] **Descriptive statistics** allow us to identify various characteristics of large groups. For example, using descriptive statistics we are able to identify differences in naturalization among male and female immigrants in our sample. *Inferential statistics* allow us to make inferences about a number of things based on our results, including the relationships between different variables, and the generalizability of sample results to a population.[5] Inferential statistics allow you to determine whether that relationship is *statistically significant, meaning that it likely exists in the population*. For example, using inferential statistics, we can employ sample data to draw conclusions about the impact of various political orientations on immigrant naturalization in the *population*. For our chapter, we relied primarily on inferential statistics because we wanted to use our sample data to draw conclusions about Latino immigrants in the United States. We will now turn to a discussion of the relative strengths and weaknesses of this approach to the study of politics.

ISSUES WITH THIS RESEARCH STRATEGY

When are statistical analyses appropriate? What are the advantages and disadvantages of this methodology? As noted earlier, statistical analysis is often used by researchers when they have a large number of observations (sample or population) that they would like to analyze. The primary advantage of working with statistics in these cases is that you can generalize the findings (based on a representative sample) to a larger population (a process referred to as **statistical inference**). For example, our study analyzes the thoughts and behaviors of 1,042 Latino immigrants (our sample); but through the use of statistical analysis, we are able to make inferences about the thoughts and behaviors of 12.8 million immigrant Latinos (the population of immigrant Latinos reported by the 2000 U.S. Census).

One of the issues that researchers relying on non-experimental data often confront is the difficulty associated with isolating causal relationships. When trying to examine a causal relationship using non-experimental methods, a common problem researchers run into is their ability to account for multiple causes of the dependent variable. Essentially, for us to be able to assert that one variable *causes* a change in another, we must be able to control for the impact of other variables (which may truly be responsible for the observed change). One of the most commonly used examples of the need to eliminate alternative explanations is the observation that both crime levels and ice cream sales tend to increase in the summer. While these variables might be associated with one another, that does not necessarily mean one is *causing* a change in the other. Instead, it is likely that some other third variable (e.g.; warm weather) is responsible for a change in both crime and ice cream sales. Thus, for us to examine whether political orientations are *causing* a change in naturalization rates among Latino immigrants, we have to deal with other variables that likely impact naturalization rates as well.

Clearly we live in a multivariate world, and it is always a challenge to identify *all* of the factors that explain political phenomena, or any phenomena for that matter. As a consequence, some scholars have greater confidence in findings drawn from experimental designs (see Chapter 10, for a discussion of experimental designs). Due to their high levels of control, experiments allow researchers to identify with greater precision and confidence the impact of one variable on another. While experiments provide the best test of causality, they are often limited in their **external validity** (or ability to generalize findings to larger populations) and are not well suited for every research question, particularly those interested in making inferences about a large population. When researchers are interested in understanding the relationship between variables for a large population, they can rely on statistical analysis to help deal with this problem, statistically 'controlling' for the impact of other variables by relying on multivariate analyses (as we do in this chapter). These analyses allow us to examine the impact of one variable on another, holding the impact of other variables constant. By statistically accounting (or controlling) for other variables which may cause variation in the dependent variable, the researcher may be more confident about the relationship they observe between their key independent and dependent variable (we will explain this in greater detail in the next section of the chapter).

While statistical analysis may help us make inferences about large populations based on relatively limited samples, and rule out alternative causes of the dependent variable, it does have some limitations. First, the use of statistical analysis (based on mathematical measures) may not allow for the kind of nuanced understanding of the subject that qualitative research might generate. Relying on aggregate summaries of large quantities of data may limit our ability to recognize individual differences in the respondents' understanding of the questions and their responses. In fact, we had to rely on qualitative research conducted by other scholars[6] to help us interpret the results of our statistical analysis because of the limitations of this type of data and method. Furthermore, examining a large number of responses together may lead us to overlook critical outliers—respondents that are very different from the mean values. We expect random variation in the data to exist, but unusual cases may tell an important part of the story that will be missed by a large-scale statistical analysis. These advantages and disadvantages will become obvious during our discussion of the results. First, we turn to a discussion of the value of comprehensive literature reviews in the research process.

THE LITERATURE REVIEW

How do we know our research question is interesting or that our approach to answering it is original? We gather and read research published by scholars on the topic we are planning to investigate. This process of gathering, reading, and summarizing research on the topic we are investigating is known as the **literature review**. Typically, scholars research topics where they have accumulated some level of expertise. This expertise comes from reading works on the topic and adding to this literature by doing original research. Since one of the areas we specialize in is Latino politics, both of us have come across literature on naturalization in graduate courses or through our own research. It is unusual for scholars to carry out research on a subject that is completely new to them. Although both of us had come across some articles on the subject of naturalization; neither of us had ever written on the topic nor had we done an exhaustive review of the literature on this topic. Thus, the first step to any research endeavor is collecting as much information as possible on the topic.

We both employed a variety of *library databases* and typed key words such as "naturalization," "citizenship," "Latinos," "immigrants," "political incorporation," "civic engagement" and a few other terms. Since we were developing a scholarly article to be published in a *peer-reviewed* or **refereed journal** we limited our search to articles published in such journals and academic books as opposed to articles in popular journals, magazines, or newspapers since these published works do not go through a *blind-review* process. Peer-review, blind-review, or refereed journals are terms describing the process an article undergoes before it is published in an academic journal. Peer-reviewed journals send submitted articles to two or more scholars in the field for review. The authors of the article do not know who is reviewing their work and the reviewers do not know who wrote the article (since the names are removed from the cover page). The process ensures that those reading the article base their evaluations, or review, on the merits of the work and not personal ties to the author(s). Based on the reviews, the editor of the journal will recommend that the article be published, revised, and resubmitted or rejected. The process is long and rigorous, but it ensures that only top quality works meeting the journal's standards are published. Works published on the internet, or non-academic journals, books, magazines, and newspapers typically do not have the same type of peer-review process.

After getting many hits from the academic databases and printing hard copies of the articles, we looked at their reference pages to see if they referenced articles that were not on our list. The next task was to read these articles and organize them into several themes. As others have pointed out in this book, the purpose of literature reviews is not to summarize the findings of every single article or book written on a topic. Given that we had over twenty articles on the subject of naturalization, summarizing each article in a single paragraph would have created a journal article with a literature review over ten pages in length! In addition, simply summarizing each article does not explain how they fit together. Literature reviews usually make up about 10 percent of an article.

As noted earlier, we hypothesized that having certain political orientations, namely a positive outlook toward voting and interest in politics, would spur naturalization among Hispanic immigrants. From the literature, we developed a definition of political orientations to be, "citizens' subjective feelings about the political system: whether they know and care about politics, desire to participate in politics, and feel capable of affecting change in the political system."[7] The literature review also allowed us to identify if the connection between political orientations and naturalization had already been made by other scholars. We found that the literature on naturalization could be divided into four themes. Each theme represented research that highlighted the importance of certain **independent variables**, the variables that predict or *cause* the dependent variable to occur. For example, we believe that naturalization (our **dependent variable**) is *caused* by (1) socio-demographic; (2) cultural; (3) contextual; and (4) transnational variables. Socio-demographic variables include an individual's level of income, education, marital status, and their age. Cultural factors include measures of English proficiency, length of residency, and ancestry group (e.g., Mexican, Cuban, and so forth). Contextual factors capture immigrants' reasons for migration, experiences with discrimination, and the characteristics of the source country such as its regime type and level of development. Finally, transnational factors are the ties immigrants maintain with the source country while residing in the United States.

The literature review not only helped us organize this vast scholarship into manageable themes, but more importantly, highlighted what previous scholars have found. Literature reviews help scholars identify what is known about a particular topic. The literature identified a number of **hypotheses** about why immigrants pursue or do not pursue naturalization. It identified the nature of the relationships (e.g., positive, negative, or non-existent) between the **independent variables** and the **dependent variable**. It also identified how these variables were **conceptualized** (defined) and **operationalized** (measured), as well as the type of data sources used. Armed with all of this information, our task, then, was to carry out the research and make a contribution to the literature by doing something different or original.

Before we had undertaken the literature review, we had some preliminary hypotheses we sought to test, but needed to confirm that these hypotheses had not been examined before by other scholars. Specifically, we believed that Latino immigrants possessing certain political orientations would more likely pursue naturalization relative to immigrants lacking these orientations. The connection between naturalization and having positive political orientations came from observing the mass immigrant rights rallies in the spring of 2006. During these rallies, many immigrants held signs that read "Today We March, Tomorrow We Vote" suggesting that many would pursue U.S. citizenship in an effort to participate in politics and vote for representatives who were sympathetic to immigrants. Thus, having an interest in American politics and desiring to participate in politics, we theorized, would lead non-citizens to pursue naturalization at rates higher than those who did not have these values. We were surprised to find that none of the previous works on immigrant naturalization considered the role of political orientations in shaping the decision to pursue citizenship. This was a gap in the literature we wanted to fill. Perhaps the absence of political orientations by previous scholars was based on the belief that immigrants did not become U.S. citizens because they desired to participate in politics. Rather, it was believed that most became U.S. citizens out of a desire to increase their economic mobility or to sponsor family members for legal residency. We set out to show that the conventional wisdom was incomplete and that many immigrants were pursuing naturalization out of a desire to participate more fully in the American political system.

The semester we began our project, one of us (Adrian Pantoja) had also assigned in the Latino politics graduate seminar, articles on gender and politics. One of the key themes from this literature is that Latinas (women) conceptualize and participate in politics differently than Latinos (men). Therefore, we believed that the naturalization decision is likely to vary by gender. In other words, we were not merely interested in determining whether Latino immigrant men and women had different rates of naturalization, but whether the factors underlying that decision differed by gender. Thus, we explicitly set out to analyze the impact of gender in our paper.

We noted in our paper that, "the existing quantitative scholarship on immigrant naturalization is lax when it comes to understanding the extent and sources of gender differences in citizenship acquisition. Many studies simply fail to control for gender in the multivariate models."[8] In addition, the effect of gender on naturalization is contradictory, with some finding women to be more likely to naturalize while others finding the opposite, leading us to write, "The dearth of conclusive evidence over the impact of gender on citizenship acquisition highlights the need for gendered approaches to the study of immigrant naturalization."[9] We had two key hypotheses that had never been examined before in the literature:

Hypothesis 1: Immigrants with positive political orientations are more likely to naturalize;
Hypothesis 2: The factors structuring the naturalization decision are going to vary by gender.
In this instance, we are dealing with several independent variables. In the first hypothesis, our independent variables are positive political orientations, while in the second hypothesis our primary independent variable is gender. Throughout the analyses, our dependent variable is naturalization.

The next task was to test whether our hypotheses were in fact correct, but first we needed a data source. Since we wanted to say something about a fairly large population, Latino immigrants in the U.S., we began searching for survey data with a large sample of Latinos. As noted before, the main advantage of using survey data with representative **samples** of the *population* (in this case the population is Latinos living in the United States), is because we can **generalize** the findings to the population in question. We will not explain the advantages and disadvantages of survey research since Chapter 7 takes up these issues in detail.

DOING THE STUDY: COLLECTING THE DATA AND DOING THE ANALYSIS

To test our hypotheses, we relied on data from the 1999 "National Survey on Latinos in America"; a survey carried out by telephone and sponsored by the *Washington Post*, Henry J. Kaiser Foundation and Harvard University. We used this survey, because at the time, it was one of the only surveys with a nationally representative sample of Latinos. The survey had an *n* (n is the letter used to designate sample size) of 2,417 Latinos. Since our focus was immigrants, or foreign-born Latinos, we needed to remove some of the respondents from the full sample. We limited our analysis to foreign-born Latinos who are either naturalized citizens or eligible for naturalization. Thus, we eliminated respondents who are born in the United States; Puerto Ricans (since they are U.S. citizens by birth); or immigrants who have resided in the United States for less than five years (the required waiting period before applying for citizenship). We also dropped individuals from our sample who were ineligible for citizenship because they were likely undocumented immigrants. We identified undocumented respondents through a question that asked why they were not pursuing U.S. citizenship. After removing these respondents, the final sample or *n* used in our analysis was 1,042 immigrant Latinos.

In Chapter 7, you learn that surveys allow researchers to collect information on a **sample** of respondents through *interviews* carried out by telephone, internet, or in-person. The responses given to each of the questions will later be converted into numbers (**operationalized**) so that researchers can measure the association between responses given to one question (usually the dependent variable) and responses given to a different question or questions (the independent variables). We will illustrate this point in the next few paragraphs by explaining how each of the *variables* we use in our paper was **operationalized** or *measured* (e.g., or simply stated, how the words or responses given in the survey were converted into numbers).

Depending on the nature of the concept, variables may fall into one of four levels of measurement: nominal, ordinal, interval or ratio. Nominal (also called categorical) variables are variables which have unordered categories (e.g., religion or gender). Interval level variables possess categories which are equidistant to one another, but the variable has no true zero (e.g. temperature). Ratio level variables possess full mathematical properties (e.g., age, income). Our **dependent variable** (Latino immigrant naturalization), is measured using an **ordinal** measure. **Ordinal measures** capture variables which have ordered (but not necessarily equally spaced) categories. For example, survey questions often present respondents with a set of responses to choose from which are ordered, such as (3) *strongly agree*, (2) *somewhat agree*,(1) *somewhat disagree*,(0) *strongly disagree*. While it is clear that a respondent who "strongly agrees" with something has a higher level of agreement than one who "somewhat disagrees," the difference in these attitudes is not mathematically precise. That is to say, differences in ordinal measures vary by intensity or strength, but the exact magnitude of the differences in the categories is unknown. To illustrate this point, we could say that the difference between 1 pound and 3 pounds is 2 pounds, or the difference between 3 miles and 5 miles is 2 miles. These differences in ratio-level variables are mathematically meaningful and precise. Conversely, it is unclear what the distance (or difference) is between ordinal categories such as "strongly agree" and "somewhat agree."[10]

In this case, the ordered categories represent immigrants' *progress* towards citizenship. Specifically, we examine whether immigrants have: no plans to apply for citizenship (coded as 0), are planning to apply for citizenship (coded as 1), were in the process of becoming a citizen at the time of the survey (coded as 2), or were already naturalized citizens (coded as 3). The *ordered measure* (0, 1, 2, 3) is preferable to a **dichotomous measure** (0 "not a citizen"; 1 "a citizen") since we believe that there is a meaningful difference between individuals who have no plans to become citizens, versus those who are planning to initiate the process, are undergoing the process, or have become U.S. citizens. To ensure that there was variance on our dependent variable, our first step was to examine how the survey respondents were distributed in their progress towards citizenship. Without variance in the dependent variable, there is little point in proceeding with our analysis since the study is concerned with why some immigrants naturalize while others do not. To examine the distribution of the dependent variable, we generate some **descriptive statistics**, which tell us something about the distribution or central tendency of a single variable, in this case, the proportion of respondents that fall into each category of the dependent variable. The results demonstrated that about half of the respondents were already citizens, approximately 16 percent were in the process of applying for citizenship, almost 26 percent were planning to apply and a little less than 9 percent had no plans to apply.

Previous scholarship has demonstrated that immigrants' nation of origin sometimes affects the speed at which they become U.S. citizens. We examined differences in the dependent variable by nation of origin or ancestry groups (e.g., Mexican, Cuban, Salvadoran, and other Latinos), relying on **Analysis of variance (ANOVA)** tests. ANOVA essentially allows us to see whether the groups we are examining are distinct through a comparison of mean naturalization rates among these different ancestry groups. Remember that when we rely on sample data to make some claim about a population characteristic or value, we are engaging in **statistical inference**. When examining samples, we often rely on statistical tests for significance to determine whether to reject the **null hypothesis** being tested. The null hypothesis, simply stated, is that there is *no* difference among various groups in the population, or that there is *no* relationship between independent and dependent variables in the population. In this example, we are using ANOVA tests to examine the probability that the null hypothesis (in this case, that average rates of Latino naturalization among groups from different countries are the same in the population) is true.[11]

The results demonstrate **statistically significant** differences in naturalization progress among the difference groups. Specifically, Cubans had the highest rate of citizenship acquisition among the three groups, with 75 percent being U.S. citizens. Salvadorans, on the other hand, had the lowest rate of naturalization, 22 percent were U.S. citizens. Mexican respondents, with 36 percent being U.S. citizens, fell between these two extremes. When we say that the difference in means among the groups in our sample is **statistically significant**, we are saying that the probability (p) that the null hypothesis is correct is quite low. In the field of political science, we often see scholars reporting multiple p-values in their articles to let the readers know what level of confidence they have regarding their results. The most common p-values reported are .10, .05 and .01. We can interpret these numbers as the probability that the null hypothesis is correct, for example, p-values of .10, .05 and .01 indicate a 10 percent, 5 percent or 1 percent chance (respectively) that the null hypothesis is correct. In this case, our results indicated that the probability (p) that naturalization rates among these groups are actually the same is less than .05 (or less than 5 percent). Thus, we are fairly confident that the differences we observed in our sample are representative of differences in the population at large.

While the results of the ANOVA tests suggest that nation of origin might explain some of the variance in the dependent variable, there are a number of other independent variables which may explain Latino immigrants' choice to naturalize. Until this point, we have yet to test *competing hypotheses* explaining naturalization. For the remainder of this analysis, we attempt to statistically identify the relationship between our independent variable of interest— political orientations—and naturalization (our dependent variable), while statistically accounting for alternative explanations of naturalization (e.g., nation of origin, socioeconomic status, transnationalism). Through the use of **multivariate analysis**, we are able to examine the impact of these competing variables on naturalization simultaneously. In section V. "Testing the hypotheses: the results" we will explain what we mean by multivariate analysis.

Before proceeding with our analysis, we needed to outline how we operationalized or measured our independent variables so that the results would be easily interpreted. Our primary independent variable—political orientations—

is measured using the responses to two different questions. The first is based on a question asking the degree to which an individual agrees or disagrees with the statement: "Voting is a waste of time." The variable, Voting is a Waste, is based on a four-point scale, ranging from 0 "disagree strongly" to 3 "agree strongly." The second variable is based on a question about political interest: "How much attention would you say you pay to politics and government?" The variable is based on a four-point scale ranging from 0 "none at all" to 3 "a lot."

While political orientations are our primary variables of interest, in order to assert that they are related to naturalization, we must control for the impact of alternate explanations. In other words, to be sure the relationship we identify is real, we have to (statistically) account for other variables which may explain Latino immigrants' choice to naturalize. How do we know which variables to include in our model? This decision is based on theoretical reasoning and previous scholarship. Recall that our review of the previous literature identified a host of different variables which impact naturalization, including respondent's nation of origin, experiences with discrimination, reasons for migration, transnational ties, age, education, income, gender, marital status, length of residency, and English-language proficiency. In our analysis, we attempt to statistically account or "control" for the impact of these predictors in order to clearly identify the independent impact of our variables of interest on naturalization.

TESTING THE HYPOTHESES: THE RESULTS

There are many different types of multivariate models which researchers use to examine the relationship between multiple variables. In this case, we chose to rely on **ordered logistic** regression (often call **ologit** for short). Ordered logistic regression is commonly used in large N analyses when the dependent variable is ordinal. Essentially, the ordered logistic regression estimates the impact the independent variables have on the *likelihood* of observations being in the next highest category of the dependent variable (in this case, progress towards naturalization).[12]

Table 6.1 displays a portion of our findings—specifically, the impact of political orientations for the full sample (male and female respondents), for Latinos (male respondents) only, and for Latinas (female respondents) only. Before discussing our results, let's review what the numbers in the table mean. Keep in mind that the statistical concepts described are typically learned in an advanced statistics course, so don't be concerned if the concepts may not be entirely clear at the moment. The key point is that the numbers on the table are mathematical properties describing (1) whether the variables are positive, negative or unrelated to the dependent variable; (2) whether the impact of the

TABLE 6.1 Ordered logistic regressions predicting Latino immigrants' progress towards immigration (truncated)

	(Full sample)		(Men only)		(Women only)	
	Coefficients (S.E.)	Min-Max	Coefficients (S.E.)	Min-Max	Coefficients (S.E.)	Min-Max
Voting is a waste	−.124(.061)*	−0.076	−.076(.087)	−.048	−.159(.087)*	−.095
Political interest	.134(.075)*	.079	.220(.104)*	.135	.026(.109)	.015
Gender (female)	.229(.136)*	.045	—	—	—	—
Sample size	997		487		510	

*p<.05, **p<.01

independent variables on the dependent variable is statistically significant; and (3) whether the impact or effect of the independent variables on the dependent variable is large, medium, small, or negligible. Nonetheless, we will use common terms used by statisticians to describe these three points. The table displays two sets of results for each model. First, we see the **unstandardized coefficients** with the **standard error** in parentheses. The **coefficients** tell us the impact of each independent variable on the *log odds* of respondents' progress towards naturalization. Specifically, the coefficient gives us the expected increase in respondent's log odds of being in a higher naturalization category for every one unit change in the independent variable, controlling for all other variables in the model. For example, in Table 6.1 (full sample), the negative coefficient for *voting is a waste* (−0.124) tells us that a one unit increase in respondents' belief that voting is a waste of time *decreases* their log odds of being in a higher naturalization category by .124, holding all other variables in the model constant. To assist with our understanding of the relationships between these variables, we present a statistic called, "*min.–max.*" (discussed later on) which helps us understand the relative impact of the independent variables on the dependent variable.

The **standard errors** for the individual coefficients are also presented. When we discuss standard errors, essentially we are talking about the accuracy of our estimates, given that we are only using a sample of the population we are trying to generalize to. In order to draw inferences about the population (in this case, Latino immigrants), relying on a sample of approximately 1,000, we have to account for the differences between our sample and what the true value of the population may be. Remember, each sample selected will vary slightly from what we would expect to see if we drew a different sample, or if we examined the entire population. The standard error captures what we call the standard deviation of the sampling distribution. In other words, the standard error captures the difference that will occur randomly between any sample and the entire population. Generally speaking, the larger the sample (and thus the greater proportion of the population being captured) the smaller the standard error.

Notice that several of the coefficients have stars (e.g., *) after them. The key below the table tells us that these stars represent the "**p" value** of the coefficient. As discussed in other chapters in this book and above, the p value refers to the statistical significance of the relationship in the multivariate model. In this instance, a p value of .05 or below gives us a high level of confidence that the relationship we're observing is not coincidental. In these instances, we refer to the exhibited relationship as "**statistically significant.**"

Aside from the coefficients, the standard errors, and p values; perhaps the most important value is the "min.–max." which helps us interpret the effect of the independent variables on the dependent variables. Again we want to know if the effect is large, medium, small, or negligible. This measure allows us to make standardized comparisons about the relative impact of the different independent variables on the dependent variable. More specifically, this statistic estimates the change in predicted probabilities of the dependent variable, given a fixed change in the independent variable from its minimum to maximum value, holding all other variables constant at their means.[13] So, for example, in the full model, the min-max value for gender (female) is .045. This number tells us that, holding all other variables in the model constant at their means, being female (rather than male) increases the respondents' probability of moving closer to naturalization by .045.

Now let's go over the results in Table 6.1. First, we examine the impact of political orientations on Latino immigrants' progress towards naturalization, using the entire sample (men and women). Both of our measures are statistically significant predictors of naturalization Specifically, the coefficients for voting (–.124) and political interest (.134) indicate that the belief that voting is a waste of time decreases the probability that immigrants will pursue citizenship, while being interested in politics increases the probability of naturalization. Thus, the statistical model shows that our expectation or hypothesis is correct, even after controlling for rival hypotheses. Our full sample model also shows that, controlling for other variables, the effect of being a woman (rather than a man) increases the likelihood of naturalization.

After observing the gender gap in naturalization, we became curious about whether the impact of political orientations on naturalization might be different for Latinas and Latinos. Qualitative research conducted by other scholars[14] indicated that men and women experience migration and naturalization in the U.S. differently. To systematically determine whether the influence of political orientations on naturalization are fundamentally different for men and women, we separate our initial sample and estimate the impact of political orientations separately for male and female Latino immigrants. Thus, we examine the impact of the independent variables on the probability of women undertaking naturalization, and the impact of the independent variables on the probability of men undertaking naturalization. The results in these models confirm our expectations—indicating that attitudes about voting significantly impact the choice to become citizens among women only, while interest in politics exerts a significant impact on pursuing citizenship for men but not women.

What do we make of these results? To understand our findings, we turn to the qualitative research on immigration and gender. Traditionally, research in this area[15] has found that women more often express interest in and knowledge about local politics, while men are more likely to express interest in politics at the national level. The results of our survey bear this out, with more Latinos expressing interest in politics than Latinas. For this reason, we are not surprised to find a weak relationship between political interest and citizenship among Latinas. Our results also demonstrate that, while both Latinos and Latinas are equally likely to disagree with the statement "voting is a waste of time," this attitude influences the choice to become citizens among Latinas only. Again, qualitative research[16] provides a guide for us. This research indicates that immigrant Latinas tend to be more active in community and local politics than Latinos. We suspect that participation in community and locally centered activities may lead women to naturalize and participate in U.S. politics at a greater rate than their male counterparts.

Lessons to Be Learned

Historically, much of our knowledge of the Latino population was based on anecdotal accounts which relied on cultural stereotypes to explain their behavior and attitudes. Social scientists who sought to challenge these ideas could only rely on in-depth interviews with a few respondents since public opinion surveys with large Latino samples were unavailable. Despite their best efforts to present an alternative narrative, their research was often challenged since the findings could not be generalized beyond the individuals interviewed. It was not until the 1989 *Latino National Political Survey* (LNPS), that social scientists could finally make general claims about the Latino population by having access to large *n* survey data. The LNPS allowed scholars to dispel many commonly held stereotypes about Latinos through the application of quantitative or statistical methodologies.

One of us (Adrian Pantoja) recalls as an undergraduate learning about the 1989 LNPS and being impressed with the fact that a handful of political scientists could shape public attitudes and policy through survey data and quantitative analysis. In this present research effort we continue in this tradition and we hope that our research makes not only a theoretical contribution but a political once as well. We believe our research question meets the criteria of theoretical and political importance and encourage the readers of this chapter (perhaps future political scientists) to pursue research questions with the same goals in mind.

In our study we empirically demonstrated that Latinos with positive political orientations would pursue naturalization at higher rates relative to similarly situated Latinos lacking these orientations. Moreover, we found that Latinas (women) pursue naturalization at higher rates than Latinos (men) and that the reasons for this pursuit vary by gender. A skeptic could take the same data set we use, replicate our methods and reach the same conclusion. Despite our confidence in our findings, we do not want to suggest that the study is not without any flaws or that any scholar knows definitively why Latinos chose to pursue naturalization. We have merely added once piece to the puzzle. But the puzzle is not solved. In the future, scholars must continue to examine this question through the use of different data, measurements, and methodologies for us to fully understand the forces driving Latino immigrants to become U.S. citizens.

Interested to Know More about the Study Discussed in this Chapter?

Consult the research publication:

Pantoja, Adrian D. and Sarah Allen Gershon. 2006. "Political Orientations and Naturalization Among Latino and Latina Immigrants" *Social Science Quarterly* 87(5): 1171–1187.

Exercise and Discussion Questions:

1. What is the *advantage* of employing a *large* **n** or **quantitative statistical** approach?
2. What is the *disadvantage* of employing a *large* **n** or **quantitative statistical** approach?
3. Why did the authors conduct a **multivariate** statistical analysis?
4. Are the **sample** and *population* the same thing?
5. Why was the LNPS so important to experts in Latino politics?

Recommended Resources:

Pew Hispanic Center (www.pewhispanic.org).
University of Washington Institute for the Study of Ethnicity, Race and Sexuality (www.depts.washington.edu/uwiser).
University of Washington Data Archive, Homepage of Professor Matt Barreto (www.faculty.washington.edu/mbarreto/data/index.html).

Inter-University Consortium for Politics and Social Research (www.icpsr.umich.edu/icpsrweb/ICPSR).

Public Policy Institute of California (www.ppic.org/main/home.asp).

Roper Center, Public Opinion Archives (www.ropercenter.uconn.edu).

Notes

1 Bobo and Gilliam 1990.
2 Andrade 2006.
3 DeSipio 1996.
4 Aron et al. 2006.
5 Aron et al. 2006.
6 Jones-Correa 1998; Hardy-Fanta 1993.
7 Quote taken from our article, Pantoja and Gershon 2006: 1172.
8 Pantoja and Gershon 2007: 1181.
9 Pantoja and Gershon 2007: 1181.
10 See Johnson and Reynolds 2005, for a deeper discussion of levels of measurement.
11 See Aron et al. 2006, for a more detailed discussion of ANOVA tests.
12 See Borooah 2006, for a more detailed discussion of ordered logistic regression.
13 Long and Freese 2006.
14 Hondagneu-Sotelo 1994; Levitt 2001; Menjivar 2000; Pedraza 1991.
15 Hardy-Fanta 1993.
16 Hardy-Fanta 1993; Jones-Correa 1998.

Survey Research

Religion and Electoral Behavior in the United States, 1936–2008

Lyman A. Kellstedt and James L. Guth

GETTING CURIOUS: HOW DOES RELIGION AFFECT VOTING?

When we sat down to write our article "Faith Transformed," we had been studying religion and American politics for almost three decades, ignoring the ubiquitous maternal advice never to discuss the two in polite society. Although religion was largely ignored by political scientists when we did our graduate training in the 1960s and 1970s, we all had a personal interest in the subject. Two of our original research group (Smidt and Green) were "preacher's kids," we were all active in Protestant churches, and we had all grown up in the Midwest, with its amazing smorgasbord of religious groups. Thus, we suspected that political scientists were missing something important by ignoring religion's impact on voting.

Real-world events finally stimulated scholarly attention to religion. The Christian Right's dramatic appearance in 1980, supporting the candidacy of Ronald Reagan, elicited a wave of studies by social scientists. We were well placed to take advantage of this new interest, as Kellstedt and Smidt were already exploring the role of evangelical voters, Guth had investigated the politics of Southern Baptist clergy, and Green was analyzing political contributors. Soon Smidt and Kellstedt were collaborating to explore religious voting, while Green and Guth studied religion among political activists and elites. By the late 1980s, we had "joined up" to study Protestant clergy, political activists, and religious interest group donors.

THE RESEARCH STRATEGY: WHAT IS SURVEY RESEARCH?

In the social sciences several research approaches are utilized to study political phenomena, including the collection and analysis of documentary evidence, ethnographic observation, experimental studies, and elite interviews—all of which we have employed at times in our work. But most of our efforts involve **survey research**, the process of asking people questions, recording their answers, and analyzing the results using statistical methods. Surveys can be conducted in several ways: by face-to-face interviews, telephone polls, self-administered mail questionnaires, and, recently, by internet contacts. Each has its advantages and disadvantages. Face-to-face interviews are valuable for establishing rapport and often allow longer questionnaires, but are costly and rarely used today, with the exception of brief "exit polls" at voting places. Telephone interviews are much more common, but face increasing public resistance and new sampling problems arising from the pervasive use of cell phones. Self-administered mail questionnaires are employed most often to study members of organizations or activist groups. Internet polling is increasingly common, but still raises questions about sampling and representativeness.

Most of our early explorations involved mail surveys of activist groups and political elites, financed by small research grants, institutional funds, and often, our own pocketbooks. Our students helped by stuffing envelopes, entering data into computer files, and doing preliminary analysis. But in studying religious voting, we were totally dependent on **secondary analysis** (analyzing data collected by someone else, perhaps for different purposes). Although a few specialized voting studies were available, the gold standard was the American National Election Study (ANES), begun with a small national survey in 1948 and continued in every presidential election since, as well as "off year" congressional elections beginning in 1958.

Nevertheless, we were quite frustrated with the way religion was measured in the ANES. At the very least, we wanted to describe how major religious groups behaved politically, but the ANES questions were extremely crude. Before 1960, ANES asked only if a respondent was "Protestant, Catholic, Jew, Other, or None." That improved somewhat in 1960 when, prompted by controversy over John Kennedy's Catholicism, a new ANES question allowed us to differentiate members of Protestant religious families (Baptists, Lutherans, Methodists, Presbyterians, etc.), but not to identify many specific denominations within those families, denominations with very different theological and political leanings.

Not until 1989 did the ANES devote one of its periodic "pilot" studies to religion, focusing on potential new questions. (New items are rarely added, as the competition for space is fierce and ANES is reluctant to drop old questions for new, untried ones.) We worked with a committee drafting new religious items and subsequently analyzing them.[1] Kellstedt (joined later by Green) developed a new affiliation code which would allow us to assign the members of hundreds of American religious groups to theoretically meaningful traditions. This task required detailed interviewer probes to produce a precise religious "belonging" measure, allowing us to differentiate, for example, between "Southern" and "American" Baptists or between members of the Lutheran Church, Missouri Synod (LCMS) and the Evangelical Lutheran Church in America (ELCA). This scheme was first employed in the 1990 ANES survey and, with minor modifications, has been used ever since. Better measurement of religious affiliation allowed us to classify voters into *religious traditions*, made up of denominations and local churches with similar beliefs and practices.

Religious traditions became our central concern in the early 1990s. Given the diversity of American religion and the small samples typical of social science research, we needed to combine members of different denominations into meaningful categories, providing a large enough "N" (number of cases) for statistical analysis. Our religious tradition classification is historically rooted, designed to capture denominations and churches with similar theological tendencies and common organizational commitments. For us, the major American religious traditions are Catholicism, evangelical Protestantism, mainline Protestantism, black Protestantism, Judaism and the unaffiliated or "seculars."[2] (Smaller faiths must usually be arbitrarily assigned to an "other" category, but can be treated individually in very large samples.) Many political scientists now use this classification scheme, and many sociologists follow a similar model derived in part from our work.[3]

Getting affiliation right was important, but religion also includes belief and behavior components. Once again, we found ANES lacking. The only "belief" item was a crude three-option question on the Bible asked in 1964 and 1968, but dropped until 1980, when it reappeared permanently, along with a query on "born-again" status. In measuring religious behavior, ANES had always asked about church attendance and, in 1980, added items on the frequency of prayer and salience of religion. Although these items were useful as far as they went, that was not very far, especially on religious belief. We had experimented with many belief and behavior questions in surveys of college students, religious activists, and political contributors in the 1980s and had worked with new measures in the 1989 ANES Pilot Study. Then in 1992 every social scientist's dream came true: we had the chance to conduct our own national survey. The Pew Charitable Trusts, after supporting our earlier exploratory work, agreed to fund a large national survey.

The actual construction of this survey proved a practical education in the intricacies of survey research. We confronted first the constraints of time and space. As we were conducting a telephone poll, it had to be relatively short (20 minutes or so) to maximize responses. Clearly, we had to make tough choices on question priority. We relied primarily on **closed-ended** items, providing response options, rather than **open-ended** questions, permitting the respondent to offer whatever came to mind. Thus, we asked respondents whether the United States should cut defense spending, and how strongly they agreed or disagreed, rather than, "What do you think about defense spending?" Although this risked forcing responses into a few categories and missing nuances of opinion, it also made coding responses much easier and ensured comparability. Wherever possible, we used "tried and true" questions already developed by respected polling organizations, in part to allow us to compare results with earlier surveys. Where such questions did not exist, we constructed new ones, trying to follow the best practices in the discipline, avoiding loaded and complex questions and emphasizing clarity in wording.[4]

Question order was also a matter of concern. We kept related questions in batteries of similar items, to reduce confusion on the part of the respondent, but at the same time we made sure that some crucial items were kept apart, so as to avoid undue mutual influence. And on political issues, we framed questions to reduce **response set**, where interviewees would simply "agree strongly" with all the statements (perhaps to get done with the survey). We also discovered that some questions were more sensitive than others and needed special placement. In our first pre-test, we found that starting the survey with religious questions produced a very high non-completion rate, as respondents simply refused to participate, or hung up soon after the survey began. When we reversed the order, putting the political questions first, the problem was solved. Once into the survey, respondents kept cooperating, even when the subject turned to religion.

Our goal was to develop **multi-item indices** of religious belief and behavior that were **reliable** (behaving the same way over time) and **valid** (showing expected relationships with other variables that should be related in theory). An index combines scores from several survey items designed to measure a single concept. For example, a religious behavior index might add responses on the frequency of church attendance, scripture reading, and personal prayer to provide a better measure of "religiosity." Such indices are vital for reducing the **measurement error** in single items. For example, a person might go to church each week under pressure from a spouse, but be uninvolved otherwise (never praying, giving money or singing in the choir). Combining answers to several questions will negate somewhat a "high" (or low) score on one item that does not reflect a "true" measure of overall religiosity. And, using a metaphor appropriate to our subject, we insist that "Measurement error is Sin."

After many fits and starts and hundreds of hours in front of our computers, we eventually produced indices of behavior and belief which were improvements over the ANES' reliance on single items such as church attendance and biblical authority. A five-item *religious behavior* index included church attendance, prayer, financial contributions, involvement in religious small groups, and scripture reading that worked across time (showing reliability) and had strong relationships with political behaviors like voting and working in political campaigns (demonstrating validity).

Developing a *religious belief* index proved more difficult. In constructing questions that went beyond the simplistic ANES Bible item, we confronted a basic issue: should we use "core" questions that could be answered meaningfully by people in almost all traditions (as well as by those with no religious faith)? Or should we design different batteries for Catholics and Protestants, Muslims and Jews? We went back and forth on this challenge. At one time or another all of us managed to be on each side of this issue, but we finally decided to emphasize common items, questions that elicited fundamental religious orientations from almost all Americans. This strategy kept surveys simple to administer (with no need for interviewers to "branch out" depending on the respondent's tradition), minimized the time required, allowed more space for other questions, and simplified the eventual analysis.

After all this experimentation, by 2006 we had developed a five-item index based on queries about the existence of God, life after death, Holy Scripture, the Devil, and evolution. Respondents had little trouble answering these questions and the index produced similar results over time (demonstrating reliability) and was meaningfully related to other religious variables and to vote choice, partisan preferences, and policy attitudes (demonstrating validity). Now we had the conceptual tools to answer our research question: how had religious factors influenced presidential voting from the New Deal era to the present?

ISSUES WITH THIS RESEARCH STRATEGY

As our discussion to this point illustrates, survey research has both benefits and costs. Asking a representative sample of people questions about their affiliations, beliefs, opinions and behaviors is usually the best, and often the only way, to determine the distribution of these variables in the mass public or some part of it. Carefully conceived standardized questionnaires allow researchers to compare responses of different groups within the mass public, and open-ended questions can be used to explore topics of interest in more depth—and in the respondent's own words. Well-done survey research also permits scholars to trace public opinion and behavior over time, providing the material for **longitudinal analysis** of the sort done in this chapter. For scholarly work on public opinion and behavior, there is no substitute for modern survey research.

But there are important costs and limitations associated with survey research. As we discovered, **secondary analysis** of data gathered by others is often frustrating, as the original researchers may not have shared a later scholar's interest or expertise in a particular field of inquiry. This often means that the questions of interest are few in number and poorly conceptualized and measured. But the very significant burden of financing one's own national survey precludes most such efforts, unless underwritten by major foundations, government or other institutions. Indeed, the prohibitive expense of in-person interviews has produced alternative strategies of phone or internet "interviewing," which still entail substantial costs and face various sampling problems. Finally, survey research requires substantial amounts of time, energy and attention for the production of valid and reliable measures of the concepts being investigated and for the efficient execution of the survey itself.

THE LITERATURE REVIEW: RESEARCH ON RELIGIOUS ALIGNMENTS IN AMERICAN POLITICS

Producing better religious measures for national surveys was not just an exercise in curiosity, but would allow us to test two competing views on religious influences on political behavior: the *ethnocultural theory* and the *restructuring theory*. We all had some training in history and were avid readers of the "ethnocultural historians" of the 1960s and 1970s, who confirmed our suspicions about the centrality of religious voting in earlier American history. We were most impressed with Paul Kleppner's argument that nineteenth-century religious groups were divided between "pietists" (mostly Protestants), who supported first the Whigs and later the Republicans, and "liturgicals" (often Catholics), who backed the Democrats. Kleppner assigned myriad ethnoreligious groups to these categories and then painstakingly analyzed precinct voting and census records. (As he focused on our home region of the Midwest, his findings may have been especially convincing.) [5] Unfortunately, ethnocultural historians did not venture far past 1896, leaving a yawning gap on ethnoreligious voting in the early twentieth century. Nevertheless, early social science studies of voting found continuing ethnoreligious divisions, with Northern Protestants supporting the GOP, and religious minorities, such as Catholics, Jews, black Protestants, and Southern evangelicals, forming the Democratic "New Deal coalition." Despite scholars' focus on the influence of social class on electoral choice after 1933, many Americans still voted on the basis of *ethnoreligious tradition*, as the 1960 election reminds us.

Although this historical literature "rang some bells" with us, we were also intrigued by a competing theory just emerging from the sociology of religion.

In 1987, Robert Wuthnow argued that American religion had been "restructured." The divisions were no longer *between* but *within* religious traditions, engaging theological "conservatives" against "liberals." His argument was not about politics, but we saw the political implications. In 1991, James Davison Hunter's *Culture Wars* built on Wuthnow's thesis, positing *political* divisions between "orthodox" and "progressive" religious camps, especially on "hot button" social issues, such as abortion. We picked up on his suggestion in "It's the Culture Stupid!" (playing off a 1992 Clinton campaign motto), in analyzing the 1992 presidential election.[6]

We showed that there was some validity in the Wuthnow–Hunter *restructuring* or *culture wars* approach, as evangelical and mainline Protestants, as well as Anglo-Catholics, were indeed dividing as these authors predicted, but some groups' voting behavior still resembled that posited by the ethnocultural model. African-American Protestants, Jews, Latino Catholics, and Latter-day Saints (to name only the most obvious) still voted as cohesive ethnoreligious communities. We were also uncomfortable with Hunter's dichotomy of orthodox and progressives, knowing that any measure of theological "orthodoxy/progressivism" would have citizens arrayed along a continuum, not clumped in two groups. In religious warfare, as in politics, people often joined up with competing camps (think Republican and Democrat), but personal experience told us that many folks were "centrists" in these theological struggles. (Think of them as religious "Independents.") Thus, if we had to simplify theological factionalism within religious traditions, we preferred three categories to two, with *traditionalists, centrists, and modernists* making up the major factions.

DOING THE STUDY: COLLECTING THE DATA AND DOING THE ANALYSIS

Thus, by 2006 we had developed the necessary concepts and measures to determine (1) how religious factors shaped presidential elections between 1936 and 2004, and (2) whether ethnoreligious politics had been replaced by culture war politics. But we still faced thorny obstacles to this project. The basic problem was simple: as we went back in time, the religious measures available on national surveys became fewer and cruder. We wanted to confirm that ethnoreligious voting behavior had characterized the New Deal, but where could we find data for an era where only one of us was alive, and not yet past bottle-sucking mode? We knew that Gallup began polling during the 1936 presidential election, and that these surveys were available at the Roper Center, a public opinion data archive. As we examined these polls, we had special requirements. We needed the most detailed religious affiliation measures possible (something better than "Protestant, Catholic, Jew, Other, None"), and we hoped (and even prayed) for some belief and practice items (only a few were found). And, quite obviously, we required questions on presidential voting and partisan preferences. We found only a few surveys with good measures of both religion and political behavior, but enough to make informed estimates.

In **operationalizing** our idea of religious traditions (developing specific empirical measures for the concept), we faced some difficult choices. For example, Gallup grouped respondents by religious families (like "Lutheran"), but we wanted to assign them to religious traditions (such as evangelical or mainline Protestant). As the largest proportion of "Lutherans," "Presbyterians" and "Methodists," were in mainline denominations, we had to assign all of them to that category, despite sizeable numbers from smaller evangelical denominations within each "family." Similarly, all white "Baptists" had to be classified as evangelicals, as most were in evangelical denominations. Despite such difficulties, the presidential voting data in Table 7.1 demonstrate that ethnoreligious voting was alive well into the 1940s, with mainline Protestants providing the strongest GOP presidential vote, and Roman Catholics and evangelicals anchoring the Democrats.

Here we should caution readers about the Gallup surveys before 1948, based on **quota sampling**. Gallup used the U.S. Census to determine the populations of various demographic groups, such as young or old, northern or southern residents, black or white, etc. Interviewers were instructed to fill quotas from each group, based on their proportions in the population. After the fiasco in 1948 when Gallup incorrectly predicted that Thomas Dewey would defeat Harry Truman for the presidency, Gallup turned to **random selection** procedures. The principle of random selection is easy to grasp. All possible respondents throughout the country have an equal, or known, probability of being selected for interview. Although random sampling involves lots of practical problems that you may have already learned about in your methods class, it has many advantages over quota sampling.

Random selection allows calculation of the **sampling error**, the difference between the sample estimate and the "real" population parameter that results from the fact that only a part of the population has been surveyed. For example, if the margin of sampling error is plus or minus 2 percent in a poll projecting that Obama will receive 52 percent of the vote, his "true" percentage could be as low as 50 or as high as 54. And random selection procedures allow one to talk about a **confidence interval**, the range of likely values for the "true" population value, given the result from the sample for a given **confidence level** (for example, a 95 percent confidence interval means that the results are likely to have occurred by chance only 1 in 20 times). As quota samples are not equal probability samples, the laws of probability do not apply and margins of error and confidence intervals cannot be determined. Thus, results from our earliest time period must be evaluated with these limitations in mind.

Our use of ANES surveys from 1948 until 1984 presents fewer problems, but still required important conceptual and operational choices. Although we did not like ANES measurement of religious affiliation, we had to use it until

TABLE 7.1 Republican percent of two-party vote for president by religious tradition, 1936–2004

Religious tradition	1936	1940	1944	1948	1952	1956	1960	1964	1968	1972	1976	1980	1984	1988	1992	1996	2000	2004	Gain/loss
Evangelical Protestant	36	46	48	38	63	60	60	38	69	84	51	65	74	69	69	67	74	78	+42
Mainline Protestant	48	58	60	55	72	71	70	46	72	75	64	70	72	64	57	55	60	50	+2
Black Protestant	35	38	32	6	20	36	32	0	4	16	7	7	11	8	10	11	4	17	–18
White Catholic	18	28	33	25	49	55	17	22	40	64	44	58	55	51	46	46	50	53	+35
Unaffiliated	28	41	39	37	56	53	45	32	46	53	44	59	57	50	34	43	36	28	0
Total sample	36	45	48	41	58	60	51	33	54	64	49	56	58	53	47	47	50	51	+15

Sources: 1936–44 Gallup polls, AIPO 0149 Forms A& B, AIPO 0208, AIPO 0209, AIPO 0210, AIPO 0211, AIPO 0308, AIPO 0335, and AIPO 0360. For all religious groups in 1948 and for evangelical and mainline Protestants in 1952 and 1956, NES 1956–60 Panel Study; 1952–84 NES Cumulative File; 1988–2004 National Surveys of Religion and Politics, University of Akron: 1992, 1996, 2000, and 2004.

we could employ our own surveys for 1988 (or use the new ANES measures available in 1990). Indeed, before 1960 the ANES had no breakdown of "Protestants" and, as a result, most scholarly work on religion and voting starts from 1960, when more detailed information was available.

We hoped to do better. We discovered that ANES had conducted a **panel study** from 1956 to 1960 (panel studies interview the same people at several time points, while **cross-sectional surveys** interview different individuals at each point in time). As we had the improved 1960 affiliation data on panel members, we could assume that affiliations did not change from 1956 to 1960—that a Southern Baptist in 1960 was a Southern Baptist in 1956. Although not universally true, the short-term stability of religious affiliation makes this a reasonable assumption. Even better, we found that the 1956 survey asked respondents to "recall" voting choices in both 1948 and 1952.

Thus, assuming continuity in religious affiliation and accuracy in recollection, we could estimate religious group voting for both earlier years. Of course, we dropped panel members too young to vote in those elections, and we could not include those who voted in one or both years but died before 1956. Nevertheless, we see no persuasive reason why these problems should distort the findings. Despite some arbitrary assumptions, the results in Table 7.1 comport with information about the 1948, 1952, and 1956 elections from other sources. In 1948 black Protestants were moving dramatically toward the Democrats, reflecting both the Truman administration's appeal to blacks and the States' Rights candidacy of Strom Thurmond. Both 1952 and 1956 are classic examples of "deviating" elections where many citizens ignored their party preference to vote for the opposition candidate. Folks did like Ike! One of us even voted for him. Note that the groups deviating the most—evangelical Protestants and Anglo-Catholics—moved strongly toward the GOP (the Republican Party) later in the century, suggesting that they were already "on the move."

Did our painstaking efforts to obtain pre-1960 data pay off? Obviously, we think so. We may be engaging in wishful thinking, having invested enormous amounts of time and energy in the project, but if our assumptions are reasonable, we did show the ethnoreligious basis of the "New Deal coalition," something scholars can only speculate about if they begin analysis in 1960. Our findings were based on less than ideal data, but they came from large-scale *national* surveys and are consistent with local studies that also documented religion's impact on voting.[7]

For the years between 1960 and 1984, we used ANES data. The 1960 ANES affiliation codes were not perfect, but we were much more comfortable with them than with the Gallup "religious family" categories used for 1936–44. And the measurement of religious tradition got better as ANES affiliation questions improved in 1990 and we could use our own surveys from 1988 to the present. As the right side of Table 7.1 demonstrates, during this period religious traditions "realigned" politically, with evangelicals becoming the strongest Republican voters, mainline Protestants and white Catholics becoming "swing" groups, divided closely between the parties, and black Protestants and seculars becoming strong Democratic constituencies. Despite differences in data sources and their limitations, Table 7.1 tells a crucial story about trends in ethnoreligious voting.

Another way to look at these patterns is by "presidential vote coalitions." Table 7.2 reports the religious composition of the two-party vote for selected elections since 1936. In the earliest years, the GOP was clearly a party of white Protestants, especially mainliners, while Democrats drew significant backing from mainliners, most Catholics and many evangelicals, as well as representation from smaller groups. By 2004, evangelicals provided the largest bloc of Republican votes, with mainline Protestants and white Catholics each supplying about one-fifth of the GOP total. The Democratic constituency in 2004 was very diverse religiously, but seculars (the unaffiliated) had a narrow lead as the largest single group, followed by equal numbers of mainliners and white Catholics, a substantial group of "all other" religions, and most black Protestants. Table 7.2 also shows the gains and losses of each religious group as a component of each party coalition over the period.

We have traced developments in ethnoreligious politics, but to test whether such alignments were giving way to culture war divisions, we had to use ANES data for the 1970s and 1980s, the critical period for this transition. Although ANES had only one belief measure (the Bible item) and one behavior measure (church attendance), we produced a crude "religious traditionalism" classification.[8] The results confirmed our expectation that the ethnoreligious model still defined voting patterns in the 1960s. By the 1980s, however, evangelicals had moved toward a culture wars model, as traditionalists were more Republican than their centrist and modernist co-religionists.[9] Given the emergence of the Christian Right, based in evangelical Protestantism, this result fit nicely with events in the political world.

With the 1988 election, we could use recall data from our own 1992 National Survey of Religion and Politics (NSRP) to assess more fully the emergence of a modified culture wars pattern. Using multi-item religious belief and behavior indices, we should have a more sensitive test of religious restructuring. In addition, NSRP samples were much larger than those in ANES, increasing confidence in the findings. For example, ANES data suggests that the culture-wars model had kicked in by 2000–2004 for white evangelicals, mainliners, and Catholics, with differences between traditionalists and modernists ranging from 10 to 18 percentage points. For the same period, however, the NSRP data in Table 7.3 show much larger gaps, ranging from 22 percentage points among evangelicals to 36 among white Catholics. Indeed, the culture wars theory explains the close party balance among mainline Protestants and white Catholics, as these traditions are the most factionalized in theological perspective. All this shows the importance of using reliable and valid indices of religious beliefs and behaviors. It may all seem a bit complex, but the results warrant the effort.

TABLE 7.2 Presidential vote coalitions by party and religious traditions, 1936–2004 (percent of total party vote)

Religious tradition	1936		1960		1984		1992		2000		2004		Gain/Loss	
	R	D	R	D	R	D	R	D	R	D	R	D	R	D
Evangelical Protestant	19	21	24	17	24	12	37	15	38	13	40	12	+21	−9
Mainline Protestant	59	37	58	25	30	16	23	16	22	15	18	19	−41	−18
Black Protestant	1	1	3	6	2	18	2	14	1	18	3	13	+2	+12
White Catholic	9	24	7	36	19	22	23	24	21	20	20	19	+11	−5
All others	5	8	3	10	7	13	7	18	8	17	11	15	+6	+7
Unaffiliated	7	9	5	6	18	19	8	13	10	17	8	22	+1	+13
Total sample	100	100	100	100	100	100	100	100	100	100	100	100		

Sources: see Table 7.1
Note: R = Republican; D = Democratic

TABLE 7.3 Republican vote for president for major religious traditions controlling for traditionalism, 1988–2004 (in percent)

Religious tradition and group	1988	1992	1996	2000	2004	Gain/loss
Evangelical Protestant	69	69	67	74	78	+9
Traditionalist	*74*	*83*	*81*	*87*	*88*	*+14*
Centrist	*65*	*68*	*58*	*63*	*70*	*+5*
Modernist	*64*	*44*	*43*	*43*	*56*	*–8*
Traditionalist/modernist gap	*+10*	*+39*	*+38*	*+44*	*+32*	*+22*
Mainline Protestant	62	57	54	60	50	–12
Traditionalist	*63*	*64*	*65*	*76*	*65*	*+2*
Centrist	*61*	*59*	*53*	*52*	*49*	*–12*
Modernist	*63*	*50*	*46*	*54*	*39*	*–34*
Traditionalist/modernist gap	*0*	*+14*	*+19*	*+22*	*+26*	*+26*
White Catholic	51	46	46	50	53	+2
Traditionalist	*51*	*54*	*54*	*61*	*74*	*+23*
Centrist	*48*	*47*	*49*	*49*	*52*	*+4*
Modernist	*54*	*39*	*37*	*39*	*35*	*–19*
Traditionalist/modernist gap	*–3*	*+15*	*+17*	*+22*	*+39*	*+36*
Total sample	53	47	47	49	51	–2

Source: National Surveys of Religion and Politics, University of Akron, 1988–2004

We labored mightily on this research, and we leave it up to our readers to assess the results. From our perspective, we demonstrated that the old ethnoreligious electoral patterns have been substantially altered since the 1930s. Although many religious minorities still display those propensities, favoring the Democrats—the traditional home of religious minorities—among evangelical Protestants, mainline Protestants, and Anglo-Catholics internal religious divisions result in very different political choices, with traditionalists favoring the Republicans and modernists backing the Democrats (as do the growing numbers of unaffiliated voters).

A final important question is whether these divisions are long-term ones, or perhaps an artifact of the politics of the 1980s and 1990s. In this respect, the extraordinary election of 2008 which produced our first African-American president might seem to have altered previous alignments. (The nice thing about studying politics is that there is always both continuity and change.) What did religious alignments look like in 2008? Table 7.4 reports findings from the 2008 NSRP. The first column shows McCain's percentage of the two-party vote and updates Tables 7.2 and 7.3. McCain virtually replicated George W. Bush's 2004 results among white evangelicals, mainline Protestants and Roman Catholics; among Protestants the culture war category differences are

TABLE 7.4 Religion and the 2008 presidential vote (in percent)

Religious Tradition and Group	McCain Vote	Republican Party ID	Democratic Party ID	GOP Vote Coalition	Dem Vote Coalition
Evangelical Protestant	76	56	28	39	11
Traditionalist	*88*	*72*	*16*	*24*	*3*
Centrist	*68*	*46*	*37*	*12*	*5*
Modernist	*54*	*38*	*36*	*3*	*3*
Traditionalist/Modernist Gap	*+34*	*+34*	*−20*	*—*	*—*
Mainline Protestant	50	42	43	20	18
Traditionalist	*68*	*51*	*37*	*7*	*3*
Centrist	*49*	*45*	*44*	*8*	*7*
Modernist	*39*	*33*	*50*	*5*	*7*
Traditionalist/Modernist Gap	*+29*	*+18*	*-13*	*—*	*—*
Anglo-Catholic	51	37	48	23	20
Traditionalist	*58*	*43*	*45*	*8*	*6*
Centrist	*63*	*44*	*44*	*10*	*5*
Modernist	*34*	*26*	*53*	*5*	*9*
Traditionalist/Modernist Gap	*+24*	*+17*	*−8*	*—*	*—*
Latter-day Saints	72	70	14	5	2
Latino Protestant	33	41	47	1	2
Latino Catholic	27	19	56	2	4
Unaffiliated	27	22	45	7	16
Jewish	23	15	66	1	3
All Others	19	18	58	1	4
Black Protestant	5	8	79	1	20
Total Sample	46	36	45	100	100

also quite familiar. On the ethnoreligious side, GOP support fell among both Latino Catholics and Protestants, disturbed by the anti-immigration stances taken by many Republicans. Black Protestants also gave McCain a much smaller vote than they had given Bush four years earlier, while other smaller groups also moved in a Democratic direction. In contrast, Latter-day Saint support for the GOP remained high, although down somewhat from 2004.

The strength of Republican and Democratic party identification within each group tells much the same story (with Independents and others omitted). The GOP's base lies among evangelicals and Latter-day Saints, with even partisan divisions among mainline Protestants and among traditionalist and centrist Anglo-Catholics. Other groups prefer the Democrats with Black Protestants leading the way. Note something missed by most scholars—Latino Protestants are much more Republican than their Catholic counterparts. This difference did not influence vote decisions much in 2008, but it did in 2004 when Bush won Latino Protestants by almost a 2 to 1 margin. All in all, the party preferences here look much like those we found in Table 7.3.

When we turn to the religious basis of the party voting coalitions (compare columns 4 and 5 in Table 7.4 with Table 7.2), very little seems to have changed since 2004. The GOP coalition is overwhelmingly white (add up the totals for white evangelical and mainline Protestants, Anglo-Catholics, and the Latter-day Saints). Seven of eight Republican votes came from these four groups. In contrast, the Democratic coalition is loaded with ethnic and religious minorities—black Protestants, Latinos, Jews—and many unaffiliated or secular folks. On the culture war side, traditionalists support the GOP in large numbers, while modernists back the Democrats. Thus, religious voting in 2008 resembles that in both 2000 and 2004, suggesting that major changes in coalition patterns are unlikely in the near future.

Lessons to Be Learned

What lessons about research have we learned? First, we suggest choosing projects that interest you and draw on your own experience. Personal interest means you will stick with the enterprise even when the work is not going well, and personal experience is often a vital source of insight. At the same time, there is no substitute for careful scholarly preparation, whether for a long-term investigation or a class project. We drew both inspiration and insight from our own experience and from the scholarship of others, not only in political science, but in history and sociology as well. Remember that the world is not really apportioned by the artificial divisions of the academy; you can garner important ideas from many sources. You also learn a lot by collaborative projects; it is safe to say that this chapter would never have been written had we not spent years exchanging and testing each others' ideas—and those of other scholars with whom we worked.

Another lesson is the importance of paying close attention to the data, whether you are using someone else's survey or constructing your own. First, know about the quality of the surveys. Were the samples chosen by random selection procedures? What were the sample sizes? The response rates? Second, how adequate were the questionnaires? Do they include measures of all the relevant variables? Do these questions really get at the concepts they are supposedly tapping? Are the questions clear or ambiguous? In the modern world, we are inundated by data drawn from polls, whether in newspapers, TV, magazines or, for that matter, the classroom. We all need to approach such data with a critical and informed eye.

The third lesson is one we learned originally in graduate school: Multiple measures of key concepts (like religious beliefs and behaviors) are almost always better than single items. Although limits on survey space often lead scholars to rely on single items, this decision usually comes at the cost of greater measurement error. Of course, any item can be worded in ambiguous fashion, and, as a result, each must be examined carefully for reliability and validity, whether it is to be used alone or as part of a composite measure.

A final lesson from our experience is that it takes a long time for scholars in any discipline to adopt the "best practice" in addressing any intellectual issue. We have been working in this field for almost thirty years and have learned a lot, abandoning many "false leads" we once followed. Yet we often see younger scholars or those new to the study of religion and politics making the same mistakes we made long ago. Eventually, most will learn through trial and error, although they could shorten that period with careful examination of previous scholarship. Of course, there are always those who draw from different theoretical traditions, or who obstinately insist on seeing the world of religion and politics in a different way than we do. They are wrong, of course, but we can still learn a lot from them!

Although years of work went into this chapter, we also had an enormous amount of fun. There is an old saw about the "loneliness of the scholar." None of us ever felt that sensation: we enjoyed endless hours thinking, arguing, and computing together (with more than a few social interludes). And we are part of a larger (and largely congenial) intellectual community engaged on a common quest to understand the nexus between religion and politics and to convey what we have learned to students, scholars, journalists, and the general public. It really doesn't get much better than that.

Interested to Know More about the Study Discussed in the Chapter?

Consult the publication:

Kellstedt, Lyman, John Green, Corwin Smidt, and James Guth. 2007. "Faith Transformed: Religion and American Politics from Franklin D. Roosevelt to George W. Bush." In *Religion and American Politics*, ed. Mark A. Noll and Luke E. Harlow. 2nd edn. Oxford: Oxford University Press.

(The authors thank Professor Noll for his gracious permission to reproduce modified versions of three tables from the original text.)

Exercises and Discussion Questions:

1. In your assessment, what are the major *strengths* and *weaknesses* of **survey research**?
2. How would you attempt to *alleviate* or *minimize* the weaknesses of such research?
3. Are any topics too "sensitive" to be studied by survey research? If so, what are they? Are there ways you might minimize this problem?
4. This chapter focuses on the impact of religion on vote choices. Are the *substantive results* of the research project discussed convincing to you? Why or why not? How could the researchers have done a better job?

5. Would you be willing to be interviewed if called on the phone? Why or why not? What does this tell you about *contemporary obstacles to survey research*?

Recommended Resources:

American Association of Public Opinion Research (www.aapor.org). Among other things, here you will find standards for the conduct of survey research.

National Polling Organizations:

Gallup Polls (www.gallup.com).
Pew Forum on Religion and Public Life (www.pewforum.org).
Pew Research Center for People and the Press (www.people-press.org). This site contains regular surveys of the American public on a vast array of issues. Data usually available for secondary analysis six months after survey date.
Mitofsky International (www.mitofskyinternational.com). This site contains data on election exit polls.

Social Science Data Archives:

General Social Surveys (www.norc.uchicago.edu/GSS+website)
Inter-University Consortium for Political and Social Research (www.icpsr. umich.edu/icpsrweb): The American National Election Studies time series and many other data sets are available here.
Association of Religion Data Archives (www.thearda.com): Many important studies of religion are available here.

Selected Scholarly Studies of Religion and American Politics:

Campbell, David, ed. 2008. *A Matter of Faith.* Washington, DC: Brookings Institution.
Layman, Geoffrey. 2001. *The Great Divide.* New York: Columbia University Press.
Putnam, Robert and David Campbell. 2010. *American Grace.* New York: Simon & Schuster.
Smidt, Corwin, Lyman Kellstedt, and James Guth, ed. 2009. *The Oxford Handbook of Religion and American Politics.* New York: Oxford University Press.

Notes

1 See Leege and Kellstedt 1993, for discussion of the 1989 Pilot Study and ANES religious measures derived from that experiment.
2 The most important classification issues involve differentiating between evangelical Protestants, more theologically conservative, and mainline Protestants, who tend to be more liberal. As "denominational families" are often split between these traditions, a detailed knowledge of religious history and theological leanings is required for accurate classification. For more detail, see Smidt et al. 2009.
3 See Steensland et al. 2000.
4 A classic and still valuable guidebook for questionnaire construction is Converse and Presser 1986.
5 For a summary of the literature we read, see McCormick 1974.
6 Kellstedt et al. 1994.
7 See Berelson et al.1954; Lazarsfeld et al. 1948.
8 As the Bible item was asked in 1964 and 1968 and only picked up again in 1980, we cannot do this analysis for 1972–76.
9 Traditionalists were those who said the Bible was literally true and attended church frequently. Modernists were those who believed the Bible was the work of man, and not God, and was of little value, while rarely or never attending church. Centrists fall between traditionalists and modernists on one or both questions. For the full results from this analysis of ANES data, see Kellstedt et al. 1994.

CHAPTER 8

Secondary Data Analysis

A Program Evaluation of School Vouchers in Milwaukee

David J. Fleming and Joshua M. Cowen

CONTENTS

▮ GETTING CURIOUS: EVALUATING PUBLIC POLICY

The citizens of Milwaukee don't often hear the names of Orville Faubus and George Wallace, but for those listening to their local radio stations in 2006 they might have. What were these names doing in the news? A radio advertisement compared Faubus and Wallace, two segregationist, southern governors from the 1950s and 1960s, to the governor of Wisconsin. The ad said, "Don't let a governor named Jim Doyle stand in the schoolhouse door, again, this time blocking hundreds of African-American students right here in Milwaukee."[1] Why were the memories of segregation rehashed fifty years later in Milwaukee, WI? The answer is school vouchers.[2]

Few social policies are as controversial as school vouchers. These programs provide publicly funded scholarships to parents that they can use for private school tuition for their children. The politics surrounding the school voucher debate is heated for a number of reasons. Questions of the separation of church and state arise. Where students attend school has been an issue linked to both desegregation and to segregation in the past. Teachers' unions and pro-market interest groups donate millions of dollars to shape public opinion and the actions of elected officials on the issue of school vouchers.

Do school vouchers improve student performance and empower parents? Do voucher programs drain support from public schools and lead to a more unequal educational system? As interest groups, public officials, and commentators make claims about the effects of school voucher plans, one wonders whom to believe. The presumptions and arguments made by advocates on both sides of the voucher debate need to be verified through a careful empirical study.

Political scientists have informed and helped to shape the school voucher debate. Official evaluations of publicly funded voucher programs in Milwaukee, Wisconsin, and Washington, DC have been led by political scientists, as was the evaluation of prominent but privately funded voucher programs in New York City, Ohio, and Washington, DC.[3] In many ways, this body of research began in Milwaukee, where University of Wisconsin political scientist John Witte served from 1990 to 1995 as the official state evaluator of the nation's first large scale, publicly funded voucher program, the Milwaukee Parental Choice Program (MPCP). During the first year of Dr. Witte's evaluation, the MPCP had 341 voucher students in seven secular private schools. After the evaluation ended in 1995, the state of Wisconsin expanded the voucher program to include religious schools. As of 2008–9, the Milwaukee voucher program enrolls almost 20,000 students in 127 different religious and secular private schools. This makes the MPCP the largest urban voucher program in the United States. Figure 8.1 shows the substantial growth in the MPCP since its inception.

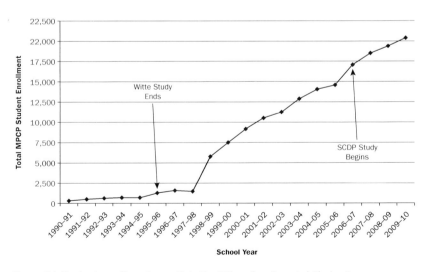

Figure 8.1 Student enrollment growth in the Milwaukee Parental Choice Program

Source: Wisconsin Department of Public Instruction

During this period of tremendous growth in the MPCP, there were no scholarly evaluations of the program after 1995. The citizens of Wisconsin had very little information on how their tax dollars were being spent. Elected officials in the state were unsure about the possible positive or negative effects of the program. Scholars, activists, and policymakers from around the country wanted to know if this experience with school vouchers was working to ameliorate the inequities and low performance that many identify in our urban school systems.

Stakeholders are now starting to get some of these answers. In 2006, the Wisconsin legislature enacted Act 125, which made a host of changes to the existing voucher law. Previously, the total number of students who could participate in the voucher program was limited to 15 percent of Milwaukee K-12 students (or about 15,000 students). This cap was lifted to 22,500 students. Voucher schools also received a new set of accreditation requirements. Finally, the state of Wisconsin instituted a new standardized testing system and evaluation program for voucher students. All voucher schools must administer standardized tests to students in grades 4, 8, and 10 and submit the test scores to the School Choice Demonstration Project (SCDP), a nationally recognized research center based at the University of Arkansas and specializing in evaluating public choice programs. Further, the state of Wisconsin directed the SCDP to conduct a five-year study comparing voucher student performance to similar students in public schools. Dr. Patrick Wolf, the director of the SCDP, asked Dr. Witte to join the evaluation team because of Dr. Witte's experience in Milwaukee and expertise in the field. As two of the researchers working with Dr. Witte in 2006, this meant that we now had the opportunity to examine the effects of the MPCP. Our work began in the fall of 2006, and the last round of data collection officially ended in the fall of 2010. The report discussed here examines the first two years of our five-year evaluation.

This research is a **program evaluation**, a type of study with a long tradition in political science. Program evaluation is "the application of empirical social science research methods to the process of judging the effectiveness of public policies, programs, or projects."[4] These social science methods can involve many of the topics discussed in this book, including content analysis, survey research and statistical analysis—some of which we also describe in our application below. However, program evaluation is characterized less by the particular research design and more by the overarching goal to which the work is directed. Evaluators are interested in making causal statements about whether the program of interest "works" as its implementers intended. For example, do abstinence-only education programs decrease teenage pregnancy?[5] Or, does Project DARE (Drug Abuse Resistance Education), a school-based drug prevention program, effectively reduce the number of students who use drugs?[6] Program evaluation is often associated with **policy analysis**. Researchers, government employees, think tanks, and others use policy analysis to examine different policy alternatives to a policy problem. If government wants to decrease the number of people who send and receive text messages while driving, what policy would be best? Should government ban texting while driving, increase education about the dangers surrounding this issue, or enhance the penalties if an accident is caused by texting while driving? Policy analysts try to answer these types of questions, and policy analysis can inform the debate about what government should do.

As such, the research process of evaluating public programs, like the MPCP, is different from other projects that political scientists do. First, the program evaluator may not get to select the research question. In our case, the state legislature decided that the School Choice Demonstration Project should examine test score differences between voucher and public school students over five years. Our research team has also examined other research questions surrounding the MPCP, but we are somewhat limited by the state statute, as schools are only required to provide us with test score and basic demographic data. Second, as the official evaluators of the MPCP, the SCDP had more authority to ensure that schools partake in the evaluation. This provided the research team with greater access and ensured more participation in the study than if we were trying to analyze the program as independent researchers. Third, our role as the state-authorized evaluators meant greater governmental oversight of our research than is typical of research done by political scientists. For example, we were required to provide yearly data to the Wisconsin Legislative Audit Bureau, a neutral oversight agency with the responsibility to examine our data and comment on our public reports. Although most social scientists expect their peers to study and critique their scholarship, few are also required to submit their work to government oversight.

For these reasons, our audience is different from the usual political science research project. The chief goal of much political science research is to get a book published or an article in an academic journal. Therefore, political scientists are often writing for other political scientists. Of course, political scientists hope to reach a larger audience with their research, but this can be very difficult. In our case, the intended audience is much broader. Our first audience is the state legislature. The legislators had authorized the study and were interested in the effects of the voucher program. As we write our reports, we are also thinking of Wisconsin taxpayers and the media. As political scientists, we want to speak to other scholars as well, but our evaluation differs from the usual political science journal article. We try to avoid technical language and academic jargon. Our report has a shorter literature review than is usual, as state representatives may not have the time or interest to read about previous work in the field. Finally, our research team wants to present our findings in the clearest way possible. This means that we may not use the most sophisticated statistical techniques in our public reports, if the same result can be demonstrated in an easier to understand manner.

After our evaluation of the voucher program is complete, we will produce academic articles in addition to the public reports. The academic articles will follow a similar structure to our reports, but they will include a longer discussion of school choice theory, as well as a more detailed literature review. As researchers, we often have to change the format of our publications to meet the needs of different audiences. Therefore, it is important for researchers to think about who will be reading their work and how to best target them.

THE RESEARCH STRATEGY: WHAT IS SECONDARY DATA ANALYSIS?

Our research strategy combined two approaches to data analysis: primary source analysis and secondary source analysis. When using **primary data analysis**, the researcher directly collects the data and observes the phenomena. Political scientists use this approach when a researcher interviews a Member of Congress, conducts a survey, or observes a protest.[7] Alternatively, **secondary data analysis** relies on indirect sources of data, as they are secondhand. Social scientists often rely on intermediaries to collect the data. This type of analysis relies on unobtrusive methods of data collection and is sometimes called document analysis.[8]

Secondary data can come from a variety of sources including autobiographies, photographs, newspaper articles, databases, and reports. Political science researchers can analyze secondary data quantitatively or qualitatively. One type of secondary source analysis is **content analysis**, which researchers can use to analyze different forms of communication (see Chapter 9). When using content analysis, researchers create a coding scheme that helps them to classify the media content. For example, researchers at the Wisconsin Advertising Project and the Wesleyan Media Project[9] track political advertisements during election campaigns and code the different images, issues, and themes of each television advertisement.

Published data are another form of secondary data. Published data are generally publicly available and have been collected by a government entity, private organization or other researchers. For example, the *Statistical Abstract of the United States* from the U.S. Census Bureau provides a host of statistics that can be used by researchers. The *Statistical Abstract of the United States*, which is published annually, is an example of a **running record**. Running records are ongoing, recurring, and often uniform sources of data. **Episodic records** are unsystematic sources of document data, such as diaries or papers from presidential administrations. Public opinion polls conducted by Gallup or other organizations, congressional roll call votes, the CIA's *World Factbook*, and the *CQ Almanac* are among the many popular sources of published data. Data archives are another popular source of published data. The ICPSR data archive through the University of Michigan and the National Opinion Research Center at the University of Chicago have publicly available data that can be used to answer many political science research questions. It is quite common for political science researchers to combine various sources of published data in their research projects. In his study of congressional elections, Dr Gary Jacobson uses secondary data from election outcomes, campaign finance reports, and members' voting records.[10]

Secondary data analysis has a host of strengths that make it a popular approach to social science research.[11] First, some research topics may be impossible to analyze using only primary or direct data sources. Say you want to examine public opinion during the Civil Rights Movement. You could try to survey people alive during those years and ask them to reflect on what their opinions were during that time. It is obvious to see the problems with that approach. Respondents may forget important events, or their experiences in the intervening years may distort their responses. A better research strategy may be to examine surveys that were conducted by others during the Civil Rights Movement. Similarly, secondary data allow the researcher to examine cross-national research questions that would be difficult to answer using primary sources. Second, researchers can use secondary source analysis to examine trends over time. Third, secondary data are usually nonreactive. **Reactivity** occurs when subjects act differently because of the study or research setting, and this can bias the results of a research study. Secondary data are often nonreactive because participants, observers, and record-keepers are usually unaware of any future research hypotheses. Cost is another important strength of secondary source analysis. Researchers can save a great deal of time and money by using existing data, rather than trying to collect the data themselves.

Many of the strengths of secondary source analysis are weaknesses of primary source analysis. However, sometimes primary source analysis is better than the alternative. A researcher may have a research question for which data are not readily available. By collecting the data oneself, the researcher will be able to ensure that the data will allow the researcher to answer the research question. When using secondary sources of data, researchers must rely on others to measure, code, and keep the data.

Given that the goal of our school voucher study was to examine differences in student achievement, we used both primary and secondary source analysis. It would have been very difficult for the research team to test all of the students in the study ourselves. Rather, we relied on the fact that public schools are required to test students in grades three through eight and grade ten. We received public student test scores and student demographic information from the Milwaukee Public School District, and these data can be considered published data. However, voucher students in the MPCP were not required to take the same test as the public school students. Therefore, the research team needed to administer the same test, the Wisconsin Knowledge and Concepts Examinations, to the voucher students in our study. Additionally, we collected data on the gender, race, and English-language proficiency of voucher students. These voucher student records can be considered primary data.

Without the published data (or a whole lot more resources), we would have been unable to do this evaluation. Given the guidelines provided by the legislature—a five-year test score comparison between voucher and public school students—we still had a large amount of flexibility in how we could perform our evaluation. We faced two big challenges. In order to isolate the effect of voucher schooling on students' test scores, we needed to create a public school student sample that was as similar as possible to the voucher student sample. We also needed to think about how we were going to examine student achievement over time.

ISSUES WITH THIS RESEARCH STRATEGY: SELECTION BIAS AND ACHIEVEMENT GROWTH

For this report, our main research goal was to examine how voucher schooling affects students' academic achievement over the first two years of our five-year evaluation. One possibility would be to compare the test scores of students in public schools to those in the voucher program. Although this method sounds reasonable, it may suffer from **selection bias**. Selection bias occurs when individuals self-select into the groups you will study in your analysis, for reasons that are also related to your outcome of interest.

Let's examine an example of the problem of selection bias. Imagine an undergraduate student, Mary Justice, who is interested in attending law school. She knows that she will need to take the Law School Admission Test (LSAT), and she will need a good LSAT score to attend her preferred law school. Ms. Justice is considering taking an LSAT class, in which she will learn about possible test topics and test-taking strategies, but she is of modest means. Should she take the class? To answer the question, she asks her friends who have already taken the LSAT if they have also taken the class. She discovers that those who took the LSAT class actually scored *lower* than the students who did not take the class.

How was that possible? Students were not **randomly assigned** to take the class or not take the class. Rather, students could choose to take the class. Examining her list of friends, Ms. Justice realizes that many of the students who decided to take the LSAT class were also those friends who were more likely to spend Friday night at a party rather than in the library. On the other hand, she noticed that those friends who were the most ambitious and the most studious did not take the LSAT class. Therefore, Ms. Justice concluded that the LSAT class did not actually lower students' scores, but rather selection bias had influenced her results.[12]

There are two strategies to deal with selection bias. One possibility is to perform an **experiment** (see Chapter 10). In an experiment, subjects are **randomly assigned** to treatment and control conditions. Previous evaluations of voucher programs have used a type of experiment, called a **field experiment**.[13]

Researchers may use this approach when there are more students applying for a voucher than there are spaces available. A random lottery then decides who will receive a voucher. This means that the lottery winners and the lottery losers will be very similar. Any initial differences between the two groups will arise by random chance alone. This is often the preferred technique to deal with selection bias. However, in our study, we did not have a situation in which there were more students applying for a voucher than spaces available. Therefore, another method to deal with selection bias was necessary.

A second way to deal with selection bias is to use a **controlled comparison** design. This is a non-experimental approach that attempts to make the groups used in the analysis as similar as possible. In a quantitative study, this is often done using **control variables** at the statistical analysis stage. Control variables are variables that are held constant during an analysis in order to isolate the relationship between the variables of interest. In our study, we used a controlled comparison design when constructing the samples. Wisconsin Act 125 stated that our evaluation should compare voucher students to a "comparable group of pupils" in the Milwaukee public school (MPS) system. We decided to use a **matching** procedure to account for selection bias. For every voucher student in our sample, we selected a public school student that was as similar as possible (keep reading to find out what we mean by "similar"). Therefore, any difference that we see between voucher and public school test scores should be because of the type of school the students attend, and not because of the different types of students in each sector.

Our first challenge was developing a strategy to select our voucher and public school samples. Our second challenge was to create an appropriate research design. According to the state statute, our evaluation will examine five years of students' test scores. This means that we will be using a **longitudinal analysis**. There three common types of longitudinal analysis. First, **trend analysis, or repeated cross-sectional analysis**, examines relationships for different samples at different time periods. If we used this approach, we would create a sample of voucher students and a sample of public school students and then compare their test scores in the first year. The next year, we would create new samples of each group and compare those students' scores, and so forth. One limitation of this approach is that the researcher is unable to examine how the test scores of individual students grow over time, since the same students may not be in the sample year after year.

The second form of longitudinal analysis is called a **before-and-after analysis**, or an **intervention analysis**. Using this approach, researchers examine variables before and after an intervention occurs in order to see how the intervention affects the variables of interest. We were unable to use this approach because the intervention, the creation of the MPCP, had already occurred. We did not have test score data from before the intervention.

We selected the last type of longitudinal research design, a **panel study**, for our evaluation. This approach is similar to a trend analysis, but the researcher examines the *same* sample at different time points. We decided to select a sample of voucher students and a sample of public school students, and then test them every year possible. Therefore, we can see how much a student's test score improves from one grade to the next.

THE LITERATURE REVIEW: HOW TO USE ONE FOR OUR REPORT

In any study in social science, it is important to consult the work that previous scholars have published. This allows us to compare our research question to similar studies in the past, and that helps us assess which methods are more or less appropriate for the specific challenges we face in our own work. In the case of the evaluation report we are describing here, there is not a long, formal review of the school voucher literature because it would not meet the needs of our audience of policymakers and the general public, but this does not mean that previous research on school vouchers did not influence our study. By reviewing the literature on school vouchers, we were able to design our study to examine some of the important questions that still exist in the field of school vouchers.

There were three main components of our literature review. First, we examined how previous evaluators of school voucher programs dealt with the issue of **selection bias**.[14] There are two possible scenarios. First is the so-called "cream-skimming" hypothesis. According to this argument, those students who are the highest achievers and with the most active and involved parents would be more likely to use a voucher to attend a private school. Therefore, if we simply compared the test scores of public and voucher school students, we would find that voucher students score higher than do public school students. However, this may occur only because the voucher students are the most motivated and not because of anything positive about the voucher program. The second scenario is called "negative selection," and it is the inverse of cream-skimming. Negative selection occurs when those students who are struggling the most in the public system choose to use a voucher. A simple analysis may show that voucher students are scoring lower than public school students, regardless of any effect of the voucher program. According to some sources, school voucher programs promote "cream-skimming" by attracting highly educated parents and highly motivated students, while other researchers show evidence of negative selection, in which low achieving students are more likely to use a voucher. These conflicting results emphasized that we needed to deal with selection bias in our research design.

We found that some studies used control variables to account for **selection bias**, while other studies employed a **field experiment design**. As we mentioned above, we could not use a field experiment approach to study vouchers in

Milwaukee. We were also concerned that only using **control variables** during the statistical analysis stage would not fully account for selection bias. The matching approach that we chose to implement is a somewhat novel design to the study of school vouchers, but it has been used in other studies of education policy.

After deciding to use the **matching method**, the research team then had to figure out what factors we would use to perform the match. We used the **literature review** to find student and parent characteristics that were related to the decision to use a voucher and to growth in student achievement. Our analysis of the previous research demonstrated that we needed to account for students' prior achievement, race, gender, and fluency in English. Our matching process did not stop there, however. As we were designing our particular matching plan, we spoke to demographers who encouraged us to consider the student's neighborhood. They argued that where students live could affect their likelihood of using a voucher, as well as their test scores. Neighborhoods could be related to a host of sources of selection bias, like social networks and access to information about schools. This is why we included neighborhood in our matching procedure. Therefore, for each voucher student, we looked for a public school student who lived in the same neighborhood, had a similar test score, was the same race, had the same gender, and had a similar fluency in English. We used the literature review, as well as expert opinion, to shape our strategy to combat selection bias.

For the second component of our literature review, we studied how the MPCP has evolved since 1990. We used Witte's earlier evaluations of the voucher program as a baseline for comparison.[15] There are distinctive policy design features to the MPCP and a unique social and political context in Milwaukee. For example, the large number of religious schools, particularly Catholic schools, participating in the MPCP meant that we should pay particular attention to how religion is related to voucher usage. By using the previous research on vouchers in Milwaukee, we were able to examine how the effects of the MPCP have changed as the program has grown.

Finally, we used the literature review to find gaps in the existing research. Although there have been a number of voucher evaluations, important questions remain. Earlier voucher studies focused on student test scores, as a measure of the effectiveness of voucher programs. While this remains an important component of our research design, we also were interested in other types of outcomes. For example, little is known about how voucher programs affect graduation rates from high school. Since this is one of the most important possible outcomes of our K-12 education system and there is little rigorous evidence on it, we decided to make high school graduation an important outcome, or **dependent variable**, in future reports. In addition, many researchers and policy advocates have questions about the participation of students with physical or learning disabilities in voucher programs. Since this is an area of great importance in America's schools today and the literature is unclear, we have made an examination of special education an important component of our evaluation.

DOING THE STUDY: COLLECTING THE DATA AND DOING THE ANALYSIS

We chose a matched panel study because it best fit our research goals and the data available. However, this approach, like any research design, has its drawbacks. We used a matched sample design in order to account for selection bias; however, unlike in an experiment, we cannot be certain that selection bias does not remain. There are two forms of selection bias: *observed* **selection bias** and *unobserved* **selection bias**. Observed selection bias is easier to deal with than unobserved selection bias because it can be directly measured and managed. For example, say that Ms. Justice finds that more women than men enroll in the LSAT course. This could be an example of observed selection bias. She could account for this by controlling for gender in her statistical analysis, or she could match students based on gender. On the other hand, unobserved selection bias is a much more difficult problem because it involves characteristics that may be difficult to measure or even define. Perhaps students who are more "motivated" are more likely to take the LSAT class. Ms. Justice can try to measure and account for motivation, but she can never be certain that this form of unobserved selection bias is not present in her non-experimental study. Similarly, despite the fact that matching techniques such as ours are considered by many social scientists to be effective strategies, it is still possible that unobserved selection bias may cloud our results. There is no perfect solution to the problems caused by bias, and as with any research of this sort, it was important to be *transparent* about the particular approach we have designed, so other scholars are aware of its strengths and limitations and can decide for themselves whether they believe we have adequately addressed these concerns.

The final consideration raised by our matched sample design is the possible tradeoff between **internal** and **external validity**. The extent to which a study is internally valid is the extent to which the causal claims made by its researchers actually reflect the truth. In our study, internal validity pertains to the confidence we have that any differences in test scores between voucher and public school students are caused by the voucher program and not some other variable that we have not taken into account. In order to receive a voucher for the first time in the MPCP, a family's annual household income must be 175 percent of the federal poverty level or less. Because of our matching procedure, almost all of the students in our study come from low-income families. This increases internal validity because it means that our voucher and public school samples are similar, so any difference we see between test scores can be attributed to the type of school the student attends. However, the amount of external validity, or how generalizable our results are, may be limited. We cannot know how low-income voucher users compare to higher-income public school students. Further, our study may not be able to predict the effects of a universal voucher system, in which there is no income limit on who can receive a voucher. Despite our concerns regarding the external validity of our study, we felt that our roles as evaluators meant that it was more important to accurately isolate and measure the effects of the voucher program in Milwaukee (internal validity) than to be able to make generalizations about how different voucher programs could work in different places (external validity).

We chose a panel study method in order to track the academic achievement of a set of the same students over five years. Although this method allowed us to answer our research question, panel studies present three additional challenges. First, **panel mortality** can occur when individuals in a panel drop out of the study because they no longer want to participate, they moved away, or for some other reason. This is problematic if those who leave the study are different than those who remain. For example, if the low performing students in the voucher program drop out of the study, it may incorrectly appear like the voucher program is having a positive effect on student achievement. Rather, the higher average scores of the voucher students are because the low scoring voucher students are no longer in the study. Panel mortality is another example of selection bias. Researchers can try to minimize panel mortality by providing incentives to subjects to keep them participating in the study.

A second challenge faced by political scientists using a panel research design is that the characteristics of subjects may *change* during the course of the study. This was a major challenge for our research design, where one particular characteristic—whether the student was a voucher or public school student—could change over time. Our goal was to compare the student achievement of voucher and public school students across five years, but what happens if a student spends two years in a voucher school and three in a public school? How should we deal with that student? Should we exclude the student from our final analysis? This problem is exacerbated in a study like ours because there are high levels of school switching in urban settings; some scholars have found that more than half of urban students move schools every three years. We have no control over when a student changes schools or what type of new school the family selects.

The third challenge is related to the previous two. Panel studies require that the same sample be followed over time. This can be a costly activity. As individuals change home addresses and phone numbers, it can be very difficult to track study participants. This problem gets worse the longer the panel study lasts. If a researcher is unable or unwilling to put their resources toward tracking panelists, it can lead to higher panel **mortality**. It often requires fewer resources to conduct a trend analysis, in which a new sample is selected at each time period, rather than having to try to follow the same subjects over time, as in a panel study.

Examining our research goals and the literature review, our research team decided to use a matched, panel study design to investigate the effects of the Milwaukee Parental Choice Program over a five-year period. For the report discussed here, our main objective was a comparison between voucher and public school students based on the growth in test scores.

Before we could perform our analysis, we needed to select our study participants. There were almost 18,000 students in the MPCP in 2006 when we began our study. We were unable to include all the voucher students, or the whole *population*, in our study. Since we were testing all the students in our voucher sample over a five-year period, it would be much too expensive and difficult to include everyone. Therefore, we needed to select a **sample** from the population of voucher students. We wanted to be sure that our **sample** *size* would be large enough to account for possible panel mortality, if students drop out of the study. We also wanted to be sure that our sample was *representative* of the population. If a sample is representative of the population, then we can make inferences about the population, which is generally the goal of this type of political science research. If done correctly, sampling can be a powerful way to make claims about populations of interest.

We wanted to make our voucher and public school samples as alike as possible, so we employed a matching strategy that included test scores. The Milwaukee Public Schools (MPS) have test score data for students in grades three to ten. Therefore, we limited our initial sample to those students in grades three to nine.[16] This has important implications for the types of inferences that we can make, as students in kindergarten to second grade and those above grade nine were not in our initial **sampling frame**, or list of possible study participants.

Based on our literature review, we were particularly interested in the effects of the voucher program on high school graduation. As a result, we included all voucher ninth graders in our study. It would be too costly to include all voucher students in grades three through eight, so we needed a sample selection strategy. We had two main options. The first is called a *simple* **random sample**. According to this approach, each possible study subject has the same probability of being included in the sample. The researcher randomly selects subjects from the sampling frame. We decided on another approach called a **stratified random sample**. Using a simple random sample, it would be possible to create a sample that did not accurately reflect the population. When researchers use a stratified random sample, they identify an important characteristic that a group shares, also called a *stratum*. For example, researchers could divide the population based on the state in which individuals live or by subjects' age. In our study, we used grade level as a stratum, so that we would get a relatively even number of sample participants in grades three through eight. Once we set up the strata, we randomly selected voucher students within each grade. Our final sample size included 2,727 voucher students. We attempted to test all of these students in the fall of 2006.

One of our main strategies to deal with selection bias is to match MPS, or Milwaukee Public School, students to our MPCP sample. For each voucher student, we essentially created a list of MPS students in the same grade. Next, using students' home addresses, we found in what census tract each student lived. We eliminated from that list all MPS students who did not live in the same census tract as the MPCP student. Then we looked for MPS students that had similar test scores on their fall 2006 tests. At this point, we often had multiple MPS students that could still be matched to our MPCP sample participant. Therefore, we finally tried to match students based on gender, race, and fluency in English.[17] By matching on neighborhood, test scores, and student demographics, we tried to account for both observed and unobserved selection bias. Our final MPS matched sample includes 2,727 students.

How good was our match? Table 8.1 compares our MPCP sample to our matched MPS sample. We also created a grade-stratified random sample of MPS students. This group allows us to see if our matching algorithm created an MPS sample that was more similar to the MPCP sample than a random sample would have been. Looking at the table, one sees that the matched MPS sample looks a lot like our MPCP sample based on these student characteristics. For example, nine percent of the MPCP sample and the MPS matched sample are white, while 15 percent of the random MPS sample is white. We also found that our MPS matched sample had test scores that were more similar to our MPCP sample than did a random sample of MPS students.

After demonstrating that our samples were quite alike when the study started during the 2006–7 school year, we wanted to examine how growth in student achievement, as measured by standardized test scores, differed between voucher and public school students. We again tried to test all voucher students in the fall of 2007 to see how their scores had improved from the previous year. We also received test score data from our public school students who were in our matched sample. Our **dependent variables**, student test scores in reading and math, are measured in terms of scale scores on the Wisconsin Knowledge and Concepts Examinations. Scale scores are scores generated from basic data

TABLE 8.1 Comparison of student demographics for MPCP, MPS matched, and MPS random samples

Sample	Black	Hispanic	White	Female	ELL
MPCP	0.66	0.23	0.09	0.55	0.11
MPS—Matched	0.67	0.20	0.09	0.53	0.10
MPS—Random	0.60	0.20	0.15	0.48	0.13

Note: Cell values represent proportions of the total sample. ELL stands for "English Language Learners." This is a measure of the proportion of students in each sample for whom English is not their first language. Table adapted from Witte et al. 2008: 11

on the number of correct answers on a multiple choice (or other) standardized test. The higher a student's score, the more the student "knows."

We first compared *mean differences* in test scores between MPCP and MPS students by grade. We examined how much students' test scores improved over the year. Overall, the amount of test score growth was generally quite similar between MPS and MPCP students; however, there was some evidence that voucher students in grades eight and ten exhibited more growth than did similar MPS students.

While suggestive of a positive effect of vouchers on student achievement, a more sophisticated analysis was needed. To isolate the effect of using a voucher, we used **multiple regression analysis**. Multiple regression analysis allows researchers to examine the unique, individual relationship between a particular **independent variable** and the dependent variable after taking the impact of other independent variables into account. We use it in our study to describe the relationship between participating in the voucher program and student test scores after adjusting for the impact of other factors, like race and gender. The results from our basic analysis are portrayed in Table 8.2. We estimated three models for both the reading and math scores. Each model is a different regression. First, focus on the MPCP 2006 row. This is our main **independent variable**, which measures if the child was a voucher student for the 2006–7 school year. Students who received a voucher were coded as a one for this variable, and public school students where coded as a zero. If voucher students scored higher than public school students did, the coefficient for the variable will be positive. If public school students performed better than voucher students, than the coefficient will be negative, as there would be a negative relationship between voucher status and test scores. As you move across that row, you will notice that the estimated coefficients (e.g., 1.43 for Model 1 Math) are positive and quite small. The Model 1 regression coefficient for the MPCP 2006 variable can be interpreted as follows: voucher students scored 1.43 points higher on the 2007 test than did public school students, while controlling for the 2006 test score. In this example, the larger the coefficient, the greater the difference between voucher and public school student test scores.

Is a 1.43 point difference a **statistically significant** difference? This question involves **hypothesis** *testing*. When we ask whether the difference we observed is statistically significant, we are asking how likely is it that we could have observed that difference if the true difference is zero. Looking at the MPCP 2006 row, one can see that none of the coefficients are statistically significant (this is why there are no asterisks). The lack of a statistically significant relationship between voucher status and 2007 test scores means that voucher students did not increase their test scores substantially more or less than did public school students from 2006 to 2007. For Model 1 Math, there is a statistically significant relationship between a student's 2006 test score and the student's 2007 score. It is a positive relationship, which means that students who scored

TABLE 8.2 Growth models of math and reading achievement, 2006–7 to 2007–8

Model	Math			Reading		
	1 Est. (s.e.)	2 Est. (s.e.)	3 Est. (s.e.)	1 Est. (s.e.)	2 Est. (s.e.)	3 Est. (s.e.)
MPCP 2006	1.43 (1.35)	1.12 (1.34)	0.02 (1.37)	1.77 (1.48)	1.59 (1.48)	0.08 (1.50)
2006 score	0.78*** (0.02)	0.75*** (0.02)	0.75*** (0.02)	0.76*** (0.02)	0.74*** (0.02)	0.74*** (0.02)
Native		−4.39 (7.22)	−4.64 (7.15)		−9.00 (15.63)	−8.71 (14.80)
Asian		−5.26 (4.92)	−5.38 (4.92)		2.17 (3.97)	1.95 (3.95)
Black		−13.63*** (2.10)	−13.25*** (2.09)		−8.13*** (2.24)	−7.63*** (2.23)
Hispanic		−7.43*** (2.21)	−7.36*** (2.19)		−2.90 (2.39)	−2.85 (2.38)
Female		2.02 (1.37)	1.84 (1.37)		1.18 (1.49)	0.94 (1.48)
Switch sch.			−7.13*** (2.68)			−9.97*** (2.84)
Intercept	119.74*** (8.31)	140.39*** (8.98)	142.62*** (8.99)	109.84*** (9.66)	122.26*** (10.25)	125.74*** (10.27)
R–sq	0.62	0.63	0.63	0.55	0.55	0.56
F	506.97***	290.41***	268.98***	317.88***	178.13***	166.01***
N	2,510	2,510	2,510	2,501	2,501	2,501

Notes: ***p<0.01, **p<0.05, *p<0.10, two–tailed. All models also include indicator variables for grades 4–8, with grade 4 as the reference category; Race variables are indicator variables with "White" as the reference category. Response weights were used. Robust standard errors are in parentheses.

Source: Witte et al. 2009: 14

higher on the 2006 test also scored high on the 2007 test, and those students that had low scores on the 2006 test also scored low on the test in 2007.

Researchers often examine different levels of statistical significance. In Table 8.2, these are evident at the bottom of the table (e.g., p<0.01, p<0.05, p<0.10). These significance levels, or **p-values**, are associated with different levels of confidence. If the researcher uses a p-value of .05, the most common p-value in social science research, this means that there is a 5 percent chance that the relationship between the independent and dependent variable would occur by chance alone, and not because a true relationship exists. If a researcher wants to be very conservative, she can set the p-value very small (e.g., $p<0.01$); however, this will make it more difficult to find a statistically significant relationship.

Besides looking at the individual relationships between independent and dependent variables, researchers are often also interested in how well the independent variables, as a group, predict the dependent variable. The R-squared statistic is one way to do this. The R-squared is the proportion of variance in the dependent variable (2007 test scores) explained by all of the independent variables (e.g., MPCP 2006 and 2006 test score) in the model. According to the R-squared in Math Model 1, our independent variables explain 62 percent of the variation in 2007 test scores. This is a relatively high R-squared for political science research, but it shows us that there are other factors that we did not include in our model that can predict test scores in 2007. The **F-statistic** tests the hypothesis that there is no relationship between any of the independent variables and the dependent variable. In all of our models, the F-statistic is large and statistically significant (see the asterisks). This means that at least one of the independent variables is related to the dependent variable.

In Model 2, we calculate the MPCP coefficient after adjusting for the impact of two additional **control variables**, race and gender. Some of these are statistically significant. For example, look at the estimated Model 2 coefficient for black students in math. The coefficient is -13.63. To interpret this result, one needs to compare it to the reference category, which is the group that was not included in the regression. According to the "note" at the bottom of Table 8.2, white students are the reference group. Therefore, the coefficient signifies the difference between black students and white students. After controlling for other factors, such as gender and voucher or public school status, black students scored 13.63 lower on the 2007 math test than did white students. The coefficient is negative because African-American students were coded as a one for the black variable, while everyone else was coded as a zero for this variable.

Two challenges with panel studies are changes in the main independent variable (voucher status) over time and panel mortality. In our evaluation, we found that many students change schools from year to year. About 75 percent of our voucher sample stayed in the same school, while only 62 percent of our MPS sample stayed in their same school from the first year to the next. Some students started in a voucher school, but then switched to a public school and vice versa. This complicates our analysis. We included a control variable called "Switch sch." in Table 8.2 that measures if a student changed schools between the 2006–7 and the 2007–8 school years. We find that school switching has a negative effect on student achievement. Students score lower on both the math and reading test after they have switched schools.

Our second major challenge is panel mortality, or study attrition. As students move and change schools, it was difficult for our research team to track them. This can be a major problem if there is differential attrition between the public and voucher sectors. We were unable to locate 290 MPCP and 201 MPS students in the second year of our study. This constitutes about 9 percent of our overall sample. To see how this panel mortality may affect our evaluation, we compared those students who we could not locate to those who remained in the study. We did not find big differences between these two groups. Then we compared those MPS students we could not locate to the MPCP students who we could not find in the second year of the study. Examining student demographics and test scores, we did not find large differences between these two groups. According to these results, panel mortality did not threaten our research design, and our sample was still representative of our population of interest.

Lessons to Be Learned

As we discussed in the introduction, school vouchers are a controversial topic. As program evaluators, we want to provide a transparent and non-ideological analysis of the effects of the voucher program in Milwaukee. Although we found few meaningful differences between voucher and public school student achievement, it has not stopped policymakers and activists on both sides of the issue from using our evaluation to support their claims. It can be frustrating as a researcher when others inaccurately portray your results. However, program evaluators should use this as a reminder to be explicit and clear about their research objectives and findings. Further, researchers should be aware of the limitations of their study and attempt to account for them in an appropriate way. For example, we realized that panel mortality is a serious threat to our analysis. Rather than ignoring it, we have tried to examine how panel mortality could affect our results. Further, we are trying to use our resources to better track students, so that we could limit the amount of study attrition. Knowing that your research could be used by policymakers and interest groups to further their agendas can make this type of research exciting, but also nerve-wracking. It requires program evaluators to be very careful and transparent in how they describe their research.

Given the research question and resources, our evaluation of the Milwaukee voucher program utilized both primary and secondary data sources. One of the greatest strengths of secondary data analysis, which may be of particular importance to political science students, is that it can be quite cost effective. It is often cheaper and easier to use data that have been gathered by someone else, as opposed to trying to collect the data on your own. Furthermore, secondary data analysis can sometimes allow the researcher to examine longitudinal questions or cross-national topics, which could be impossible using other data sources. However, secondary data analysis is not without its weaknesses. Since the researcher is relying on others for data collection, it is often likely that the variables or measurements will not be ideal for the research question. For example, our research team would have preferred to have test score data for all grades, rather than only in grades 3–8 and grade 10. Similarly, we would have liked to examine more subjects beyond math and reading, like science and social studies. Nevertheless, we were only able to use the data on public school students that were available from the State of Wisconsin. Additional primary data from the public school and voucher students could have allowed us to examine these other issues.

It is imperative that users of secondary data analysis fully understand how the data they are examining were collected, measured, and kept. Researchers must ask if the data are representative of the population of interest, and social scientists often face the challenge of incomplete data.[18] Incomplete data may arise from **selective survival**, which means that some documents may survive longer than others. Furthermore, record keepers often do not keep or preserve all records. For example, if a political scientist is examining the memoirs of presidents, she may notice that negative stories about the presidents are often overlooked and not included in the documents. This is an example of **selective deposit**, which are biases that are related to what type of information is available in documents. If history is written by the victors, researchers must be aware of the possibility of bias in the written record.

Official program evaluators have a constituency beyond their academic peers. While many policy-makers view evaluations as a way to inform their decision-making, others see evaluations as a way to avoid or postpone difficult decisions. At the same time, legislators often want answers quickly. Although our final evaluation of the MPCP has not been completed, some observers have already made conclusions about the effects of the program. This is a common challenge. Finally, policymakers may have goals for the evaluation that are different than those of the researcher. In our evaluation, lawmakers are primarily concerned with the effects of the MPCP on standardized test scores. We believe this is an incomplete approach. In other reports, our research team examined how the MPCP affects parents' views of safety and discipline in their children's schools and how the voucher program has affected taxpayers. In future reports, we will analyze graduation rates and parental satisfaction. It is our view that the effects of a public program should not be reduced to a test score alone.

Performing an evaluation of a public program is often different than other forms of political science research. Legislative mandates and oversight can be quite challenging to researchers. However, we view our participation in this evaluation as a form of public service. According to the Wisconsin Department of Public Instruction, the Milwaukee voucher program costs over $130 million per year. Policymakers and taxpayers deserve to know the effects of public policies. Our experiences with the evaluation of the Milwaukee Parental Choice Program have taught us that political scientists can play an important role in informing citizens and shaping public policy.

Interested to Know More about the Study Discussed in this Chapter?

See the official evaluation for the State of Wisconsin:

Witte, John F., Patrick J. Wolf, Joshua M. Cowen, David J. Fleming, and Juanita
    Lucas-McLean. 2009. "The MPCP Longitudinal Educational Growth Study:

Second Year Report." School Choice Demonstration Project, University of Arkansas, Fayetteville, AR, SCDP Milwaukee Evaluation Report #10, March.

Exercise and Discussion Questions:

1. If the researchers had been able to **randomly** assign students to the Milwaukee voucher program, how may some of the problems with **selection bias** have been avoided further? Can you think of any problems associated with **selection bias** that may have remained (hint: can policymakers force students to attend private schools?)

2. The researchers argue that including students' neighborhood location as part of the matching process accounts for many interesting **variables** that explain the decision to attend a certain school. Can you think of some examples of these variables? What *other reasons* for attending a particular school may still be unaccounted for in this design?

3. The researchers discuss a *tradeoff* between **internal** and **external validity**. Imagine you are an advisor to a United States Senator or to a state governor. It is your job to advise this policymaker on whether certain programs (like school vouchers) are worth supporting. In assessing the available scholarly evidence for whether a particular program "works," how might you weigh the trade-off between internal and external validity? Is it more important to provide precise, unbiased estimates of a program effect (internal validity), or more important to be able to describe the results as relevant to other groups that could be affected by similar programs (external validity)?

4. One of the major questions in American politics is what explains how Members of Congress vote. Political scientists have used both **primary** and **secondary sources** to examine this question. What methods could you use to answer this question? What are the *strengths* and *weaknesses* of using primary source versus secondary source analysis? Do you think that the type of analysis you use would affect the conclusions that you would make? What does that say about political science research?

Recommended Resources:

School Choice:

SCDP Evaluation Website (www.uark.edu/ua/der/SCDP/Milwaukee_Research. html).
Pro-School Voucher Website (www.edchoice.org).
Anti-School Voucher Website (www.aft.org/issues/schoolchoice/vouchers).

Student Mobility:

Students interested in reading more about student mobility in urban schools should read:

Kerbow, David, Carlos Azcoitia, and Barbara Buell. 2003. "Student Mobility and Local School Improvement in Chicago." *Journal of Negro Education* 72(1): 158–164.

Alexander, Karl L., Doris R. Entwisle, and Susan L. Dauber. 1996. "Children in Motion: School Transfers and Elementary School Performance." *Journal of Educational Research* 90(1): 3–12.

Rumberger, Russell W., Katherine A. Larson, Robert K. Ream, and Gregory J. Palardy. 1999. *The Educational Consequences of Mobility for California Students and Schools*. Berkeley, CA: Policy Analysis for California Education.

Sources of Secondary Data:

Education data (www.nces.ed.gov).

Statistical Abstract of the United States (www.census.gov/compendia/statab).

U.S. Federal Executive Branch datasets (www.data.gov).

Library of Congress (www.thomas.gov).

CIA's World Factbook (www.cia.gov/library/publications/the-world-factbook).

Wisconsin Advertising Project (www.wiscadproject.wisc.edu) and Wesleyan Media Project (www.election-ad.research.wesleyan.edu): These sites contain campaign advertising data.

Poll results (www.pollingreport.com).

Data archive (www.icpsr.umich.edu/icpsrweb/ICPSR): ICPSR at the University of Michigan.

Notes

1 Borsuk 2006.

2 Fleming 2009.

3 Howell et al. 2006; Witte 2000; Wolf et al. 2009.

4 Langbein and Felbinger 2006: 3.

5 Trenholm et al. 2008.

6 Ennet et al. 1994.

7 For other examples of primary source analysis in this volume, see Chapters 5 and 7.

8 For more examples and information on the difference between primary and secondary data, see Cole 1996; O'Sullivan and Rassel 1999.

9 See the end of this chapter for web-links to these projects and other sources of secondary data.

10 Jacobson 2001.

11 Singleton et al. 1998.

12 It is also possible that selection bias could work in the opposite direction. Perhaps Ms. Justice finds that those who have taken the LSAT class score higher than those who do not take the class. She also notes that the best and most conscientious students are more likely to take the LSAT class. Those students who did well on the LSAT will also have taken the class, but their high scores could be due to their hard-working mindset, not the effects of the LSAT class.

13 For examples of the use of field experiments to analyze the effects of school vouchers, see Howell and Peterson 2006; Wolf et al. 2009.

14 Students interested in these scholarly studies should read Witte 2000; Greene et al. 1999; Rouse 1998, for work on Milwaukee vouchers; Howell and Peterson 2006, for studies in New York City, and Dayton, Ohio; and Howell and Peterson 2006; Wolf et al. 2009, for separate studies of vouchers in Washington, DC.

15 Witte 2000.

16 We did not initially select tenth-grade students into our sample, because we wanted at least two years of test scores for each participant in our study.

17 We used a method called propensity score matching to do this. Propensity score matching involves estimating the probability that a subject is exposed to a particular condition (here, participating in the voucher program) based on a set of observable characteristics about that subject. In our case, these characteristics involved race, gender, prior test scores, and the student's first spoken language.

18 Singleton et al. 1998.

CHAPTER 9

Content Analysis
Local Media and Congress

C. Danielle Vinson

CONTENTS

GETTING CURIOUS: HOW DO LOCAL MEDIA COVER CONGRESS?

On any given day, Congress and its members do a lot. A few headlines illustrate the point: some have national implications ("House deals symbolic blow to raising debt ceiling");[1] some are strictly local ("Charleston would have to compete for port funding under [Senator] Graham proposal");[2] and some border on bizarre ("Rep. Weiner Gored by Goat in Washington").[3] The options of what to cover about Congress are endless.

So, how do local media cover Congress and its members? You might reasonably ask, "Who cares?" In 1992, I discovered that suddenly I cared. While working on a research paper for a media and politics course in graduate school, I found myself confronted by a contradiction between what scholars said about how local media covered members of Congress and my own observations of the local news. The scholarly research claimed that members of Congress enjoyed frequent and mostly favorable coverage from their local press.[4] However, most of the local reporting I had seen on one of my senators was much more critical than favorable. And I could not remember the newspapers or television stations in my parents' congressional district where I had lived for twenty years saying much of anything at all about their local representative. I doubted that my experiences with local congressional coverage in two states would be that different from local coverage anywhere else in the country. That meant that there was a serious disconnect between what scholars thought they knew about local media and Congress and the reality of local coverage of Congress. My observations suggested that local media coverage of Congress was not well understood.

As I looked more closely at the existing research, I began to see why it might not fit with reality. Most of the studies on local media coverage of Congress were at least ten to twenty years old.[5] Perhaps politics, the nature of local media, and the relationship between politicians and reporters had changed since those studies were done. A second problem for the existing research was that it only focused on newspapers. It seemed likely that local television or weekly papers might cover different stories than daily newspapers, and even when all organizations reported the same story, they might focus on different aspects of it. Finally, existing studies did not take into account the variations across media markets that might affect congressional coverage. Some small media markets cover only one or two congressional districts. In contrast, large urban markets could cross all or part of as many as thirty districts, and the media there could not possibly give frequent attention to all those members of Congress.

At this point, you might be inclined to ask, "Okay, so we don't know much about how local media cover Congress, but does that really matter? Why do we need to know this?" If I was going to spend what turned out to be nearly ten years researching local coverage of Congress, I first needed to answer what social scientists often call the "so what" question. I had to consider the *significance* of my research—why it was important to know how local media cover Congress and how that knowledge might add to our understanding of Congress and the American political system.

Coming up with an answer to these questions required not only reading about Congress and the media but also *thinking* about it. From my media and politics course, I remembered we had focused on the media as a watchdog over government that helped citizens hold elected officials accountable by informing them. We had also looked at how political leaders used the media to help communicate with the public, particularly their constituents. The reading I had done on media and Congress made it clear that most members of Congress received little if any attention from the national press, meaning national media were not particularly useful as a watchdog or a channel of communication for most members of Congress.[6] Furthermore, at least in the early 1990s, more people received their political news from local television and newspapers than any other source. If this was true, then perhaps the local media might be better suited to serve as a watchdog and channel of communication for congressional members. And if they were not serving those roles, then there was a potentially serious deficiency in our political system. The only way to find out was to understand what local media covered about Congress and how they did it. My research question seemed sufficiently significant for me to proceed with trying to answer it.

THE RESEARCH STRATEGY: WHAT IS CONTENT ANALYSIS?

Interested in a research question and convinced it was significant, I now needed to put together a **research design** or strategy for studying my question. For me, the method of research was quite obvious—**content analysis**. To understand how local media cover Congress, I needed to *systematically* examine and analyze local reporting on Congress.

Content analysis is a way to use categories to systematically analyze written or broadcast records. The process allows us to convert verbal or visual non-quantitative (non-numerical) content into data that can be measured quantitatively. We first choose what content we want to analyze. Almost any written, oral, or visual material can be subjected to content analysis—including media coverage, speeches, press releases, political ads, cartoons, and photos—but the content should be appropriate for investigating the researcher's question. In most cases, we do not have enough time or sufficient manpower to analyze all the material that might be relevant to our research question, so we must choose a subset of the material, what we call our **sample**. For example, I could not examine congressional coverage in all local television or newspapers; I had to pick a small number over a specific time period to analyze.

Once we have selected what we want to analyze, we create *categories* that measure the aspects of the content we want to investigate. For example, suppose we want to understand what makes coverage of Congress negative. We would select as our content a sample of media stories on Congress. To construct our categories, we would consider what aspects of coverage might make it negative. Thus, our categories might include several measures. We might evaluate the overall tone of the story—is it positive or negative? Second, we could look at the congressional activity being covered—was it about constituent service or credit-claiming, which would be positive, or floor debates and votes, which might highlight partisan conflict, or scandal, which is inherently negative. We could also consider any visuals (photos, cartoons, or video) accompanying the story. Together these aspects of the coverage might help explain why it was perceived as negative.

Choosing categories and defining them requires careful thought and planning and a fair amount of trial and error. Categories need to be both *exhaustive* and *mutually exclusive*. Exhaustive means that the categories must cover all possibilities, and mutually exclusive means all the content must be able to be assigned to a single category and cannot fit more than one. Suppose we want to look at the tone of coverage of a member of Congress. Can tone only be positive or negative? What would we do with an article that includes both positive and negative information about the member? We would need more categories to insure that they are exhaustive and cover all possibilities for the tone of the article. Continuing this same example, we might also want to know the sources of this coverage to help us determine which sources are more likely to be positive and which negative. We might create categories of possible sources that include the congressional member, his or her staff, members of the opposing party, scholars, and political experts. The potential problem with these categories is that scholars and experts might overlap. Some political experts might not be scholars, but political scholars are experts. The categories are not mutually exclusive. We could solve the problem by replacing the two confusing categories with more clearly defined ones such as academic political experts and non-academic political experts.

Once we have created our categories, we need to determine our **unit of analysis**—that is, the level of the content we will analyze. For example, we can analyze an article as a whole, or we can look at each paragraph or sentence. The unit of analysis will depend in part on what we want to know and the categories we have created. If we want to know what makes coverage negative, it makes sense to use the story as the unit of analysis. But if we want to know if one member is covered more negatively than another, it might be better to code each sentence of the story rather than the story as a whole.

Having now chosen the content we wish to study, created and defined the categories for doing so, and selected our unit of analysis, we need to compile the categories in a *content code* (see Figure 9.1). We can use the content code to analyze each unit of analysis, recording the answers for each in a spreadsheet or appropriate statistical program. Once we are done, we will have a full record of how often each category occurred in our content sample, and we can begin to perform a number of statistical operations described in more detail later in the chapter.

A. Story ID number _____

B. Type of media
1. daily paper
2. weekly paper
3. early evening newscast
4. late evening newscast

C. Primary congressional actor
1. local representative/senator
2. other rep./senator in the state
3. congressional party leader
4. other representative/senator

D. Primary congressional activity
1. committee hearing
2. committee vote
3. floor debate
4. floor vote
5. constituent service
6. credit-claiming
7. scandal

E. Orientation of coverage
1. Favorable
2. Unfavorable
3. Ambiguous
4. Neutral

Figure 9.1 Partial content code for local coverage of Congress

ISSUES WITH THIS RESEARCH STRATEGY

Content analysis offers several *advantages* to researchers. First, it can be applied to a wide variety of content and messages. We can analyze not only the written and spoken word from sources including news media, government documents, speeches, and television shows, but we can also examine visual content in photos, cartoons, television, film, and art. For example, some scholars of Congress have examined the photos and mementos that congressional members display on the walls in their Washington offices to see what messages they are communicating to visitors to their offices. The ability to analyze so many different types of content is particularly valuable when studying new media such as a congressional member's website because they combine written and spoken words, visual images, and non-verbal sounds. Furthermore, the applicability of content analysis to such a wide range of content makes it useful for studying nearly any subject, not just American government. In international relations, it has been used to study foreign policy leadership.[7] One well-known example from comparative politics is the Comparative Manifesto Project—a content analysis of European political parties' election programs since 1945 that provides data to study parties within specific countries or across countries.[8]

Second, many of these sources of content are increasingly easy and inexpensive to *access* and search. Many newspapers from around the world are readily available on the internet and are archived in electronic databases. Likewise, abstracts (summaries) or transcripts of television news shows, political talk shows, and radio shows are also available online. The internet has expanded our access to transcripts of government hearings, legislative debates, and presidential speeches. Elected officials often maintain their own websites where they post their speeches, clips of radio and television interviews, and press releases.

A third major advantage of content analysis is its suitability to both **quantitative** and **qualitative** analysis. The primary purpose of content analysis is to transform written or visual non-quantitative data into quantifiable categories that make **quantitative**, or statistical, analysis possible. As we count the occurrence of each category in our units of analysis, we can determine the *frequency*, or how often something occurs. For example, if we look at campaign ads, we can determine whether the tone of each is negative or positive. When we are done coding our entire sample of ads, we can see how many were negative. Content analysis also allows us to see how often certain categories are *correlated* with each other or other variables—that is, how often they occur together—and how they *co-vary*—whether they increase or decrease as other categories or variables increase or decrease. We might, for example, look to see if the number of negative ads in a congressional race is higher in those races that are close or if they increase as election day gets closer. Depending on the nature of our categories, we may be able to perform sophisticated statistical analysis on our data, as we will see later in this chapter.

But content analysis is not limited to quantitative analysis. It can also enable us to do more in depth **qualitative** examination. For example, while we can look at political ads to see how often candidates go negative, we can look at qualitative categories to analyze what makes an ad negative. We might look at the specific language or images candidates use. The ability to extract qualitative data and examples from content analysis often helps to illustrate the patterns we find in the quantitative analysis and makes our presentation of it more interesting.

Despite the benefits of content analysis, it is not without its costs and challenges. One important concern is the **validity** and **reliability** of our categories. Validity is whether the categories measure what we claim they do. For example, when we code news content as negative or positive, are we measuring how the story was covered or the coder's opinion of the issue being covered? Our content code needs to be clear about how we have defined negative and positive to ensure validity. Reliability is whether someone else following our definitions and procedure would arrive at the same coding decisions. In content analysis, these two issues are often connected. For objective categories such as the date a news article appeared in the paper, the measure is clearly valid and reliable. But on more subjective matters such as the tone of a news article, there may be more room for the coder's own judgment to play a role. Researchers must be careful that their own *selective perception*—the tendency to filter and interpret what we read or hear through our own ideological preferences—does not bias the analysis. Suppose we are analyzing the tone of a news article that reports that "Republicans plan to try to stop passage of the President's bill." Is that statement favorable or unfavorable to Republicans, or is it neutral reporting? If my analysis depends on whether I like the President's bill, then we have a problem with validity and reliability because I am now reading my own views into what the reporter actually said (a problem for the validity of the measure), and I cannot be certain that another person would arrive at the same interpretation (a problem for reliability).

Content analysis must provide clear definitions of categories that can be applied consistently and with the same results regardless of who does the coding. To guard against subjective measures, we typically conduct *inter-coder reliability* tests. We enlist a second person to code a small sample of our data and measure the level of agreement or discrepancies between the two coders. On objective categories, we would expect complete agreement. On subjective categories, we look for agreement on more than 80 percent of the cases. If inter-coder reliability falls below 80 percent, it may be an indication that the categories and definitions are problematic and need further clarification.[9]

One additional challenge in content analysis is the practical problem that this method can be labor intensive and time-consuming. It takes time to search databases to find the appropriate content to analyze, and the actual analysis can take even longer. In my own research on local coverage of Congress, once I gained access to local newspapers and television newscasts, I had to search them for stories about Congress. Then I had to read or watch nearly 2,000 stories and code 16 aspects of coverage for each story. Many scholars who do large-scale content analysis rely on graduate students to help with the coding. Some have turned to computer-assisted content analysis.

Software programs that aid in content analysis allow the researcher to download the material she wants to code and create a lexicon or dictionary that the computer will then apply to the downloaded content. Essentially, the computer searches for the words, phrases, or concepts of interest to the researcher and counts how often they occur. These innovations are useful, but they too have limits, particularly for studies in which the context of a word or phrase is important. For example, computer assisted content analysis would be quite helpful for learning how media references to the pro-life and pro-choice movements have evolved over time by counting the occurrence of labels such as "pro-life," "anti-abortion," "pro-choice," or "pro-abortion" from media coverage over a long period of time. But this would not necessarily tell us whether the coverage of the movement is favorable or unfavorable or who actually used these labels to refer to the movement. That might require more labor intensive human coding.

Even if we are able to overcome the challenges posed by content analysis, we must recognize its limits. Analyzing content alone may not help us explain the causes of content or determine its effects. For example, we might study news coverage of a member of Congress and find that it is mostly unfavorable and that the member is rarely quoted in the coverage. We might conclude that the press has treated the member unfairly. But there is an alternative explanation—the member might not return reporters' phone calls, leaving reporters with only one side of the story. We have no way of knowing which explanation is accurate from the content analysis alone. If we want to explain the content or learn the effects it has on readers or viewers, we must combine content analysis with other methods such as elite interviews or surveys of public opinion. This use of multiple methods to study a research question is called *methodological pluralism*.

For my own research question, content analysis was the only method that could help me understand how local media cover Congress and its members. But before I could make decisions about what media to analyze and what categories to include in my analysis, I needed to conduct a literature review of the existing scholarly research that was relevant to my topic.

THE LITERATURE REVIEW

The existing research on local media coverage of Congress was sparse, limited in its scope, and questionable in its findings as I mentioned at the start of the chapter. There were no books on the specific subject, and the research that was available looked primarily at local newspapers.[10] Furthermore, it considered coverage for only short periods of time—usually centered around campaigns and elections. What I discovered was not so much gaps in the literature but a big gaping hole.

Despite the lack of literature on local coverage, there was some research on national coverage of Congress, and there was plenty of research on how both local and national media decide what to cover. These studies proved to be valuable in constructing my content analysis and in explaining the significance of my research. There was a consensus in the research on national coverage of Congress that most members did not receive much attention from the national press, and those that did tended to be party or committee leaders in Congress or mavericks who bucked their own party regularly. When the national press covered Congress, it focused more on the institution of Congress—the House and Senate, committees, or parties—rather than on the individual members.[11] In designing my own study, I would need to see if the same held true for local media.

The literature on how media decide what to cover provided explanations for the concept of newsworthiness and also noted the importance of organizational and structural considerations—for example, the amount of news space, the number of reporters, and the presence of a Washington bureau—in determining what media cover.[12] Some scholars pointed out that political elites could have a role in shaping coverage through their press relations efforts.[13] Others considered the profit-making role of the media and its impact on content.[14] All of these studies helped me figure out that there were three main areas of coverage I needed to consider—the amount of coverage of Congress, the substantive content (who and what were covered), and the tone of the coverage. They also suggested that different types of media might cover Congress differently and that media markets of varying sizes would approach congressional coverage in distinct ways. It was time to design my study.

DOING THE STUDY: COLLECTING THE DATA AND DOING THE ANALYSIS

The first issue I had to resolve was *what media coverage* I would use for my analysis. I wanted to include a variety of media from each market in my study. I decided to look at daily newspapers, television (both the early and late evening newscasts), and at least one weekly newspaper. I opted for two television newscasts because the late evening news often included more national news than the early newscast, and the two evening newscasts typically draw the largest audiences. I selected the daily newspaper and the television station with the largest audience in each market. For the weekly papers, I had to consider a different issue. After consulting a few congressional press secretaries, I learned that weekly newspapers serve vastly different audiences—some geographical, some ethnic or racial, some religious, and some, a specific interest group. The press secretaries suggested that I focus on geographically or racially defined readerships because these weeklies were the only ones to cover Congress with any frequency.

The next issue was to figure out the *time period* for following coverage. Here the limits of my access to certain types of media constrained my options. In 1993 when I was gathering data, electronic databases were not as readily available even for newspapers as they are today. I could get daily newspapers on microfilm, but I would have to subscribe to the weeklies, and there was no way to obtain local television news except to record it when it aired. Thus, retroactive retrieval of the news was expensive if not impossible. For these reasons, I had to choose dates in the future.

I wanted routine coverage of Congress, but with no crystal ball to see into the future, I had to find a way to minimize the likelihood that I would pick a time period that turned out to be atypical. The solution was to pick nonconsecutive weeks over several months. I chose four weeks between September 1993 and January 1994. These included times when Congress was in session and when it was on recess and the end of a congressional session and the beginning of a session. I settled on four weeks as a sufficient but manageable number to analyze. I later added two additional weeks of coverage during the 1994 fall congressional campaigns to deal with the impact of campaigning on coverage. Even when retroactive retrieval is possible, using nonconsecutive days or weeks can be a good tactic for minimizing the effects of a single event or issue and providing a more representative and manageable sample of content.

This strategy worked well, but there were a few deviations from normalcy. Forest fires or mudslides dominated one week of coverage in two media markets, and there was a major sports story in one of the markets that took up space usually reserved for regular news. A couple of congressional scandals erupted during the weeks I collected data. All these unusual occurrences confirmed the wisdom of my decision to look at nonconsecutive weeks of coverage.

Although technology and electronic databases have made retroactive retrieval of content easier and less expensive, researchers still have to make tough decisions about what content and time periods they will study. If we fail to make choices to limit the sample, the content analysis can quickly become overwhelming and the data unwieldy.

The final decision I had to make about gathering data was *which media markets* to use. The decision was governed primarily by three considerations. Because I hypothesized or theorized that market–district congruence or the fit between media markets and congressional districts would affect how local media cover Congress, I needed to make sure I chose markets that would provide contrasts in congruence. I wanted low congruence markets that covered all or part of a large number of districts and high congruence markets that covered all or most of just one or two districts as well as some markets in between. Second, I wanted coverage from around the country to make sure that there were no regional differences in coverage. And the final consideration was practical: I had to be able to find someone who could tape the evening news during the study. I looked at media markets where I had family, friends, and friends of friends and then selected the markets that provided differences in congruence and regional location. In the end, I settled on eight media markets—two high congruence (Santa Barbara, CA and Charleston, SC), four moderate congruence (Atlanta, GA; Columbia, SC; Raleigh, NC; and San Antonio, TX), and two low congruence (Los Angeles, CA and Philadelphia, PA).

Then I waited for the weeks I had chosen to gather my news to arrive and held my breath that all would go well. Mostly it did. A few VCRs were set incorrectly or were affected by power outages, causing a few missed newscasts. And on one occasion, a World Series Game between Philadelphia and Toronto ran well past midnight on CBS as both teams, exhibiting neither pitching nor defense, scored in double figures, and one of the people taping news on that network fell asleep before the news came on—another missing day and a reminder that social scientists often do not have complete control over the collection of their data.

My plan was to analyze the content of all news stories, editorial and opinion pieces, letters to the editor, features, and political cartoons that mentioned Congress or its members during the weeks I chose. I decided the story as a whole should be the **unit of analysis** so that I could look at the amount and detail of coverage, the substance of what was covered, and the favorability or orientation of the coverage toward Congress. Smaller units of analysis such as paragraphs within a story would not have provided this big picture. At the end of the process, I had 1,853 stories to analyze.

The next step was to create my *content code*. I had to devise *categories* to measure the aspects of coverage I was most interested in—amount of coverage, substantive content, and evaluative content. Here, I will focus on the categories I used to analyze the substantive content of local congressional coverage. To answer what was covered, I looked at several aspects of the substantive content—the issues, the congressional actors, the congressional activities, and the sources reporters used. For each of these aspects of coverage, I had to create a list of categories that would encompass all the possibilities of what the media could cover about Congress. In some cases, content codes from existing scholarly research offered a starting point for creating categories. I could modify them to fit my particular interests rather than starting over from scratch.

I was particularly interested in the extent to which local media localized or put a local spin on their coverage of Congress. Where possible, I tried to create categories that would help capture that. I also created an overall measure of localization. If there was no content in the story explicitly relevant to the media market, I categorized it as national. At the other extreme, if the story was of concern only to the market in which it ran, I labeled it exclusively local. Stories that included information of interest to both a national and local audience were coded as mixed.

For the issues, I started with broad categories such as foreign policy and scandals, and then divided those to create more specific categories if issues within the broad divisions were given substantial coverage. For example, Congress was considering passage of the North American Free Trade Agreement (NAFTA) during the fall of 1993, and this received extensive coverage. I made it a separate category from the other foreign policy issues. Through a little trial and error, I settled on 30 issue categories. If I were just beginning this project today, the comprehensive issue categories used in the Policy Agendas Project, now available online, would be a useful starting point.[15]

Determining whether the issues were local or not required more qualitative analysis because some issues, depending on the focus of the particular story, could have been local or national. NAFTA, for example, was a national story if the report only looked at how likely the agreement was to pass in Congress. However, if the story considered the impact of NAFTA on the local textile industry, it was a local story.

In addition to the issues, I wanted to look at whom the media focused on as the participant in congressional activity. My list of congressional actors included both individuals and institutions (House or Senate committees, the House, the Senate, Democrats, and Republicans). I divided the individuals into several categories—the local representative or senator, other representatives from the state, congressional leaders, and other members of Congress not from the state. These categories could be aggregated or combined into two larger divisions—local actors and non-local actors.

Looking at the possible congressional activities that could be reported, I was also able to divide them into local and non-local activities. The local activities included appearances or speeches in the district or state, campaign activities, and then three types of actions that existing research on Congress talks about being important for members of Congress in seeking reelection—casework for constituents, claiming credit for legislative accomplishments, and taking positions on issues of importance to constituents. The non-local activities included committee hearings or votes, floor debate, floor votes, interaction with the executive branch, relations with interest groups or lobbying, and scandal.

Finally, I considered the sources that reporters cited in their stories. One way reporters might put a local angle on the stories is by using local sources. I included among my categories of sources the local representative or senator, other representatives from the state, and non-congressional sources from the state. Non-local sources included other members of Congress, the president or other members of the executive branch, experts, and a category labeled "other" to capture any additional possibilities.

Once I had coded all the stories, I could begin to analyze the data. First, I wanted simply to describe the coverage. I did this by conducting frequency analysis of each category—that is, how often it occurred in the coverage or how many of the news stories in my sample included a specific category. For example, I conducted a frequency analysis on the overall measure of localization and found that 66 percent of the stories were national and 16 percent were exclusively local. While the frequencies did allow me to know more about what is covered in Congress and how much of the coverage provides a local angle, I also wanted to understand the variations in coverage across media markets and types of media. This would help me explain and perhaps even predict coverage. For that I needed to conduct more complex analyses.

I began by doing **crosstabs** to see if categories related to other variables like congruence or the type of media as I expected they would. Crosstabs look at two or more variables to see how often they occur at the same time. For example, I looked at the degree of localization in each type of media and found significant differences across the types of media. Daily papers, black weekly papers, and late night television newscasts all had mostly national coverage (more than 60 percent of their stories). Early evening newscasts had the most exclusively local news at nearly 40 percent. Community-based weekly papers had the most localized content with 26 percent of their stories exclusively local and another 57 percent mixed. I also examined the differences in localization across market–district congruence. Moderate congruence markets had the most purely local stories and the least national stories. Low and high congruence markets had somewhat less local coverage and slightly more national coverage.

Having confirmed that there were differences across media and markets but that all local media included at least some localization of Congress from time to time, I wanted to see how these local media environments accomplished that localization. To do this, I ran a series of **logit regressions**—a statistical method that allows us to see the impact of several **independent variables** on a **dependent variable** that is dichotomous or has only two possible values. In my first regression, the **dependent variable**, the aspect of coverage I wanted to explain, was whether or not the story used a local member of Congress as the primary actor. The **independent variables**, what I thought would explain the dependent variable, included the market–district congruence, whether the news organization the story came from had a Washington reporter, whether the provider of the story was local (a local reporter, for example) or national (a wire service), and then the type of media. To measure the type of media, I used **dummy variables**—a variable that equals one if it is in a particular category and zero if it is not—to indicate if the story was from an early evening newscast (coded 1) or not (coded zero), from a late evening newscast (coded 1) or not (coded zero), and so on for the different types of weekly newspapers. The results appear in Table 9.1.

The regression analysis revealed that stories from higher congruence markets, early evening newscasts, community weeklies, and a local provider are more likely to focus on local congressional actors. We know this because the

TABLE 9.1 Who localizes by covering local congressional members?

Variable[a]	Coefficient	Standard error	First differences[b]
Congruence	.3726*	.0927	.159
Washington reporter	.0077	.1797	.001
Early evening news	1.0841*	.2773	.256
Late evening news	.3417	.2852	.075
Community weekly	1.6845*	.4188	.398
Black weekly	.3411	.3654	.076
Local provider	1.7958*	.1352	.381
Constant	−2.3863*	.2461	

Notes: N = 1, 853; X2 = 25.2795*; df = 6; *significant at p<.001; [a] the dependent variable was whether or not the story used a local member of Congress as the primary actor (1 if yes, 0 if no); [b] first differences indicate the increased or decreased likelihood of the dependent variable if we raise the independent variable from its minimum to its maximum while holding the other variables at their mean.

Source: Reprinted with permission from Vinson 2003: 80

coefficients for these variables were all **statistically significant**. Their p-values were all smaller than .05, meaning the probability of these patterns in the independent variables and the dependent variable occurring randomly if there were no relationship between the variables was less than 5 percent. We can also see in the last column in Table 2 the **first differences** or the likely increase or decrease in the dependent variable if we raise each independent variable from its minimum to maximum value while holding the other variables constant. Thus, going from a low congruence market to a high congruence market increases the likelihood that the story will cover a local member of Congress as the primary congressional actor 15.9 percent, all else being equal. The story occurring on an early evening newscast as opposed to daily papers increases that likelihood by 25.6 percent.

There are several numbers below Table 9.1 that are commonly reported in statistical analysis. N is the number of cases used in the analysis—in my study that was the 1,853 stories on Congress. Below that is X^2 or **chi-square statistic** and the *degrees of freedom* (df). Together, these statistics allow us to determine if the model or relationship between the independent variables and the dependent variable is statistically significant. In this case, the computer computes the chi-square statistic and degrees of freedom and uses them to arrive at the p-value, which is less than .001, suggesting that the probability of the relationships in this model occurring randomly is very low, and thus the model is significant.

Using the same independent variables, I ran similar regressions using local activities and local sources as the dependent variables. I learned that local activities are more likely to be reported on late evening news and in community and black weeklies than in daily newspapers and early evening newscasts. They are more likely to be in stories from a local provider. Interestingly, congruence had no effect on the kinds of activities covered. The use of local sources for congressional coverage was more likely in television news and weeklies than in the daily papers. And it was more likely as market–district congruence increased. These findings confirmed my hypotheses that the different types of media would cover Congress in different ways and that market–district congruence would also affect coverage of Congress. Of particular importance was the discovery that all media in all markets did localize at least some congressional coverage, but they went about it in very different ways. Some, particularly in moderate and high congruence markets, focused on the local members of Congress and local sources, while others in low congruence markets found local angles in the issues being covered.

Overall, the study confirmed my expectations. Different media do indeed cover Congress and its members differently, depending on the resources of the media outlet, its purpose and its audience, and the fit between the media market and the congressional districts it covers. The differences in coverage were predictable, and they helped explain the disconnect between the existing research on Congress and local media and my own observations of local coverage that prompted my research.

Lessons to Be Learned

Apart from the substantive findings, there are several things we can take away from this study. First, it is okay to challenge the existing scholarly literature if it does not appear to provide adequate descriptions or explanations of what we observe in the real world. In the social sciences, limitations in our methods make it difficult to completely close the book on a research question. We should always scrutinize existing descriptions and theories in light of their accuracy and ability to explain current events and behavior. Second, in the realm of content analysis, we must accept the fact that we cannot control everything in the research (in my case, other events during the time periods I studied, missing days of coverage, or types of media I could not access). We need to acknowledge our deficiencies and try to minimize their effects.

Finally, I learned that **quantitative** and **qualitative** analysis can be *complementary*. In my case, much of my analysis was quantitative, but systematic qualitative examination of the coverage often corroborated the statistical findings and made the research much more interesting. For example, to support my findings on how different media in different markets localized their congressional coverage, I did a qualitative case study of how NAFTA, which received attention in all my media markets, was covered, specifically looking to see if the patterns I saw in the statistical analysis appeared in the coverage of this issue. The qualitative findings backed up the statistical analysis.

Now, look around you. There is a world of content that has an impact on politics and society. What research questions can you think of that would be appropriate to study with content analysis?

Interested to Know More about the Study Discussed in this Chapter?

Consult the research publication:

Vinson, C. Danielle. 2003. *Local Media Coverage of Congress and Its Members: Through Local Eyes*. Cresskill, NJ: Hampton Press.

Exercises and Discussion Questions:

1. What are the weaknesses of content analysis, and how might you overcome these problems?
2. Try to devise a way of determining whether content is negative or positive that is not dependent on your own ideology or preferences.
3. What challenges might new media (internet, blogs, twitter, or other social media) pose for doing content analysis that we don't encounter with traditional media?

Recommended Resources:

On Content Analysis:

(www.academic.csuohio.edu/kneuendorf/content): Online companion to *The Content Analysis Guidebook* by Kimberly Neuendorf. It includes content analysis resources, bibliographies of studies that use content analysis, and links to message archives that could be used for content analysis.

Sources of Content that Could Be Analyzed:

(www.presidentialrhetoric.com): Includes transcripts of recent and historic presidential speeches.

(www.presidency.ucsb.edu/sou.php: includes): Includes transcripts of state of the union addresses, recordings of presidential radio addresses, and a wide range of presidential documents including signing statements and executive orders.

(www.tvnews.vanderbilt.edu): Provides abstracts of all network television news from 1968 to present.

(www.tweetcongress.org): Provides information about which members of Congress use twitter and links to their twitter pages. It includes live-stream channels of tweets broken down by Senate, House, Congress, and both parties.

(www.manifestoproject.wzb.eu): Comparative Manifesto Project. It provides content analysis of European party election programs since 1945. The website provides codebooks and data for the project.

Notes

1 Mascaro 2011.
2 Clark 2011.
3 "Rep. Weiner Gored by Goat in Washington," myFOXphoenix.com, June 11, 2010.
4 Bagdikian 1974; Vermeer 1995.
5 Bagdikian 1974; Robinson 1981.
6 Hess 1986; Robinson and Appel 1979; Tidmarch and Pitney 1985.
7 Walker et al. 2011.
8 "Manifesto Project Database," Accessed June 2, 2011, http://manifestoproject. wzb.eu
9 Lombard et al. 2010; Neuendorf 2002.
10 Bagdikian 1974; Clarke and Evans 1983; Tidmarch and Pitney 1985.
11 Cook 1989; Hess 1986.
12 Gans 1979; Shoemaker 1991.
13 Cook 1998; Kedrowski 1996.
14 Kaniss 1991; McManus 1994.
15 "Policy Agendas Project," Accessed June 1, 2011, www.policyagendas.org

Experimental Research

If Bill Clinton Were a Woman?

Elizabeth S. Smith

GETTING CURIOUS: ARE WOMEN DISCRIMINATED AGAINST?

"I did not have sexual relations with that woman, Miss Lewinsky. I never told anybody to lie, not a single time; never. These allegations are false. And I need to go back to work for the American people. Thank you." It was January 26, 1998 and our sitting president just denied having an affair with a 22-year-old intern by the name of Monica Lewinsky. The year that followed would be a whirlwind of accusations and he-said, she-saids. It would end in the impeachment of President Clinton, only the second time ever in our nation's history when a president was impeached. And, yet, though he was impeached, Clinton was not removed from office as the Senate failed to convict him with the charges of perjury, obstruction of justice, and abuse of power.

Sex scandals were nothing new to Bill Clinton. He had been elected president in 1992 after allegations (with tape-recordings of Clinton and his accuser) of a long-term affair with a woman named Genifer Flowers. The Lewinsky scandal broke in large part because of accusations by a woman named Paula Jones of sexual harassment by Clinton when he was governor of Arkansas and she was a state employee. That case ended in 1998 when he agreed to pay $850,000 in a court settlement. And, yet, despite that case, the Flowers scandal, and the Lewinsky scandal, Clinton ended the year of 1998 with some of the highest approval ratings a president has ever had at the end of his second term. How could that be? Why did the American public not punish him for his scandalous behavior? And, how would the public react if a female politician had been engaging in such shenanigans?

The notion of a double standard for males and females, especially male and female politicians, was of particular interest to me when I decided to pursue this research project. Are women held to a higher standard than men? Would female politicians be able to operate like Bill Clinton did and still keep their political office and their high approval ratings? The anecdotal evidence suggested otherwise. In fact, it was during the Clinton administration's first term that Zoe Baird, a female attorney who was nominated by Clinton to be Attorney General, was forced to withdraw after it was discovered she had hired an illegal alien to be her nanny and failed to pay the taxes. Similarly, his second nominee was also a female, Kimba Wood, who had in fact paid the taxes on her nanny (who was also not a U.S. citizen) and who was forced by the similarities of the controversy to withdraw her name. While these were not sex scandals like Clinton's, it could be argued that these females' situations were less nefarious than Clinton's and, yet, they ended up derailing both of their chances to become Attorney General.

But, anecdotal information that females are judged more harshly than males involved in scandal is not scientific information. Anecdotal hunches depend on the handpicked 'data' one uses to make the best case. I would need to devise a strategy to figure out if in fact voters held male and female politicians to a different standard. One way I could do this, I thought, would be to gather systematically all of the political scandals of male and female politicians and examine the reactions by voters. However, how many cases of female politicians involved in a scandal would I be able to find?

In 1998, when I began this research, women made up only 11 percent of Congress and that was an all-time high. In addition, how would I make comparisons when all things were not similar between the various cases? For example, how can one really compare the nanny-gate episodes to the Monica-gate and other Clinton-sex scandal episodes and say that the results were different simply because it was a male or female politician who was involved? In one case, the offender was the president (or presidential candidate); in the other, the offenders were relatively obscure female attorneys. In one case, the offenses were sex scandals; in the other cases, the offenses had to do with hiring illegal nannies. In order to test whether voters held men and women to different standards when it came to involvement in a scandal, I needed cases where the only thing different was the gender of the politician. What I needed was *control* over all other factors. And, thus, I decided that an *experiment* where I could hold constant the specifics of the scenarios and *manipulate* the gender of the candidate would provide me with the kind of clear evidence I would need to be able to show whether or not the gender of the politician mattered. The primary benefit of the experimental method over all other research methods is the ability to have this control.

THE RESEARCH STRATEGY: WHAT IS THE EXPERIMENTAL METHOD?

Experiments are most often associated with the hard sciences. Based on careful observations of the world around them, scientists begin with a hypothesis, or educated guess, about a relationship between two or more variables—e.g., sunshine is needed to make grass grow. The causal variable(s) (in this case, sunshine) is known as the independent variable and the thing which is affected by it (the growth of the grass seed) is known as the dependent variable. In order to confirm the hypothesis, scientists must *manipulate* what they believe to be the causal variable (amount of sunshine) and observe the effects of this manipulation on the dependent variable (the grass seed). So, a scientist would create in this very simple example two conditions manipulating whether sunshine was present or absent. The scientist would then observe whether the grass grows in the first condition (with sunshine present) but not in the second, *ceteris paribus*. Ceteris paribus literally means all other things being equal and reflects the essential need in an experiment for *control*. So, in this example, in order to confidently make a **causal** *inference* that sunlight causes grass to grow, the scientist would want to be able to make sure the two conditions differed in no other way than whether the grass was exposed to sunlight or not. Relevant controls would include using the same grass seed in both conditions, the same soil, planted in the same container with the same amount of water. If all other things are equal, the scientist can feel confident that the independent variable, sunlight, caused the effect on the dependent variable (growth of the grass).

The scientific method is used to test causal relationships in other disciplines as well. Psychologists, educational specialists and many others have used experiments to test their hypotheses. The most simple version of an experiment is that reviewed above—which reflects what is known as the classic **pre-test/post-test design**, where an observation (pre-test) is made of the dependent variable (grass seed) before the manipulation, the manipulation is introduced (the sunlight), and the effect is observed (post-test). This classic design is illustrated in Table 10.1.

Political scientists interested in finding out the effects, for example, of negative campaign advertisements might assign one group of people to exposure to negative advertisements while another group was not exposed to any negative advertisements.[1] To assess the effect of the negative ads, the researcher might do a pre-test asking the participants how likely they think they are to vote in

TABLE 10.1 Classic pre-test/post-test experimental design

	Pre-test	Manipulation	Post-test
Experimental group	O_1	X	O_3
Control group	O_2		O_4

the next election and then do a post-test after the experimental group was exposed to the negative ads asking the respondents now how likely they are to vote in the next election. An essential aspect of creating control in an experiment like this is **random assignment** of participants in the study to each of the conditions. If participants are randomly assigned, probabilistically speaking they should be on average about the same and therefore we can feel more confident (but not 100 percent certain) that any differences between the groups in the post-test were due to the manipulation and not to inherent differences between the groups themselves.

ISSUES WITH THIS RESEARCH STRATEGY: THREATS TO INTERNAL AND EXTERNAL VALIDITY

However, this classic design is not without its problems (as we have seen throughout this textbook no method is entirely perfect). There are threats both to the **internal** and **external validity** of this study. Internal validity threats have to do with whether the manipulation was really what was responsible for the difference between the groups (between group difference) as well as for the change from the pre-test to the post-test within the group (within group differences). Scholars have identified a number of threats to internal validity. For example, **history effects** are when something else (besides the manipulation) occurs between the pre-test and the post-test that is the cause of the change from time one to time two, not the manipulation. **Maturation effects** occur when there is a change in the respondents themselves from time one to time two that has nothing to do with the manipulation. If there is a significant period of time between the pre-test and the post-test, both history and maturation effects may be responsible for the changes. **Testing effects** are also internal validity threats—asking someone about their voting behavior may make them sensitive to this and after more careful thought they may then give a different answer in the post-test, not because of the manipulation but because of the pre-test itself. **Social desirability effects** might make respondents more likely in the post-test to say they are likely to vote since that may be perceived as the socially desirable response. Or, respondents might say they are less likely to vote just because that is what they think the researcher desires to hear. In addition, some participants might decide they no longer want to participate in the study after the pre-test—the effects of some people dropping out are also threats to internal validity and are known as **mortality effects**. Consider perhaps if some group of students were offended by the ads and decided they just did not want to participate anymore. Since we cannot make people stay in a study, those who drop out might differ in some systematic way from those who stayed in so we do not know for certain that the differences within groups and between groups in the post-test are due to the manipulation or to the differences in the people now participating. **Instrumentation effects** are when the instrument itself (for example, the question of whether they are likely to vote) changes in some way. So, even if the same question is asked in the pre-test and post-test, imagine if at time one it was administered orally by a shy, nervous graduate student to the participants and in time two it was administered orally by a confident, boisterous graduate student. Changes from time one to time two might be the result of who administered the instrument not the manipulation. Fortunately, random assignment of participants to both a control and an experimental condition helps to ensure that any of these threats to internal validity will, on average, (but not always) affect both groups equally. Thus, we can feel confident that differences between the experimental group and the control group are due to the manipulation and that we are making an appropriate causal inference about the effect of the independent variable on the dependent variable.

External validity refers to the extent to which the findings are generalizable to the real world (rather than only holding true in this artificial, experimental setting). Threats to external validity in this example might be *implementation-related*—that participants were forced to sit in some lab and watch ads undistracted which does not mimic how voters usually are exposed to ads (in their home environment, while watching TV and doing the dishes, etc.). Threats to external validity might also be *people-related*—typically college students are recruited for experiments and, even though they are randomly assigned to conditions, college students, especially chosen from one particular locale (a *place-related* threat), may be fundamentally different from the rest of the population. Finally, threats to external validity might be *instrument-related* (which can also be a threat to internal validity as discussed earlier). Pre-testing the participants and their awareness of their involvement in a study may make them subject to *guinea pig effects*, also called the **Hawthorne Effect** (named after an experimental study done on workers at a company by the name of Hawthorne)—their behavior cannot be generalized to the larger population because as participants in a study who are aware they are being studied, they act differently than they would in the real world.

One way scientists have dealt with some of these problems is to create other kinds of experimental designs. For example, the post-test only design attempts to address the problem of testing effects by eliminating the pre-test. Thus, a post-test only design looks as depicted in Table 10.2:

TABLE 10.2 Post-test only experimental design

	Manipulation	Post-test
Experimental group	X	O_1
Control group	–	O_2

Post-test only designs are actually quite common in political science and political psychology. An example would be an experiment where researchers were interested in understanding how the wording of a question on a survey might affect responses.[2] Asking participants in a pre-test and post-test two different versions of the same question would be awkward (participants would wonder why they are being asked essentially the same question) and likely reactive (the response on the pre-test would very likely have an effect on the response on the post-test). So, in a post-group only experimental design such as this, one group would be given one version (the old version, for example) of a survey question and the other group would be given a different version (the new formulation of the question). The researcher would then be interested in examining not the difference within the groups from time one to time two (since no pre-test was administered) but, instead, the difference between the two groups in their responses to the questions.

Occasionally, researchers also use **multi-group experimental designs** (these can be either **pre-test/post-test designs** or **post-test only**). For example, suppose a researcher was interested in the effects of congressional communications on constituents.[3] Researchers might want to see how many mailings by a member of Congress it takes to make voters aware of the Congresspersons' position on an issue. The experimenter might have a control group who got no information about the Congressperson's position, one experimental group where the participants got one mailing, another where the participants received two mailings, etc. In a pre-test, the experimenter would measure knowledge of the Congressperson's position on an issue before the communication and then after. Such an experiment would look as depicted in Table 10.3 (the pre-test could be eliminated here as well and just the differences between groups compared):

TABLE 10.3 Multi-group experimental design

	Pre-test	Manipulation	Post-test
Experimental group$_1$	O_1	X_1	O_4
Experimental group$_2$	O_2	X_2	O_5
Control group	O_3		O_6

Sometimes experiments occur naturally (*natural experiments*) or are performed in natural (real-world) settings (**field experiments**). An example of a field experiment would be if voters in one county were given a sticker that said "I Voted" while voters in a similar county were not given such a sticker. The researcher could observe voter turnout in both counties in the prior election and voter turnout in the election where the stickers were introduced in the one county and observe whether turnout was higher from time one to time two in the county where the sticker was provided and whether voter turnout differed between the two counties. Of course, in field and natural experiments, the study is no longer plagued by the problem of an artificial setting. However, the researcher also loses a lot of control so it makes it more difficult to know if the manipulation itself was responsible for the effect.[4]

I decided that my study on the effects of the gender of a politician involved in a scandal on voters' evaluations would best be assessed with a **multi-group**, **post-test only design**. Before I explain how that design was chosen and created, let me first discuss the next logical step in my research process—the literature review.

THE LITERATURE REVIEW

I had an idea of what research *method* I wanted to use to explore my question. And, I had a clear research question: Do voters evaluate male and female politicians involved in scandal differently? But, before I could go any further with the project I had to find out if anyone else had already answered this question. Was there research already done in political science or psychology perhaps that addressed this topic? Was there research that would help me support my **hypothesis**, or educated guess about the relationship between my main **independent variable**, sex of the politician, and my **dependent variable** which was voters' evaluation of the politician?

What I needed to do now was what scholars call a **literature review**. A literature review is a systematic examination of the extant scholarly literature in the field and related fields that is relevant to your research topic. Typically, the process of completing a literature review begins with searching a library database with certain key words related to your topic. In my case, I searched for books and articles, for example, using such terms as political scandals, gender politics, impression management, political ethics, and gender bias. I searched political science databases in order to learn especially what political scientists had learned about political scandals as well as psychology databases as I needed to be able to confirm that gender bias existed and to find out how it manifested itself. The goal of writing a literature review, which is found in the first section of one's research paper and constitutes about 5–10 percent of the entire paper, is to engage with others in the scholarly conversation. In a literature review, the author acknowledges what other scholars have discovered about this topic as it relates to the research question at hand. Literature reviews are *not* comprehensive summaries of everything that has ever been done or said about the topics but instead highlight commonalities in findings as well as areas where there may be disagreement among scholars. Typically, literature reviews group past research along common themes and, perhaps most importantly, highlight gaps in knowledge that the present study is intending to address.

So, the first thing I examined was the research on political scandals. And, I found that scholars had spent a considerable amount of time considering how politicians extricated themselves from blame when they were involved in a scandal. A number of very interesting studies had been done on the effectiveness of various "blame avoidance strategies."[5] While I was not initially interested in this aspect of scandals, as I read on, I began to see that these blame avoidance strategies were inextricably linked to how voters ultimately evaluate the politician. Politicians involved in scandals have to react in some way to their constituents. What is the most effective reaction? Should they deny involvement in the scandal as Bill Clinton is doing in the quote which began this chapter? Or, should they provide an explanation? A justification? I decided that in order to address my research question appropriately I would need to manipulate in the experiment the kind of account that was offered by the politician and see which one "worked" best for him/her, thus this was the first indication that I would need a multi-group design.

In my literature review, I also discovered that no one had directly addressed the question of whether male and female politicians involved in a scandal were evaluated differently. So, I knew I had something to contribute with this particular study. Examination of the women and politics literature did confirm that voters generally think female politicians are more honest and ethical than male politicians. And, the psychology research I reviewed provided mixed findings about whether people were more likely to judge harshly when someone failed to meet their expectations or were more likely to downplay or ignore information that did not meet their expectations—so this was an area of disagreement in the research into which my research could provide some insight. Research also confirmed that there were stereotypes surrounding male and female issue area competencies—certain issue areas were deemed to be 'female,' such as family and social issues, and certain issues were associated more as 'male,' such as economic issues, so I also decided that these stereotypes were important in considering the type of scandal in which a politician was involved.

DOING THE STUDY: COLLECTING THE DATA AND DOING THE ANALYSIS

Based on this review of the literature, we developed our experimental design. We created an experiment that would evaluate (1) the effect of the sex of a politician, (2) the type of account strategy used (denial, excuse, or justification), and (3) the gender stereotypes surrounding the issue the scandal involved (economic scandal, sex scandal, nanny scandal, etc). Note that "I" has now become "we." In fact, it was around this time that I was joined on this project by my co-authors, Ashleigh Smith (now Powers) and Gus Suarez, both of whom were undergraduate students at Furman University at the time. Collaboration in scholarly research is quite common and my experience has always been that two (or more) heads are better than one when approaching a research problem.[6] Both Ashleigh and Gus were very bright undergraduates and I could not have done this project without them. Gus and Ashleigh were particularly clever at coming up with the hypothetical scenarios we would use. In all, we developed two scenarios that we thought represented stereotypically *female* scandals, one involving the hiring of an illegal alien to be a nanny and one involving sex with a superior for the purposes of career advancement. We created two stereotypically *male* scenarios, one involving illegal gifts from contributors, the other involving sex with a subordinate. For each scenario, we altered only the sex of the politician and the account strategy used (justification, excuse, denial). The scenarios are presented in the Appendix at the end of this chapter. As you can see, my simple idea very quickly grew into a quite complex study now with twelve different groups.

Our dependent variable was the respondent's overall evaluation of the politician. Borrowing from past research (which is a common technique and useful for the purposes of comparison across studies), we used a scale developed by one of my graduate school professors and her colleagues[7] that measured respondent's assessments of the politician's competence, likeability and the general impact of his/her account. In total, we had nineteen Likert-items that we used to create a **Likert scale**. A likert item is nothing more than a response scale with seven point options ranging from 1 to 7—for example in this case, in one question, marking a 1 indicated one thought the politician was very incompetent and marking a 7 indicated one thought the politician was very competent. To create a Likert scale, the responses on the items were averaged into a composite evaluation score with high scores representing positive evaluations. To ensure that all items are related to one another and 'hang together' as a meaningful measure, scholars will compute a statistic called a **reliability coefficient**, or *Cronbach's alpha*. The reliability coefficient can range from 0 (representing no correlation among the items) to 1 (measuring perfect correlation). Typically, a Cronbach's alpha of at least .65 allows one to say that the scale is sufficiently reliable as a measure of a concept. In our case, the

Cronbach's alpha was about .88 so we felt we had a good measure of evaluations of candidates using these items.

We administered our experiment to 240 people, 164 of whom were undergraduates at our university and 76 of whom were people from our community. Before we could do this, however, we had to secure approval from our university's **Institutional Review Board**. Institutional Review Boards are designed to ensure that scholars are doing ethical research that preserves the dignity of the participant in the study and does not violate their rights. Institutional Review Boards became commonplace at universities after several unethical studies came to light such as the Tuskegee Syphilis study (see Box 10.1). Institutional Review Boards assure that participants in a study give **informed consent**, meaning they know the risks and benefits to them of the study, before participating and that no unnecessary deception or risks are involved.

You may have noticed that our **sample size**, also called our N (for number of participants in the study), was relatively small at 240. How can we say anything generalizable (or, in the language of scientists, how do we know our study has **external validity**?) with such a small sample size and especially one that includes so many undergraduates? We probably cannot. As we discussed earlier, experiments are limited in that the findings may or may not be generalizable to the population. Unlike surveys, experiments typically do not include **random samples** or samples where every member of the population of interest has an equal chance of being included. Instead, as discussed above, experiments often involve **convenience samples**, or samples which include people willing and available to participate in the study (most often college students).[8] The strength of experiments, however, as we reviewed earlier, is that because the researcher has control over the variables being manipulated, experiments have **internal validity**, meaning that one can feel confident that there is a cause and effect relationship between the independent variable(s) and the dependent variable. While experiments do not typically involve random

Box 10.1 The Tuskegee Syphilis study

The Tuskegee Syphilis study was a study which began in 1932 involving 600 African-American men, about half of whom had the debilitating and deadly (at that time) disease of syphilis. The men were offered incentives for participation (such as free medical exams and food) and were not told that they were part of an experiment. Many received inadequate or no treatment for the disease and the study continued until it was brought to light in 1972, despite the fact that in 1947 penicillin had been discovered as a treatment for the disease.

samples, **random assignment** of participants to the various conditions (in this case to the different scenarios) assures that, on average, any differences found between the groups after exposure to the manipulation is in fact due to the different manipulations (because probabilistically speaking, on average, if the groups are randomly assigned they should be about the same at the beginning).

To analyze our findings, we used a statistical technique called **ANOVA**, or analysis of variance. ANOVA is not much more than examining if there are differences in the averages, or *means*, of the dependent variable (in our case, a composite score evaluation of the politicians which was computed by averaging the scores on the various evaluation questions) between the groups. In our case, we were able to examine the main effects of the manipulation of the gender of the politician as well as any interaction effects between the sex of the politician, the type of account offered, and the stereotypicality of the offense, as well as whether the sex of the respondent mattered. We calculated whether there is any statistically significant (large enough given the sample size and degree of variability in the responses) differences between the groups.

And, what did we find? Table 10.4 presents the results of our analysis in a table. Learning to read and create a *table* is an important part of understanding research results and presenting one's research clearly. If you look at the first line of the table in Table 10.4, you can see that, surprisingly, we found no support for our main hypothesis that females would be evaluated more harshly than males when involved in a scandal. In fact, the mean overall evaluations of the male and female politicians were essentially identical (see the first line of the table, Ms (meaning "means") = .46 and .46). But, what do those "Fs" and "ps" represent? The "F" represents how the variations in the means for what we actually "f"ound differ from the variations in the means if the **null hypothesis** (the hypothesis we always are testing against which is the hypothesis that there is no relationship between the independent and dependent variables) were true. If there was no relationship between the dependent and independent variables, then one would expect the F to be small, approaching 1. The larger the "F" the greater your certainty that there is a significant difference in the groups, or, said in another way, that the independent variable influences the dependent variable. The numbers in parentheses besides the "F" in the table represent degrees of freedom. The first number represents the number of groups minus 1 (each participant read two scenarios) and the second number represents the number of participants minus the total number of groups. A savvy reader will see that this second number, 209, is less than the 240 we said were involved in the study. This is because we had to omit participants who had too many missing items or questions they did not answer in the study because their scores would not be comparable. Degrees of freedom make a difference as the number of groups and participants will affect the calculation of the **statistical significance** of the F value. **Statistical significance**, represented by the "**p**," or p-value, in the table tells us what the "**p**"robability is that we would find these means in the population randomly if in fact there was no relationship between the independent

TABLE 10.4 Results from 2 x 2 x 3 x 2 (politician's sex x respondent sex x account x stereotypicality of scenario) ANOVA: mean evaluations of politicians

Main effects

Sex of politician		Male	Female
		.46	.46

$F(1, 209) = .002$, *ns*

Sex of respondent		.48	.45

$F(1, 209) = 13.86, p < .05$

Account	Excuse	Denial	Justification
	.41	.49	.50

$F(2, 209) = 13.86, p < .001$

Scenario stereotypicality		Male	Female
		.44	.49

$F(1, 209) = 16.44, p < .001$

Specific interaction effects

	Scenario Stereotypicality	
Sex of politician	Male	Female
Male	.42	.51
Female	.45	.47

$F(1, 209) = 7.21, p < .01$
Scenario

Stereotypicality	Account	Sex of respondent	
		Male	Female
Male	Excuse	.44	.37
	Denial	.45	.43
	Justification	.47	.45
Female	Excuse	.41	.43
	Denial	.57	.46
	Justification	.53	.54

Note: $F(2, 209) = 3.38, p < .05$

and dependent variables. Generally speaking, scholars say that a p-value of less than .05, which means there is less than a 5 percent chance one would have found these differences randomly, gives us a pretty high level of confidence that we have found some meaningful differences between the groups.

So, back to our findings. We found, then, that politicians were not judged more harshly because of their sex—a very important finding, perhaps even more so because it was not what we had expected to find. In addition, we can see from the next line in the table that females evaluated politicians more harshly than did males, although the differences were not large (Ms = .45 for females and .48 for males). We did find, however, support for our hypothesis that the type of explanation or account offered mattered. Participants found excuses for a transgression to be the most objectionable form of account (Ms = .41 for excuses, .49 for denials, and .50 for justifications). This is what previous studies had found as well. And, we found that respondents were more forgiving when politicians were involved in those scenarios we labeled stereotypically female (hiring of an illegal nanny for domestic work and having sex with a superior) (Ms = .49) rather than in the stereotypically male scenarios (accepting illegal financial bribes, having sex with a subordinate) (Ms = .44).

Finally, the table shows some of the interactions we examined in our analysis. Contrary to our expectations, we found that respondents were more forgiving when politicians were involved in a counter-stereotypical scenario. We also found an unexpected three-way interaction between the account offered by the politician, the stereotypicality of the scenarios, and the sex of the participant. Thus, it was not as we expected that the sex of the politician affected the acceptability of the account, but, in fact, that certain kinds of accounts resonate more for men than they do for women in certain scenarios.

Lessons to Be Learned

So, what are some take-away lessons from this study for you as you approach your scholarship? First, findings contrary to your hypotheses are still interesting—perhaps even more so as they challenge preconceived notions. Second, be sure to keep your study simple. Even a very simple study examining the effects of politician sex on voter evaluations can quickly become complicated as one includes such additional factors like account strategy and scenario stereotypicality and their interactions. Third, be sure to consider how your research engages in the scholarly conversation. Our findings regarding the lack of effect of politician sex are in fact supported by other gender research which has shown that, all other things being equal, voter bias is not all that prevalent. Finally, realize the limitations of any analysis. Our study was merely a drop in the scholarly bucket in considerations of gender bias, scandals, and politicians. One study using just one methodology, in this case experiments, cannot come to definitive solutions or answers to a problem. Further study using different methodologies like surveys, content analysis, and in-depth interviews would provide even greater insight into this subject. This is why research is so fun. There are always next steps to be taken and acknowledging in one's paper the limitations of one's research as well as the new questions the research raises is the sign of a good scholar.

Interested to Know More about the Study Discussed in this Chapter?

Consult the research publication:

Smith, Elizabeth, Ashleigh Smith Powers, and Gus Suarez. 2005. "If Bill Clinton Were a Woman: The Effectiveness of Male and Female Politicians' Account Strategies Following Alleged Transgressions." *Political Psychology*, 26(1): 115–134.

Exercises and Discussion Questions:

1. What do you see as the primary *strengths* of the *experimental methodology*? What are its primary *weaknesses*?
2. Identify a *research project* discussed in this textbook that does not use the experimental method and develop a proposal for an experiment which would provide further insight into the **research question** being asked.
3. Find out how the **Institutional Review Board** (or its equivalent) works on your campus. Who sits on the board? How do they define their mission? How do they keep tabs on the scholarship being conducted on your campus?

Recommended Resources:

Kinder, Donald R. and Thomas R. Palfrey. 1993. *Experimental Foundations of Political Science*. Ann Arbor: University of Michigan Press.

Time-Sharing Experiments for the Social Sciences (www.tess.experiment central.org): This website is the location for a project funded by the National Science Foundation to allow scholars to conduct experiments that include a very large, diverse sample, thus allowing for greater certainty of the generalizability of one's findings. The experiments are conducted through the internet on a random sample of the population and include "time-sharing" whereby different research questions posed by different scholars are considered in the same experiment. Scholars interested in using this service must submit a proposal for consideration. You can access the projects that have been conducted and the data that has been collected to examine and analyze for yourself.

Appendix: Scenarios

Stereotypically Female Scenarios

HIRING OF AN ILLEGAL ALIEN

State Representative Carolyn (Phil) Winthrop appeared in front of Michigan legislators yesterday to answer charges that she (he) knowingly hired an illegal alien to care for her (his) children in March of 1988. Under the 1986 Immigration Reform and Control Act, federal regulation prohibits the hiring of illegal aliens. The illegal alien, Consuella Rodriguez, was employed by Carolyn (Phil) Winthrop for approximately six months before she returned to her native country of Guatemala.

Representative Winthrop's appearance yesterday before her (his) colleagues was in response to allegations brought against her (him) by challenging electoral candidate Jerome Howard. Mr. Howard has since withdrawn from the race citing personal conflicts. Incumbent Representative Winthrop is now the only candidate for the district five election next month.

After hearing Representative Winthrop's statement yesterday, the Michigan State Legislature recommended a special task force to further investigate her (his) actions. The task force, scheduled for selection later this week, will include a bipartisan panel of Winthrop's fellow legislators.

Justification: Representative Winthrop said in a press conference yesterday that she (he) indeed had known about Ms. Rodriguez's illegal alien status prior to her employment. However, she also explained that Ms. Rodriguez had applied for legal alien status.

"Ms. Rodriguez wanted to be—was actively trying to become—an American, and in hiring her, I committed no wrongdoing since she had technically begun the process of naturalization."

Excuse: Representative Winthrop said in a press conference yesterday that her (his) husband (wife) hired Ms. Rodriguez and handled all terms of the employment. "My husband (wife) was completely responsible for Ms. Rodriguez's documentation," she stated. "I expected him (her) to go through the proper legal channels, and I should not be held responsible for his (her) actions."

Denial: Representative Winthrop said in a press conference yesterday that she was not aware that Ms. Rodriguez was an illegal alien until shortly before her deportation in September.

"I had no idea that Ms. Rodriguez was in the United States illegally. My infraction was completely accidental—an innocent mistake."

SEX WITH A SUPERIOR

Headline: "Sexual Scandal Engulfs Two Kansas State Reps"

The Kansas legislature was stunned yesterday amid new allegations of a sexual scandal involving two well-respected Kansas politicians, Rep. Stephanie (John) Williamson and Representative John (Stephanie) Starling. Numerous sources within the Kansas State House have reported that Rep. Williamson may have traded sexual favors with Rep. Starling in exchange for a position for her(him)self on the State Budget Committee.

A close confidant of Rep. Stephanie (John) Williamson speaking on the condition of anonymity stated yesterday that Rep. Williamson approached Rep. Starling, the chairman (woman) of the State Steering Committee, about securing a position within the State Budget Committee—a position considered by many political analysts to be one of the most influential in the state. Sources claim that shortly after this initial encounter, Ms. (Mr.) Williamson began a sexual relationship with Starling in the hopes that it would secure her (him) a position within the committee. "Stephanie (John) saw this relationship as a long term investment towards an important position within the legislature," the source said.

Representative Williamson responded to the charges stating:

Justification: "While the allegations concerning me using sexual favors to attain a position in the State Budget Committee are completely untrue, Representative Starling and I have been involved in a relationship for some time. As two consenting adults, we feel that this relationship is not improper in any way. However, I must make clear that I did not receive the position on the committee as a result of this relationship."

Excuse: "During the two years, Representative Starling and I have worked closely together on a number of projects. As a result of the large amount of time we spent together, a close relationship occurred. Neither of us expected this relationship to develop, it just happened. I never meant to bring this notoriety to myself or my district."

Denial: "These charges are outrageous lies. I have never been involved in a sexual relationship with any of my colleagues, nor would I ever do so in order to gain an important appointment. I achieved the position on the Budget Committee because of my past experiences in the budget process, not because of a sexual tryst."

Stereotypically Male Scenarios

ILLEGAL GIFTS FROM CONTRIBUTORS

Headline: "Further Scandal Allegations Against Rep. Richardson"

A number of questions concerning State Representative Anthony (Jennifer) Richardson's use of public funds have arisen after a budget investigation revealed a number of suspicious transactions. Michael Windsor, a senior official in the State Budget Office, disclosed yesterday that the recent statewide audit uncovered a number of discrepancies in Rep. Anthony (Jennifer) Richardson's 1998 financial records. Mr. Windsor further stated that the "inconsistencies ranged from minor mathematical mistakes, to more serious charges possibly involving illegal activities" but refused to elaborate further.

Sources close to the investigation have revealed that the Iowa legislator may have improperly accepted gifts from a number of social and interest groups. These gifts range from small personal gifts—including books and products—to thousands of dollars in campaign contributions. Furthermore, the sources claim that the evidence, which includes receipts, bank statements and tape recordings, is overwhelming and "points to direct involvement by Mr. Anthony (Jennifer) Richardson."

Rep. Richardson responded to the charges by stating:

Justification: "While my acceptance of these contributions may have been improper, I was assured by my legal counsel that acceptance of these gifts would have been appropriate and legally sound. The current laws governing contributions by interest groups are rather vague and obscure, and this contributed to my oversight."

Excuse: "I am deeply troubled by the accusations that have arisen concerning improper contributions. Let me make it clear that this egregious error was caused by an oversight by my staff and that I was in no way directly involved. I will do everything in my power to make sure the problem is resolved, and that justice is done."

Denial: "These false accusations are yet another attempt by the opposition to discredit me for all that I have tried to do for the people of the state of Iowa. When will the other side realize that the people are sick and tired of partisan politics and personal attacks."

SEX WITH A SUBORDINATE

Headline: "Sexual Allegations Against State Rep. Stillwell"

The Illinois statehouse was rocked yesterday amid allegations of an improper sexual relationship between State Representative James (Betsy) Stillwell and a state employee, Betsy (James) Whitley.

Ms. (Mr.) Whitley, a former legislative aide to the representative, revealed in a press conference that she was involved in an "illicit sexual relationship" with Rep. James (Betsy) Stilwell, lasting from December 1996 until early this year. Ms. (Mr.) Whitley claimed that her alleged sexual relationship with the representative began when Mr. (Ms.) Stillwell made sexual advances towards her (him) following a 1996 Christmas party.

Sources close to the representative's office have revealed that Rep. Stillwell may have promised Ms. Whitley a better job in exchange for sexual favors. When questioned about the possible quid pro quo connections, Ms. Whitley declined to answer on the advice of her attorney.

Various key political figures, including Minority Leader Steve Alverson, have called for an investigation of the charges. "This represents a possible case of sexual harassment, and should be investigated as the law demands," Rep. Alverson stated.

Representative Stillwell responded to the allegations by stating:

Justification: "The truth of the matter is that Ms. (Mr.) Whitley and I became deeply involved in a close personal relationship. However, since I was currently going through a divorce and Ms. (Mr.) Whitley was single, I found our relationship to be quite proper, as it was between two consenting adults. I am saddened that our relationship has been disclosed in this manner, but I firmly believe that no wrongdoing has occurred as a result of our relationship."

Excuse: "While it is true that Ms. (Mr.) Whitley and I did engage in a sexual relationship, I must make it clear that the relationship was openly initiated by Ms. (Mr.) Whitley following an office Christmas party in 1996. At that time, I was undergoing marital difficulties. Ms. (Mr.) Whitley made it abundantly clear—through her (his) actions and language—that she (he) openly welcomed a close intimate relationship."

Denial: "These rumors are absolutely untrue. While I have been going through some marital difficulties, I have never been unfaithful to my wife (husband). I am not quite sure why Ms. (Mr.) Whitley is doing this, but I hope that she (he) clarifies this situation to everyone by stating the truth—that nothing happened between us."

Notes

1 See, for an example of such a study, Ansolabehere and Iyengar 1995.
2 See, for example, Sullivan et al. 1979.
3 See Cover and Brumberg 1982 for such an example.
4 See Niven 2006; Panagapoulos and Green 2008, for examples of field experiments.
5 McGraw 1990, 1991.
6 In fact, this research started around 1995 with a germ of an idea when I was in graduate school working with some of my peers. Little did we know our preliminary discussions on this topic would become so relevant once the Clinton scandal broke. Thus, you can see research is a long and ongoing process and you never know where a conversation about certain ideas might take you.
7 Gonzales et al. 1995.
8 Although surveys with random samples also are limited to those who are willing and available to participate.

Formal Modeling
Cultural Icons of U.S. Foreign Policy

Stephen G. Walker

GETTING CURIOUS: WHO MAKES FOREIGN POLICY DECISIONS AND HOW?

In this chapter I investigate U.S. foreign policy decision-making by Presidents Theodore Roosevelt and Woodrow Wilson. I am curious about their impact on decisions for war and peace as leaders and as *cultural icons* of two traditions in U.S. diplomatic history. By cultural icons I mean that they are representatives of two sets of cultural norms in the conduct of American foreign policy. One is the *Realist* tradition in which the immediate sources of foreign policy are beliefs in balance-of-power principles and national interests as guides to making decisions in a political universe of hostility and conflict. The other is the *Idealist* tradition in which beliefs in principles of international law and peaceful dispute resolution are the proximate basis for making decisions in a political universe of friendship and cooperation.[1]

In the conventional account of American diplomatic history, Roosevelt is the Realist icon while Wilson is the Idealist icon. Together they represent a tension between two larger historical forces in the form of collective beliefs of larger social formations such as the Republican and Democratic political parties in American society. A focus on the beliefs of these two leaders and their political descendants is one path to a better understanding of the general political forces for peace and war that shape the world in which we live today. Depending on whether a U.S. president is a Realist or an Idealist, s/he may be more or less inclined to use force as an instrument in the conduct of American foreign policy. Therefore, who leads matters in understanding such U.S. foreign policy decisions as the "war of necessity" in Afghanistan or the "war of choice" in Iraq following the 9/11 attacks by Al Qaeda on the United States.[2]

THE RESEARCH STRATEGY: WHAT IS THE FORMAL MODELING METHOD?

A cultural approach to understanding decisions for war and peace defines a research question that "is essentially a psychological one: what are the underlying beliefs—realist, idealist, or some combination" of the leaders who make them?[3] In this chapter I shall employ *game theory* as our source of **formal models** of Realists and Idealists who make foreign policy decisions.[4] A "formal" model is distinguished from an "informal" model by being more explicit and logical in representing the elements (concepts, assumptions, propositions, and conclusions) of a theory.[5]

For example, as a student of history I may have a psychological theory (explanation) for how and why a particular leader makes a decision for war. Implicit in my theory are the concepts of decision maker (leader), decision (war), and causes (beliefs) that together may provide a causal story of how and why a particular U.S. president, e.g., Woodrow Wilson, decided on America's entry into World War I. If I simply state that Wilson made the decision as a U.S. president to enter World War I because he was an Idealist, then my theory remains an informal model.

In order to represent my theory as a formal model, it is necessary to consider explicitly and state logically whether or not other U.S. presidents with some other beliefs would have decided to enter the war. Game theory offers such a formal model of these possibilities. If it is possible to consider politics as a series of decisions in a "game," then game theory can provide an explanation as a formal model of those decisions. The word *game* has a somewhat frivolous meaning in everyday language, referring to "an activity providing entertainment or amusement," or "a competitive activity or sport."[6] Drawing parallels between politics and games has some face validity, however, as both activities may involve players as winners and losers in such contests as wars between competing states or elections between competing candidates for the same office.

Game theorists distinguish between games of chance and games of strategy. In the first instance, players in a *game of chance* win or lose according to the mathematical laws of probability. Each player places a "bet" (guess) on the outcome of the game and wins a certain percent of the time, as in a lottery or other gambling activities such as dice or roulette games in which the outcome does not depend on direct interactions between the choices of the players. In the second instance, players in a *game of strategy* make joint decisions that interact to generate the outcome of the game and who wins or loses, e.g., in card games such as bridge or poker or the board games of checkers or chess. Information in the form of each player's beliefs about the situation on the chess board and whether or not the other player's decision will depend on one's own decision can influence a player's subsequent decisions and the outcome of the game. A final constraint on decisions that make their interaction a game of strategy are *rules of play*, e.g., the rule in chess or checkers that players alternate their decisions rather than making simultaneous choices leading to a final outcome.

Two simple examples from the child's games of "scissors and stones" and "tic-tac-toe" illustrate these features of a game and the distinctions between a game of chance and a game of strategy. In the competitive game of entertainment called "scissors and stones," there are two players with three choices, "scissors, rock, or paper," and each player chooses simultaneously to determine the outcome of the game. Additional rules of play to determine the winner are that "scissors cuts paper," "rock crushes scissors," and "paper covers rock." After comparing their choices, one player "wins" and the other "loses" unless both players simultaneously made the same choice leading to a "tie" outcome. These possibilities appear in Figure 11.1, which lists the Row player's choices down the left side, the Column player's choices across the top, and the outcomes for the possible intersections of their choices in the cells of the game matrix. This matrix is a formal model of the game, because it represents and explains all the possible outcomes or "states" in the game.

A single play of this game is a game of chance in which each player "bets" (guesses) that his/her best choice is scissors, rock, or paper. There is no single, "best" choice or strategy as a solution to this game. As Figure 11.1 shows, the

		Column player				**Columns**		
		Scissors	Rock	Paper				
	Scissors	T, T	L, W	W, L		X_1	O_8	O_2
Row player	Rock	W, L	T, T	L, W	**Rows**	O_6	X_3	X_5
	Paper	L, W	W, L	T, T		X_9	X_7	O_4
		Scissors, rock, paper game*				**Tic-tac-toe game****		

Figure 11.1 Games of chance and games of strategy***

Notes: *Outcomes: W = Win, T = Tie, L = Lose in each cell of the game for Row, Column players, **X = move by player X and O = move by player O. Each move is numbered in the order that it occurred. *** Scissors, rock, and paper is a game of chance while tic-tac-toe is a game of strategy

chance of winning a single play of the game is always 33 percent (1 out of 3) for each player. According to the menu of choices and the rules of play, each player always has one chance out of three to "win" (W) v. "lose" (L), or "tie" (T) when her choice intersects simultaneously with the other player's choice. In repeated plays of the game, however, the players may be able to transform the game into a game of strategy with beliefs about each player's choices in preceding plays of the game.

For example, if Column displays a tendency to choose "rock" more frequently in repeated plays, then Row should choose "paper" more frequently, based on the belief that the new information indicates that it is a winning strategy because there is now a chance greater than 33 percent that Column will choose "rock." In choosing "paper," Row is thinking rationally, i.e., purposefully (goal-oriented), mindfully (means-oriented), and empathetically (other-oriented). Therefore, she is making a strategic choice, i.e., her choice is based on the other player's choices as well as on the goal of winning with the most efficient and effective means.[7]

The game of "tic-tac-toe" is a game of strategy and not a game of chance. Its rules of play dictate the alternating choices of the players, based on an initial "state" followed by intermediate states leading to a final outcome. The sequence of states or phases is defined by each player's previous choices. An example is shown in Figure 11.1 where each player chooses to enter either an "X" indicating Player X's choice or an "O" indicating Player O's choice. The competitive goals in this game are also W > T > L, i.e., for one player either to "win" (W) by aligning three Xs or three Os along a row or column or diagonal of the game matrix or to at least "tie" (T) by denying the other player such an alignment in order not to "lose" (L). The game's final outcome is determined by a maximum of nine alternating moves by each player (corresponding to the nine cells) or until one player aligns three of his or her moves along a row, column or diagonal of the matrix. Again, this matrix is a formal model of the game, because it represents and explains all the possible outcomes or "states" in the game specified by the rules of play.

In Figure 11.1, Player X moves first by placing an X_1 in the upper-left corner of the grid and Player O moves next by placing an O_2 in the upper-right corner of the grid. Then they alternate subsequent moves, $\{X_3, O_4, X_5, O_6, X_7, O_8, X_9\}$, and the final outcome of the game ends in a tie. Following these moves as they occur, it's clear that: Player X attempted (X_3) to align along the diagonal from upper-left to lower-right; Player O blocked (O_4) this attempt with a move to the lower-right corner; Player X attempted (X_5) to align along the middle row; Player O blocked (O_6) this attempt with a move to the middle-left cell; Player X attempted (X_7) to align along the middle column; Player O blocked (O_8) this attempt; Player X then moved (X_9) to the lower-left corner, reaching the maximum of nine moves and ending the game in a Tie. Neither player achieved their best outcome of a win (three moves aligned along a row, column, or diagonal), but both players also avoided the worst outcome (Lose).

The information available to each player in this game is "two-sided," i.e., both players have the same information, which consists of the rules of alternating play, the rank order of each player's preferences for the different possible outcomes (win > tie > lose), and the previous moves by each player before making his or her own next move. It is possible in principle, therefore, to calculate the correct move for each player at a given state in the game in order to achieve a win or at least avoid a loss with a tie. A failure to make this calculation accurately becomes a mistake that may also lead to a lower-ranked outcome unless the other player also makes a mistake that cancels out the first player's mistake.

With the aid of computers and enough time, these calculations can also be made for more complex games that involve two players, e.g., checkers.[8] However, with more than two players or more than two choices, these calculations become virtually impossible (even for computers). For example, both humans and computers playing chess only adopt "rules of thumb" (rough approximations as heuristics) that may increase the chances of winning the game, because the mathematics necessary to solve chess are too costly and complex. Even solving checkers took several years and multiple computers to calculate a relatively weak solution of just the possible moves left with only ten pieces on the board.[9]

Therefore, it is not surprising that game theorists are more successful in capturing features of games of strategy with formal models by representing the choices and outcomes of much simpler games with only two players and two choices. They often use a game matrix like the ones shown in Figure 11.2. As a mathematical model, a *game matrix* of rows and columns is abstract enough to apply to the analysis of a variety of decisions in different situations. In order to make its abstract features concrete enough here to model U.S. foreign policy decisions, I label the two players as either Realists or Idealists, specify their two choices as either Cooperation or Conflict, and stipulate as an additional rule of play that the players make alternate rather than simultaneous choices. I also provide them with information in the form of beliefs about each other's

		Idealist				Realist				Realist	
		CO	CF			CO	CF			CO	CF
	CO	**4,4**	1,2		CO	**3,3**	1,4		CO	**4,3**	1,4
Idealist				Realist				Idealist			
	CF	2,1	3,3		CF	4,1	2,2		CF	2,1	3,2
		Idealist game				Realist game				Hybrid game	

Figure 11.2 Three types of 2 x 2 games*

*Notes:*Choices are CO = Cooperate; CF = Conflict. Preferences for players are ranked (4 = highest…1 = lowest) separated by a comma for Row, Column players. An Idealist player ranks settlement highest while a Realist player ranks domination highest. The mutually best solutions for both players are in bold

preferences for the different outcomes generated by the interaction of their alternating choices. With this information and rules of play, therefore, I have created in Figure 11.2 a formal model of the possible initial, intermediate, and final states for games between two Realists, two Idealists, or a Realist and an Idealist.

The game matrices show two decision makers with two possible choices, Cooperation (CO) or Conflict (CF), and ranked preferences based on either Idealist beliefs or Realist beliefs. The consequences of their intersecting choices are ranked as outcomes for each player in the cells (4 = highest to 1 = lowest) where each player's decision intersects with the other player's decision. The four possible outcomes are settlement (CO, CO), deadlock (CF, CF) domination or submission (CF, CO or CO, CF) as consequences for each player. By convention the Row player's ranking for each outcome is first in each cell and separated by a comma from the Column player's ranking for the same outcome.

ISSUES WITH THIS RESEARCH STRATEGY: ARE FORMAL MODELS WORTH DOING?

While this formal representation (model) of possible decisions and outcomes in a mathematical universe may seem intimidating to the casual observer, inserting features of the political universe into this artificial world enables us to better understand their relationships. Is it really worth doing, however, or are formal models just "elegant models of irrelevant worlds"?[10] According to Fiorina, the benefits of this effort are "the precision and clarity of thought which these models require, and the depth of argument that they allow" (ibid.). Assumptions and concepts that are implicit are made explicit. Their logical implications are easier to see and check. It is possible to follow an argument more deeply to its final conclusions if it is stated in mathematical language than in everyday language.

The costs may include making assumptions that are not realistic (with a small r), i.e., they do not correspond to known observations. The assumptions in formal models of game theory are that leaders follow rational choice procedures in making decisions instead of taking shortcuts. They clearly identify goals and alternative means, plus they take account of constraints imposed by the actions of others before acting. However, it may be the case that decision makers are responsive rather than purposive. They can make decisions in accord with external norms, such as roles based solely on others expectations, rather than on the basis of internal goals or means selected by the individual.[11]

The game theory models of rational choice in Figure 11.2 make the two-sided information assumption that both players know their own preference rankings and the preference rankings of the other player for the different outcomes,[12] In the discussion of formal game models as a research strategy above, the key assumption is that each player will exercise its agency (the power to make choices) under the constraints of all of this information. However, in the real world decision makers may instead choose among alternatives based on biases, faulty calculations, or false information about the available alternatives and their consequences.[13]

The analytical dilemma deepens further after taking into account more deeply the abstract nature of formal models. It is inherent in the definition that such a model will "abstract" (take out) for consideration some features of the phenomenon that it represents while omitting other features. Even if the fit between the abstract model's subsequent predictions and empirical observations of relevant cases is good, this correspondence may not reflect the actual operation of the phenomenon and its causal logic. In the case of rational choice models of decision making, the landscape is littered with articles and books decrying the lack of fit between the features of rational choice models and the features of actual decisions and their sources.[14]

In response, I argue that the effort to construct and understand formal models of foreign policy decisions and their sources is worth doing if the model resembles important features of the actual political universe and the beliefs of the leaders who make decisions in it. A sensible approach to take regarding these issues is first to understand that decision makers decide under constraints and incentives that allow or propel them to be rational in varying degrees, depending on those circumstances.[15] Second, ask whether the case or cases under investigation meet the requirements for different degrees or *levels of rationality* in decision making: Are they purposeful (do they have preferences for different goals)? Are they mindful (do they consider different alternatives for reaching their goals)? Are they empathetic (do they take the preferences and decisions of others into account)? Third, follow up by making observations (to the extent possible) as to whether the decision makers respond to those constraints and incentives in making the actual decisions under consideration. I shall follow these steps in the analysis of Theodore Roosevelt and Woodrow Wilson as cultural icons of U.S. foreign policy by systematically observing their political universe and the basis for their decisions.

THE LITERATURE REVIEW: BELIEFS AS CAUSES OF FOREIGN POLICY DECISIONS

The investigation of Theodore Roosevelt and Woodrow Wilson as cultural icons of U.S. foreign policy engages three different research literatures: applications of game theory to the analysis of foreign policy decisions;[16] biographical and diplomatic accounts by historians of the lives and times in office of U.S. presidents;[17] analyses of strategic culture and the belief systems of political leaders.[18] We have already introduced the most relevant literature regarding game theory with our previous discussion of 2 x 2 games as formal models. Here we narrow this focus to one of these theories, the Theory of Moves (TOM) formulated by Steven Brams to model the logic of sequential games.[19] This theory is distinguished by its more realistic assumptions of alternating (sequential) rather than simultaneous moves and by repeated rather than single plays of the family of 2 x 2 ordinal games identified earlier by Rapoport and Guyer.[20]

TOM's rules of play also make the *two-sided information assumption* that *each* player knows the ranked preferences of *both* players and *the rationality assumption* that they will act to maximize their gains and minimize their losses. According to TOM, a game begins from an initial state (one of the cells in the game) and ends after both players either choose "stay" at the initial state or move sequentially with alternating moves until both choose "stay" at one of the other cells. In making these decisions, TOM also permits each player to engage in pre-play communication before making their choices. One player may threaten to "move" unless the other player chooses "stay." Both players also calculate "two, three, or four moves ahead" before making their choices.[21] In this account, the leaders of states make alternating foreign policy moves in a game with rules of play similar to such familiar board games as checkers or chess.

The record of the moves of U.S. presidents vis-à-vis other players in world politics is well known and makes American diplomatic history the second relevant research literature. Roosevelt is noted by diplomatic historians and biographers for his decisions to "walk softly and carry a big stick" in dealing with other nations in the Western Hemisphere, his machinations to build and control the Panama Canal, and his mediation of the Russo-Japanese War that won him the Nobel Peace Prize.[22] Wilson's involvement in the Western Hemisphere was marked by intervention in the domestic affairs of Mexico, attempts to remain neutral when World War I began in Europe, and his decision to enter the war in order to "make the world safe for democracy" and create the League of Nations organization for the peaceful resolution of disputes between states.[23]

The controversy in the literature that is the focus of our research project is not what each leader decided in their terms of office as the U.S. president. The focus is instead on the belief systems of each leader that guided these decisions. Specifically, "the controversy in the historiography of American foreign relations . . . is not over the behavior of the two leaders. It is whether and how their behavior was motivated by Realist or Idealist beliefs and preferences."[24] Simply put, the research question specified by introducing beliefs into the formal models of game theory is: do the beliefs of the two leaders indicate that they were playing variations of the Idealist, Realist, or Hybrid Games in Figure 11.2?

The answer to this research question brings together the research literature dealing with Realism and Idealism and the literature on strategic culture and the belief systems of leaders as sources of foreign policy decisions. In the context of U.S. diplomatic history the Realist and Idealist traditions emphasize the different themes of balance of power and national interests v. international law and peaceful dispute resolution as cultural norms on which to base American foreign policy decisions.[25] More generally, Realists and Idealists make different assumptions about human nature, the sources of conflict and cooperation in world affairs, and the ability of leaders and states to exercise control over historical development.[26] It is both a theoretical and an empirical issue as to which of these doctrinal belief systems is actually "realistic" (with a small "r"). The causal analysis of conflict and cooperation, manifested most dramatically as war and peace, remains an unfinished research agenda for historians and social scientists.

However, it seems clear that the proximate or immediate causes of war and peace are the decisions of leaders to choose cooperation or conflict and escalate or de-escalate those decisions over time. It is also relatively transparent that both cooperation and conflict at any level of intensity is a social phenomenon that requires two agents in order to occur. Based on these two assumptions it looks worthwhile to examine the beliefs of leaders about the self and others in order to understand their decisions for war or peace in dealing with one another. By their very nature strategic beliefs focus on both the actions of the self and others plus environmental features such as the distribution and exercise of power between the self and others in the political universe.

Collectively, these strategic beliefs constitute the *operational code* of beliefs and intentions for the decision-making unit of a state, which may be an individual, a group, or a set of governing institutions.[27] If these beliefs are shared by decision makers within a state, they make up elements of its strategic culture, which may be monolithic or be divided into subcultures. Often these sets of beliefs echo the traditions of Realism and Idealism in different historical and geographical contexts. For example, Johnston has identified Confucian (Idealist) and Parabellum (Realist) subcultures in the history of Chinese strategic culture.[28] Kagan distinguishes between Venutian (Idealist) and Martian (Realist) strategic cultures within different states in the European Union.[29] Similar distinctions are noted by scholars of other historical eras and geographical regions in both Western and Eastern civilizations.[30]

DOING THE STUDY: COLLECTING THE DATA AND DOING THE ANALYSIS

Previous analyses of operational codes and strategic cultures have distinguished between philosophical beliefs that the decision maker uses to diagnose the nature of the political universe and instrumental beliefs about the utility of different means for protecting and achieving strategic and tactical goals. This distinction gives operational code analysis a focus on the decision maker's process of strategic rationality as the decision maker takes into account goals, means, and the actions and capabilities of others in making purposeful, mindful, and empathetic decisions.

George sharpened the focus on these elements of a decision maker's operational code by asking a set of research questions about philosophical and instrumental beliefs.[31] He identified the following kinds of questions about philosophical beliefs: (P-1) Is the nature of the political universe friendly, mixed, or hostile? (P-2) Are there optimistic or pessimistic prospects for realizing fundamental political goals? (P-3) Is the political universe relatively predictable or unpredictable? (P-4) Is the degree of control over historical development by self relatively high or low compared to others in the political universe? (P-5) Is the role of chance in determining political outcomes relatively high or low? His questions about instrumental beliefs included the following kinds: (I-1) Is cooperation or conflict the best strategy for realizing fundamental political goals? (I-2) Is escalation or de-escalation the best tactic? (I-3) Is it better to accept or avoid risks in pursuing goals? (I-4) Is it better to be flexible or firm in executing strategies and tactics? (I-5) What is the relative utility of different means for exercising power?[32]

Several scholars have identified and classified answers to these questions in the form of various types of belief systems or operational codes, defined as different sets of philosophical and instrumental beliefs that are interdependent and consistent with one another.[33] The types of belief systems in Figure 11.3 are defined according to differences in key beliefs (I-1, P-1, and P-4). The upper two Types A and C represent Idealist belief systems in which the political universe of others (P-1) is friendly (+) and the self's strategic orientation (I-1) is cooperative (+). The lower two Types B and D represent Realist belief systems in which the political universe of others (P-1) is hostile (–) and the self's strategic orientation (I-1) is conflictual.

Differences in P-4 beliefs permit a distinction between the Pragmatic v. Dogmatic style of each leader in an Idealist or a Realist game, in which their respective top-ranked preferences remain the same but the next-ranked preferences are in a different order. The variations reflect differences in the relative historical control of the self v. others. If Self's historical control (P-4) is higher (>) for an Idealist, then domination is Self's second-ranked preference after settlement followed by deadlock and then submission. If Self's historical control (P-4) is lower (<), then the second and third preferences are reversed. A similar logic governs the rankings of Realists. If Self's historical control (P-4) is higher (>), then deadlock is ranked second after domination followed by settlement and submission. If Self's historical control (P-4) is lower (<), then the second and third preferences are reversed. A simple Theory of Inferences about Preferences (TIP) with the following four propositions states these rankings as propositions for either Self or Other in the four games in Figure 11.3:[34]

Prop. 1. If Self (I-1, P-4) or Other (P-1, I-4) is (+, <), then the rank order of preferences for Self or Other is Settle > Deadlock > Dominate > Submit.

GAME OUTCOMES

Other

	CO	CF
CO	Both players settle	Self submits/ Other dominates
Self		
CF	Self dominates/ Other submits	Both players deadlock

PURE IDEALIST GAMES

Type A (Pragmatic)			**Type C** (Dogmatic)		
Other			**Other**		
	CO	CF		CO	CF
CO	**4,4**	1,2	CO	**4,4**	1,3
Self			**Self**		
CF	2,1	3,3	CF	3,1	2,2

Self: I–1, P–4 = +, <   Self: I–1, P–4 = +, >
Other: P–1, P–1 = +, <   Other: P–1, P–1 = +, >

PURE REALIST GAMES

Type D (Pragmatic)			**Type C** (Dogmatic)		
Other			**Other**		
	CO	CF		CO	CF
CO	**3,3**	1,4	CO	2,2	1,4
Self			**Self**		
CF	4,1	2,2	CF	4,1	**3,3**

Self: I–1, P–4 = –, <   Self: I–1, P–4 = –, >
Other: P–1, P–4 = –, <   Other: P–1, P–4 = –, >

Figure 11.3 Beliefs and intentions of pure Idealist and Realist operational codes*

Notes: *Key beliefs are friendly (+) or hostile (?) for P-1 and cooperation (+) or conflict (?) for I-1; low (<) or high (>) for P-4. Intentions are ranked as preferences from (4 = highest…1 = lowest) for Self (row) and Other (column) in each game. Mutually best solutions are in bold

Prop. 2. If Self (I-1, P-4) or Other (P-1, P-4) is (+, >), then the rank order of preferences for Self or Other is Settle > Dominate > Deadlock >Submit.

Prop. 3. If Self (I-1, P-4) or Other (P-1, P-4) is (–, <), then the rank order of preferences for Self or Other is Dominate > Settle > Deadlock > Submit.

Prop. 4. If Self (I-1, P-4) or Other (P-1, P-4) is (–, >), then the rank order of preferences for Self or Other is Dominate > Deadlock > Settle > Submit.

By extension it is possible as well to infer the corresponding propositions regarding intentions for hybrid belief systems by identifying the corresponding hybrids of beliefs about Self and Other. For example, the hybrid Idealist–Realist belief system in Figure 11.2 is Self = (+, <) and Other = (−, <), constituting an Idealist (Self) in a Realist (Other) political universe. Proposition 1 specifies Self's preference rankings and Proposition 3 specifies Other's preference rankings. Together the two propositions specify the game between Self and Other shown in Figure 11.2 as an A–D game between a Type A (Pragmatic–Idealist) Self and a Type D (Pragmatic–Realist) Other.

With the assistance of these four propositions and the typology of belief systems in Figure 11.3, it is possible to identify the independent and dependent variables in our analysis of the operational codes of Roosevelt and Wilson. The independent variables are the pairs of key beliefs for Self (I-1, P-4) and Other (P-1, P-4), which distinguish the different types of belief systems in Figure 11.3. The intervening variables are the different *subjective games* that we can infer for the two leaders from observations of their key beliefs, which may vary over time or across regional domains. Two leaders may have the same subjective game, or one leader may have a Type A belief system and subjective game while another leader may have a Type D belief system and subjective game. These types may also shift over time for the same U.S. president from their first term to their second term, as the attention of Presidents Roosevelt or Wilson shifted from regional issues in the Western hemisphere to global issues outside the Western hemisphere in their respective terms in office.

Finally, it is possible for two leaders to make strategic decisions toward one another based on either convergent or divergent subjective games. If they are playing the same game, then their *actual game* corresponds to their respective subjective games. If not, then their actual game (the external pattern of behavior in the world of events) may not be the same as their subjective game (the internal pattern of beliefs in their minds). Therefore, our explicit focus in the following analysis is only on measuring the subjective game for Self, constructed by measuring the beliefs of Roosevelt or Wilson, and its ability to explain the decisions of each president. Omitted is the more complex task of measuring and analyzing the subjective games of other players in the political universe. To sum up, the dependent variables are the choices and outcomes for each president, and the independent variables are the particular operational codes of key beliefs and intentions attributed to Self and Other by each U.S. leader.

In order to test the rival claims by diplomatic historians regarding the Idealist and Realist beliefs of these two leaders, I advance the following hypotheses regarding the key beliefs (P-1, I-1, P-4) and subjective games of Roosevelt and Wilson.[35] According to the conventional historical account, Roosevelt's operational code should be a Realist (Type D or Type B) belief system. Wilson's operational code should be an Idealist (Type A or Type C) belief system. The revisionist historical account advances counter-hypotheses that qualify the conventional account in two ways. One is to reinterpret the beliefs of both leaders in an Idealist direction, and the other is to portray

Wilson as more of a realist than Roosevelt: The revisionist account contends that, "Roosevelt never really understood the implications of modernity while Wilson grasped its implications for modern warfare by 1917 as America entered World War I."[36]

The revisionist account is also more nuanced regarding the beliefs and actions of both leaders than the conventional account, taking explicitly into consideration the possible contributions and the interaction between agent (leader) and structure (context) to explain the sources of their foreign policy decisions. It is a more dynamic interpretation as well, which allows the leaders to evolve over time as their beliefs adapted to changing circumstances and stimuli from the environment. According to the revisionist account, "Their beliefs shifted toward Idealism in the case of Roosevelt and toward Realism in the case of Wilson."[37]

The conventional and revisionist historical accounts suggest the following hypotheses and counter-hypotheses. The first two hypotheses are derived from the conventional historical account, in which the belief systems of the two leaders are static over time and across regions. The other three hypotheses are derived from the revisionist historical account, in which the belief systems of the two leaders are more dynamic and change over time as their attention shifts from the Western Hemisphere, where America is a hegemon, to Asia or Europe where the United States is one Great Power interacting with other Great Powers.

H-1. Roosevelt's key beliefs will be consistent with a Realist (Type D or B) belief system.

H-2. Wilson's key beliefs will be consistent with an Idealist (Type A or C) belief system.

H-3. Roosevelt's key beliefs will be consistent with Idealist beliefs in his first term in office (1901–4) and remain consistent with Idealist beliefs in his second term in office (1905–8).

H-4. Wilson's key beliefs will be consistent with Idealist beliefs in this first term in office (1913–16) and change to be consistent with Realist beliefs in his second term in office (1917–20).

H-5. The beliefs of both Roosevelt and Wilson regarding the ability to control historical development will be significantly lower in their second terms than in their first terms in office, which means that:

a. Roosevelt will change from a Type C Idealist in his first term to a Type A Idealist in his second term;

b. Wilson will change from a Type C Idealist in his first term to a Type D Realist in his second term.

Indices for the key beliefs of each president are constructed from a content analysis of their annual messages to Congress regarding foreign affairs. The total observations (codable verbs) retrieved from these sources average approximately 1,095 per president per term, which is about the size of a typical national public opinion survey of political attitudes.[38] An automated content analysis system machine-coded each message to retrieve verbs attributed to Self or Other by the President regarding the exercise of power in the form of words or deeds of conflict or cooperation.

The indices for the three key beliefs (P-1, I-1, and P-4) were calculated for each leader during both terms in office and then divided into scores for each term. The P-1 and I-1 scores are balanced proportion indices between the cooperation and conflict verbs attributed to Other (P-1) and the cooperation and conflict verbs attributed to Self (I-1); the P-4 score for Self and Other is a simple proportion (percentage) index of the total verbs in each case. For the first two indices the difference between these pairs of attributions is also divided by their sum to make them into percentages, too. These steps are done to make the three indices comparable with one another by expressing them in percentages as a common metric (range of values) between .00 and 1.0 in absolute terms.

The indices for P-1 and I-1 range from +1.0 to −1.0 with positive values indicating more attributions of cooperation behavior, negative values indicating more attributions of conflict behavior, and values close to zero indicating a pattern of mixed or balanced behavior between cooperation and conflict. The index for P-4 ranges from .00 to +1.0 for Self or Other: values close to .50 indicate a balanced distribution of cooperation and conflict attributions between Self and Other; values close to .00 or +1.0 indicate an imbalance in total attributions.

In order to make these indices more comparable across leaders, they are recalculated as standard deviations (distances) from the mean scores for a norming sample of thirty-five leaders from different countries, regions, and historical eras. This step transforms the scores for a particular leader into a common metric for comparison with other leaders, which is expressed as a comparison of each leader's score with the mean (average) scores for all of the leaders in a group. According to Walker and Schafer, "A norming group for interpreting the scores of particular leaders is desirable because almost all leaders generally present themselves and their states as cooperative (I-1) with a relatively modest level of historical control (P-4) in a friendly political universe (P-1) . . . The norming group scores for these three beliefs (I-1, P-1, P-4), therefore, are used as midpoints to distinguish leaders whose beliefs are either above or below the scores of the average world leader."[39] This transformation for all three indices gives those scores below the mean a negative sign and those scores above the mean a positive sign in standard deviation units, which may range from .00 to greater than + 1.0.

The results are displayed in Figure 11.4, which show the results for the two U.S. presidents for both terms and then for each term in office. Roosevelt remained an Idealist no matter whether the results are combined for both terms or divided into first and second terms. Wilson was an Idealist in his first term and a Realist in his second term, making the Realist results for both terms spurious when the analysis controls for the effects of time and space as Wilson's attention shifted from inside to outside the Western Hemisphere. The subjective games for each leader in Figure 11.4 are constructed from their normalized key belief indices below each game and the four TIP propositions that specify each leader's preferences for the different outcomes in the game matrix.

GAME OUTCOMES

	Other	
	CO	CF
Self CO	Both players settle	Self submits/ Other dominates
CF	Self dominates/ Other submits	Both players deadlock

ROOSEVELT GAMES

	First Term (Idealist Game)		Both Terms (Idealist Game)		Second Term (Idealist Game)	
	Other		**Other**		**Other**	
	CO	CF	CO	CF	CO	CF
Self CO	**4,4**	1,3	**4,4**	1,3	**4,4**	1,2
CF	2,1	3,2	2,1	3,2	3,1	2,3

First Term — Self: I–1, P–4 = +.30, –1.43; Other: P–1, P–4 = +.55, +1.43

Both Terms — Self: I–1, P–4 = +.78, –1.29; Other: P–1, P–4 = +.37, +1.29

Second Term — Self: I–1, P–4 = +1.04, .00; Other: P–1, P–4 = +.26, .00

WILSON GAMES

	First Term (Idealist Game)		Both Terms (Realist Game)		Second Term (Realist Game)	
	Other		**Other**		**Other**	
	CO	CF	CO	CF	CO	CF
Self CO	**4,4**	1,2	3,2	1,4	3,2	1,4
CF	3,1	2,3	4,1	**2,3**	4,1	**2,3**

First Term — Self: I–1, P–4 = +.26, +.43; Other: P–1, P–4 = +.47, –.43

Both Terms — Self: I–1, P–4 = –.04, –.29; Other: P–1, P–4 = –.29, +.29

Second Term — Self: I–1, P–4 = –.39, –.86; Other: P–1, P–4 = –.63, +.86

Figure 11.4 Idealist and Realist operational codes* for Roosevelt and Wilson

Notes: *Normalized belief indices compared to the average world leader for P-1 are friendly (+) or hostile and for I-1are cooperative (+) or conflictual (–). Normalized belief indices for P-4 are low (–) or high (+) historical control. Intentions are ranked as preferences from (4 = highest…1 = lowest) for Self (row) and Other (column) in each game. Roosevelt's second-term P-4 score equals the mean world leader's P-4 score. Nash equilibrium outcomes are in bold

Source: Walker and Schafer 2007

Roosevelt's subjective game in each term of office is an Idealist game, indicated by the positive signs for I-1 and P-1 below each game. He shifts from a pragmatic leadership style in the first term toward a dogmatic leadership style in the second term as Self's P-4 score changes from below the midpoint (–1.43) in the first term to reach the average world leader's score (.00) in the second term. Wilson's subjective game shifts from an Idealist no-conflict game (I-1 and P-1 have positive signs) with a dogmatic leadership style (Self's P-4 > zero) in his first term to a Realist conflict game (I-1 and P-1 have negative signs) with a pragmatic leadership style (Self's P-4 < zero) in his second term. This shift corresponds to his decision for war in 1917, as he abandoned the previous U.S. position of neutrality in his first term. He entered the war against Germany and Austria on the side of Britain, France, and Italy after German submarines repeatedly violated U.S. neutrality by sinking American commercial ships.

These results support the revisionist account of Roosevelt and Wilson as cultural icons of U.S. foreign policy. The only revisionist hypothesis that was not confirmed is H-5a, which predicted that Roosevelt's belief in Self's historical control (P-4) would decrease when, in fact, it increased to equal the average world leader's (P-4) score. Therefore, I identified his second-term game according to this trend, as defined by Prop. 2 (+, >) for Self and Prop. 1 (+, <) for Other from the Theory of Inferences about Preferences.

The formal logic of Wilson's decision making is shown in Figure 11.5. When Germany violated American neutrality from an initial state of (3,2) by choosing "move" (→) to (1,4) and then choosing to "stay" at (1,4), Wilson eventually responded in a repeated play of the game by choosing "move" (↓) from the new "initial state" to (2,3); both the United States and Germany then chose "stay" at (2,3) as a final outcome. This cell as the final outcome is the *Nash equilibrium* for this game (named after the mathematician John Nash who proposed it). A Nash equilibrium is an outcome from which neither player

	Germany			Column			Germany	
	CO	CF		CO	CF		CO	CF
CO	3,2	←"3,2"	CO	Both Settle	Col. Dom/ Row Sub	CO	3,2	"1,4"
USA	↓	↑	Row			USA	↑	↓
CF	4,1	→ 2,3	CF	Row Dom/ Col. Sub	Both Deadlock	CF	4,1	← 2,3

Figure 11.5 Strategies for Germany and USA in Wilson's Realist game*

Note: *Alternative choices are CO = Cooperate; CF = Conflict. Preferences for players are ranked (4 = highest…1 = lowest) separated by a comma for row, column players. Initial state is in quotation marks; the final state is in bold. Sequential choices are to choose "move" (→) or "stay" (→|). Game outcomes are Settle, Deadlock, Dominate (Dom), Submit (Sub) for each player. Column's strategy is to choose "stay" at (1,4) while Row's strategy is to choose "move" to the final outcome of (2,3) from an initial state of (1,4). Nash equilibrium outcome is in bold

Source: Walker and Schafer 2007

can move strategically without risking domination by the other player as a final outcome (1,4 for USA or 4,1 for Germany). Therefore, strategic interactions between America and Germany stayed at deadlock (2,3) until the Western Allies finally defeated Germany and Austria by force of arms in 1918. The German unconditional surrender moved their interactions from (2,3) to (4,1), ending the war with a final military outcome of domination by the USA and submission by Germany.

Lessons to Be Learned: Cultural Icons and Foreign Policy Decisions

What is to be learned from this exercise in using formal models? First, the answer to our main research question is that the sources of U.S. foreign policy decisions can be represented by the use of formal models. Second, formal models offer clear and precise contrasts between alternative answers to this particular question regarding the cultural icons of U.S. foreign policy. Third, we find that the revisionist answer with respect to this question is empirically more consistent with the evidence of presidential strategic beliefs and intentions contained in the annual messages on foreign affairs sent by Roosevelt and Wilson to the U.S. Congress. Fourth, a dynamic formal model (the revisionist account) is a better fit than a static formal model (the conventional account), which did not take into account changes in beliefs over time and across regions in making foreign policy decisions. Fifth, there is apparently a convergence in the evidence from contemporary public sources such as presidential addresses available to political scientists and archival evidence such as private correspondence and classified government documents available to historians long after the events under analysis have occurred. Sixth, the abstract nature of formal models does not preclude them from being sufficiently realistic to explain important features of political decision making.

Finally, it appears that formal models need to be used in an alliance with other methods of analysis in order to fully assess their contributions. Formal models organized and analyzed the data on presidential beliefs, but those data needed to be collected and indexed systematically in order to test the models. Survey research and content analysis methods for collecting data worked together with statistical methods and historical interpretations in constructing indices and displaying the results in this chapter. Such allies make formal models of game theory more than plausible causal stories resting on casual empirical investigations.[40] A combination of game theory, psychological theory, and historical interpretations guided the use of these different empirical methods.[41] The general lesson here is that such alliances are often desirable and even necessary in order to solve conceptual and empirical problems in social science.

Interested to Know More about the Study Discussed in this Chapter?

Consult the publication:

Walker, S. and M. Schafer. 2007. "Theodore Roosevelt and Woodrow Wilson as cultural icons of U.S. foreign policy." *Political Psychology* 28: 747–776.

Exercises and Discussion Questions:

1. Scientists have long realized that numerous *models* can fit any set of observations.[42] How many alternative games can you construct from the simple Theory of Inferences about Preferences in this chapter? Can you think of an *alternative explanation* for America's entry into World War I that does not rest on Wilson's operational code? If you use your new theory to specify a formal game theory model of his decision making, what rankings do you assign to Self and Other regarding preferences for the outcomes of domination, deadlock, settlement and submission? When you apply your new theory, do you get a different game than the Realist Game in this chapter for Wilson's second term? For example, do you get a hybrid game in which he remains an Idealist Self but faces a Realist Other? Do you get a different final outcome (equilibrium) for this game than the one for Wilson's Realist game?

2. The logic of each game can be extended to define a class of events, which meets the criterion for a *formal model* to be *logically exhaustive*. If you were to take the time to figure out all the possible combinations of rankings and intersections making up the general class of 2 x 2 ordinal games, the answer is 78 possible games, which also meets the other criterion for a formal model to be *mutually exclusive*.[43] The 78 games divide into two subsets of no-conflict and conflict games. Twenty-one of the games are no-conflict games in which both players rank the same outcome highest and include all of the Idealist games. Fifty-seven are conflict games in which the players do not rank the same outcome highest and include all of the Realist games plus the hybrid Idealist–Realist games as a subset of mixed-motive games within the set of conflict games.[44] When we distinguish either between individual games or between no-conflict and conflict games, we are identifying differences in the structure of the decision-making setting in which the players exercise agency in making choices.

Recommended Resources:

Fiorina, Morris. 1975. "Formal Models in Political Science." *Midwest Journal of Political Science* 19: 133–159: This is a good discussion of formal modeling. If your library subscribes to JSTOR, it is available on line.

Walker, Stephen G. and Mark Schafer. "Operational Code Theory: Beliefs and Foreign Policy Decisions." In *The International Studies Encyclopedia*, ed. Robert Denmark, (8): 5492–5514. Chicester, UK: Wiley-Blackwell: This is a good discussion of operational code theory (the encyclopedia is available online, by library subscription, from blackwellreference.com).

Brams, Steven. 2002. "Game Theory in Practice: Problems and Prospects in Applying It to International Relations." In *Millennial Reflections on International Studies*, eds. Michael Brecher and Frank Harvey, 392–404. Ann Arbor: University of Michigan Press: A good, brief description of game theory as a formal model of international relations.

Walker, Stephen G., Akan Malici, and Mark Schafer. *Rethinking Foreign Policy Analysis: States, Leaders, and the Microfoundations of Behavioral International Relations*. New York: Routledge: This is an extensive application of sequential game theory and operational code analysis to the study of foreign policy and international relations. This book tackles the complex problem of measuring the intersections of agents with different subjective games and understanding the decisions and outcomes that are generated. It is available online from Amazon Kindle.

Notes

1 Walker and Schafer 2007, 747–748.
2 Haass 2009.
3 Walker and Schafer 2007, 748.
4 Brams 2002; Walker and Schafer 2007.
5 Fiorina 1975.
6 *American Heritage Dictionary* 1994: 346.
7 Walker 2011: 13.
8 Schaeffer et al. 2007.
9 Brams 2002; Schaeffer et al. 2007; see also, Feynman 1995: 24–5; Walker et al. 2011: 10–12.
10 Fiorina 1975: 138.
11 Fiorina 1975: 150–151.
12 Brams 1994.
13 Fiske and Taylor 1991; Lau 2003.
14 Fiorina 1975; Geva and Mintz 1997; Green and Shapiro 1994.
15 Bueno de Mesquita and McDermott 2004; Lupia et al 2000; Suedfeld et al 2003.
16 Brams 1994; Stein 1990.
17 Bailey 1958; Cooper 1983.

18 Johnson 1995a; Walker and Schafer 2010.
19 Brams 1994.
20 Rapoport and Guyer 1966; see also, Brams 1994: 2002.
21 Brams 2002: 395.
22 Bailey 1958; Cooper 1983.
23 Cooper 1983; Walker 1995.
24 Walker and Schafer 2007: 770.
25 Claude 1962; Morgenthau 1985; Osgood 1964.
26 Waltz 1959.
27 Walker and Schafer 2010.
28 Johnson 1995b.
29 Kagan 2003.
30 Larus 1965.
31 George 1969.
32 Walker and Schafer 2010: 5496.
33 Walker and Schafer 2010.
34 Walker and Schafer 2007: 760.
35 Walker and Schafer 2007: 754–755.
36 Walker and Schafer 2007: 750.
37 Walker and Schafer 2007: 755.
38 Walker and Schafer 2007: 756, n. 13.
39 Walker and Schafer 2007: 759, n. 15.
40 Fiorina 1975.
41 Elman and Elman 2001; Walker 2003; Walker and Schafer 2010.
42 Fiorina 1975: 138.
43 Brams 1994; Rapoport and Guyer 1966.
44 Brams 1994: 215–219.

CONTENTS

Normative and Ethical Considerations of Political Science Research

Elizabeth S. Smith and Akan Malici

In the 1960s, a sociology graduate student by the name of Laud Humphreys conducted a study of homosexual behavior in public places. Unknown to the subjects of his field research study, Humphreys, a gay man himself, identified men having homosexual encounters in public bathrooms. He obtained the license plate numbers of these men and then went to their homes (disguising his own appearance so he would not be recognized) under the guise of conducting a "social health survey" and asked them questions about their personal life. He discovered that many of these men were in heterosexual marriages and living very traditional lives. In the era in which his research was done, the information he gathered was remarkable as it fundamentally challenged notions of what was normal behavior and led to a deeper understanding of human sexuality. However, on many fronts, his study violated the most important ethical standards for research. Humphreys did not obtain informed consent from his subjects, deceived them regarding the purpose of his survey, and he also infringed on their privacy by coming into their homes under false pretenses. Because of these ethical violations, he was denied his Ph.D. degree by his university.[1]

Because you are a college student, you may find at least equally disturbing the research conducted by Mary Henle and Marian Hubbell in the 1930s. These two psychologists focused on egocentrism in adult conversation (how often adults make reference to themselves as opposed to others when they speak). Specifically, they wanted to know whether there is a decrease in egocentrism as a person matures from childhood into adulthood. Their methodology was simple: They would carefully listen to conversations and count egocentric words or phrases in the conversations. Obtaining such relative frequency counts for their sample of young adults would allow them to compare their results to the results from samples of children's conversations. In order to be particularly unobtrusive, they did not shy away from secretly invading the privacy of the subjects being observed. Here is how they describe their procedure:

> In order not to introduce artifacts into the conversations, [we] took special precautions to keep the subjects ignorant of the fact that their remarks were being recorded. To this end [we] concealed [ourselves] under beds in students' rooms where tea parties were being held, eavesdropped in dormitory smoking-rooms and dormitory wash-rooms, and listened to telephone conversations.[2]

You may rightly be shocked, and it is good to know that this type of research would not be permissible any longer. Standards have changed over time and become more stringent to protect subjects participating in a research project. Normative and ethical questions and concerns must be considered at every stage of the research process in any field. Political scientists, like others, must consider the ethics of the research questions they ask as well as the methods by which they gather the answers to those questions. **Institutional Review Boards** (IRBs) are now present at all universities and any research using human or animal subjects (even research conducted by undergraduates) must be approved as ethical by these boards before it is conducted.

Throughout the chapters of this book, we have seen the struggles and the joys surrounding the research process and particular research methods. Though this is the final chapter of this book, ethical and normative considerations should not be considered afterthoughts in this process. In fact, these considerations are at the forefront of any good scholarly work. So, what are the ethical and normative considerations any good scholar should take into account?

Normative considerations are value considerations concerned with how things (politics) should or ought to be. The Democratic Peace Theory that we discussed in Chapter 2, for example, carries very strong normative implications. If democracies indeed do not fight each other, then the normative implication would be to want democratization in countries where it is lacking.

Ethical considerations are concerned with how one ought to act (as a researcher) morally speaking, with the rightness or wrongness of the researcher's actions, and the right and wrong ways to treat other living beings. The means that Henle and Hubel used to conduct their study on egocentrism in young adults just intuitively seem to be wrong and not ethical. The wrongness of our research activities may, however, not always be as obvious and so one must be very careful here.

Both normative and ethical considerations should matter to good scholars and they should be considered during every aspect of the research process: When one is choosing a research question and the appropriate or conducive methodology to study and answer it, when one is actually conducting the research, and finally when one is considering the meaning and implications of one's findings and conclusions.

ISSUES WHEN CHOOSING ONE'S TOPIC

Perhaps, the most important part of the research process is choosing an appropriate topic and research question. At the heart of this choice is considering the normative issue of whether this topic is important. When considering their **research question** and topic, good scholars ask themselves: Does this question really matter? Does it address some fundamental problem or issue in our world? Does it contribute to making the world a better place? Does it challenge us to address in some way the fundamental question of how things ought to be in the world? Is it based on truthful premises and is it fruitful in suggesting answers to other problems? These are **normative questions**. While these questions seem lofty and the goals high, the ultimate purpose of any research project is to contribute in some way to understanding the world a little bit more in the hopes of making it a little bit (or a lot) better for all.

Certainly, the choice of topic depends in part on what you as an individual scholar think is important or significant or what should be considered as important by more people. However, as reviewed at the beginning of this book, excellent research is about revealing scientific knowledge, not promoting personal bias or opinion. While some research directly answers challenging questions, more often research contributes to just a portion of our understanding of the big picture. But, a good researcher should always be able to articulate an answer to the "so what?" question regarding the significance of their topic.

We believe that it is a good practice to use one's colleagues as bouncing boards for one's research ideas. As humans we are often guided by our own and very unique senses of curiosity. Led by our own curiosity, it often happens that one comes up with a particular (research) question and subsequently develops a blind passion for it, not seeing the limited usefulness or applicability of any answer to it. This is where colleagues can be helpful in giving us a reality check. Our colleagues, like ourselves, are experts on what we intend to study, particularly those who work in the same field as we do. They may be able to give a more objective answer to the "so what?" question.

Colleagues may also be helpful in another area. No matter how great our expertise in any given area may be, ultimately, we are still limited. Elizabeth Smith, for example, did not read every article and book on female discrimination in particular or women and politics more generally. Similarly, Akan Malici did not read all articles and books on foreign policy decision making, his area of specialization. The questions we ask may have been asked and answered already, yet we may not be aware of it. Colleagues may save us a lot of time and obsolete engagement. If, however, our question is worth pursuing, colleagues may be helpful in suggesting literature that can in significant ways aid our research.

There are also other challenges when deciding on a research question. Consider, for example, issues faced by scholars we met in this book when they were considering their particular topic of study. In chapter eight, for example, authors David Fleming and Joshua Cowen took on a particularly contentious topic in their decision to research the school voucher issue. Passionate, partisan debate surrounds this issue with stakeholders like parents, the public and private school systems, the state and federal governments, and important political leaders having vested interests in certain outcomes. While this particular study was authorized by the state of Wisconsin, the legislature did not provide any funding to carry it out. These scholars then were forced to seek funds from various foundations and organizations. At the same time, however, they had to be sure they were not beholden to these groups to "find" certain outcomes or did not appear biased to outsiders because of these funding sources. This was an *ethical* challenge and it is a common problem when research is funded by private organizations which, of course, may have their own ideologies, interests, and agendas and may want to see these supported by scholarly research, which rightly tends to be perceived as credible and authoritative. It is important for scholars to remain mindful of these challenges. Fleming and Cowen explicitly drew our attention to this challenge. Yet, because they were mindful of them, they were confident that they could "handle" them while pursuing the very important question of whether these expensive and varied approaches to educating young people in a democracy were in fact efficacious.

The choice of topic for study also created particular ethical and normative dilemmas for two of the scholars who discussed their qualitative research in this book. In Chapter 4, Kate Kaup discusses her study of the treatment of ethnic minorities in China. The Chinese government, a **normatively** important entity for study precisely because it has been described by various commentators as a repressive regime, directly blocks access to information it deems politically sensitive, like research on human rights violations. Chinese scholars who dare to research such sensitive topics regularly find themselves imprisoned, as Ph.D. candidate Tohti Tunyaz discovered when he was sentenced to ten years in prison for his work on Uighur history.[3] It has also been in the experience of Western researchers who criticize the Chinese government that they can be denied visas to conduct future research. Given the often oppressive and, at times, dangerous research climate surrounding politically sensitive issues, the researcher may understandably opt to pursue issues less critical of the government. But, according to Kaup and other scholars in similar positions, it is important that regimes like the Chinese government are not allowed to shape the research agenda as that would mean research is only done on sanitized political issues and presents a distorted view of these governments and their politics.

In Chapter 5, Kristina Thalhammer discusses her interviews with individuals who were subject to extreme regime violence and repression under the military junta in Argentina from 1976 through 1982. Her choice of topic was also clearly **normatively** important—when, how, and why are people willing to resist unjust political authority? However, we should not fail to ask: Was it *ethically* responsible to go out and ask very sensitive and emotionally difficult questions of those who were involved? It is important to remember that loved ones of those asked were brutally tortured and/or were disappeared forever by the regime. Such a choice of topic required many participants to relive painful memories from their past or to confront their own lack of action in the face of injustice. A researcher must carefully weigh such costs against the potential benefits of pursuing a particular topic. The benefits of providing insight into political resistance and the fruitfulness of such a research pursuit for understanding other circumstances (like rescuing behavior during the Holocaust or government whistleblowers) were benefits that most would say outweighed the potential costs. Although, she could not be entirely sure, it was Thalhammer's sincere assessment that her questions would not inflict enduring pain on the participants.

Some have argued that certain topics are off limits **normatively** speaking because they begin by suggesting premises that are biased or subjective, or they are not fruitful in providing us the potential to address other questions. Disagreements among scholars have been centered around (research) questions which ask, for example, "Did the Holocaust occur?" Such a question begins so far from a truthful premise, most would argue that it is illegitimate to ask. Or, for example, take the controversy surrounding the (research) question: "Are their genetic explanations for the differences between men and women in success in science?" Or, similarly, "Can we explain differences in educational achievement between blacks and whites based on innate traits?" Such topics are similarly considered by many **normatively** and **ethically** inappropriate in large part because they are reductionist about human behavior, suggesting that what we do and how we act can be explained by simplistically examining categories assigned to us by birth rather than the totality of our experiences as humans and, in the asking, suggest no solution to the social problem.

There is clearly room for disagreement about the appropriateness of a choice of research question. A sincere and honest engagement with one's motivations for asking potentially controversial or offensive questions is a first step for serious scientific research as opposed to sensationalism or demagoguery. Once again we also find that it is smart to consult with one's colleagues. Talking to others, sharing one's ideas and taking suggestions and possible warnings seriously is always a good measure toward success as a reputable researcher.

ISSUES WITH ONE'S RESEARCH STRATEGY

In 1971 a team of researchers led by Stanford University psychologist Philip Zimbardo conducted what came to be known as the (in)famous *Stanford Prison Experiment*.[4] You may remember that we mentioned this study in the very first chapter of this book. The researchers were interested in studying abusive prison situations. They randomly selected two dozen students to live in a mock prison of the Stanford psychology building and they assigned to them randomly the roles of prisoners and guards. Zimbardo himself took the role of "Prison Superintendent." After a very short time (one day) participants adapted scarily well to their assigned roles. The guards displayed authoritarian attitudes and some went even so far as to display truly sadistic behaviors. As one form of punishment, for example, the guards would remove the prisoners' mattresses, so that they would be made to sleep on the concrete floor. Equally shocking, some prisoners were forced to be nude as a form of punishment. At times, guards also did not allow the prisoners to urinate or defecate in a restroom, which contributed to deplorable sanitary conditions. The prisoners, on the other hand, adopted passive attitudes and endured physical abuse and, at the request of the guards, they went even so far as to inflict punishment on their fellow inmates.

In the aftermath of the experiment, critics charged Zimbardo with losing sight of his true role as a psychologist as he permitted the abuse to continue for several days. This was an **ethical** charge. Indeed, it was only when a shocked graduate student entered the situation and objected to the conditions of the mock prison that the experiment was terminated. At the time Zimbardo's study was cleared by the Ethics Code of the American Psychological Association. They did not anticipate that it would not only violate the dignity of the participants, but also cause them actual harm. It became evident that a research proposal on paper can look quite different from the actual conduct of the study. Moreover, it also became clear that the general "do no harm" principle established by IRBs is not a guarantee for the research process to unfold accordingly.

When scholars choose experiments as their research methodology, **ethical** questions are especially apparent. This is also the case for interviews and surveys. All these research methodologies involve human beings in very direct and immediate ways. Of utmost concern in any of these methodologies should be that the subjects of study are treated with dignity and respect, that their interests are protected and that the potential costs of any study to the participant are weighed carefully against the potential benefits of the research to furthering knowledge and understanding. While IRB reviews are not a guarantee for an ethical research process, they, no doubt, are nevertheless a crucial necessity as they do formalize certain standard criteria that must be met to ensure the protection of the interests of those being studied.

The IRB review looks at several standard criteria in evaluating the appropriateness and ethics of a research study. Participants must give what is called **informed consent** to be included in an experiment, survey, interview, etc. Informed consent means that the subject is told that they are part of a research study; they are told what the general topic and purpose of the study is; they are told how the results of the study will be used (for example, published in a scholarly article that includes their name or maintains their anonymity); they are informed of the potential risks or costs to them as well as the benefits of participation in the study; and, finally, they are told they may discontinue their participation in the study at any time.

The goal of IRBs to protect the rights of those being studied is particularly important in cases where the subject of study is considered technically unable to give consent (for example, when minors are studied (as was the case in the school voucher study discussed in Chapter 8) or when, for example, the mentally disabled are studied). True consent also depends on a participant not being provided inducements to participate that are so great that they are unwilling or really unable to say 'no' to participation. For example, large monetary incentives for participating in an experiment or a survey are typically not allowed by IRBs as they present so much coercive power to participate that the individual may not think clearly about the costs and benefits. One of the authors of this chapter (Elizabeth), for example, had a friend in college who agreed to participate in a medical experiment that subjected him to a treatable, but very disagreeable, bacterial disease because he needed the $500 they offered for his participation in order to pay his rent that month. The incentive very likely made him participate in a study he normally would have found too risky and costly.

Similarly, issues regarding full consent come to the forefront when the researcher holds some kind of power over the participant. For example, when a professor is conducting experiments and using some of her college students as participants as Elizabeth Smith did in her experiment on political scandal, students may feel obligated to participate because they do not want to lose the favor of a teacher who may be grading them. Or, in the case of the school voucher study, for example, schools (both public and private) may feel unable to resist participation when they are strongly encouraged to participate by a state legislature that controls some valuable purse strings. Careful consideration must be given to provide fair but not overly coercive inducements or pressure to participate.

The costs or risks to a participant in a research study must be carefully assessed by the scholar conducting the study. Sometimes the subjects of the study themselves might not recognize the potential risk they face. For example, peasants in a Chinese village may unwittingly expose themselves to government backlash by sharing information with a Western researcher. Or, participants may be unwittingly confronted by survey or interview questions they did not expect to be asked and subsequently these questions cause them psychological distress.

Respecting the dignity of participants being studied means also that, whenever possible, participants should be given the opportunity to learn more about the study and the final findings. In the case of experiments, such as the one Elizabeth Smith discussed in Chapter 10, it is commonplace for participants to be *debriefed* at the end of the experiment. Usually in an experiment and often even with survey research and interviews, the researcher does not want to tell the participants at the beginning the full purpose of the research or the hypotheses going in as they do not want that information to affect the participants' responses. For example, the experiment in Chapter 10 would not have produced valid results if participants had known that the researcher was interested in finding out if the sex of a politician affected their evaluations of the politician's scandalous behavior. Similarly, in her interviews with survivors of the Argentinean military junta, Thalhammer in Chapter 5 did not want her interviewees to know that she was interested specifically in resistance because, as she said, she did not want them to tailor their answers to support (or disprove) her hypothesis.

Debriefing the participants after a study has been conducted on what the full purpose of the study was or sharing the published work with them respects their contribution to and sacrifice for the project and indicates to the participants the valued role they played in furthering knowledge. At the same time, it also allows them to benefit from the knowledge gained. In the case of the school voucher study, for example, schools, state governments, and non-profit organizations can use the results to help them consider the most effective educational policies to implement. Similarly, participants in a survey or in in-depth interviews may gain greater self-knowledge or understanding of how their opinions are similar to or different from others.

Occasionally, sharing the results of a study with participants can be difficult. For example, a researcher might present critical or unflattering information about a subject. In most cases, however, if a participant has given informed consent, has been allowed to maintain their anonymity of their own choosing, has not been unfairly coerced to participate, and the research has been conducted in a professional and objective manner, participants feel respected in the process and recognize the value of the knowledge gained by the study. Fair and respectful (even if critical) treatment of participants is important as well because scholars are part of a community of researchers. If one of us fails to treat our participants ethically and with respect, we burn bridges for other scholars. As a result, scholars will then find it more difficult to get cooperation in their future projects and, thus, to continue to contribute to the scholarly body of knowledge.

We want to conclude this section with an emphasis on *objectivity* as a **normative** requirement placed upon the researcher. Maintaining objectivity is a main imperative in doing research. It is easy to see how objectivity, as a principle, applies to all research methodologies whether it involves human beings in direct and immediate ways or not.

From the outset, of course, objective collecting and handling of the data is essential. It is especially important that scholars do not "cherry pick" the data or the participants in a study to support a particular hypothesis. For example, in Chapter 9 on content analysis of local media coverage of members of Congress, because of time and resource constraints, Danielle Vinson could not include all local coverage of all members of Congress. However, to assure her sample was not biased, she carefully created a **random sampling** procedure, whereby no one type of media outlet or geographical location was more likely to be selected for her analysis than any other. Random sampling is similarly important in survey research. Chapter 6 on statistical analysis discusses the Latino National Political Survey. It illustrates well how valuable such a data set was as all prior studies had been done on only small, non-random groups of immigrants and, thus, the results were not generalizable regarding why some immigrants choose to go through the naturalization process while others do not. Scholars of case studies, such as those discussed by Kai He in Chapter 3, must be particularly sensitive because of the small samples they often use to make sure their selection of cases is based on objective criteria of interest not just because they will help support some preconceived hunch, opinion or the researcher's hypothesis or theory.

Objectivity also requires the researcher to maintain a certain level of scholarly detachment from the subject of study. For example, especially in intense or personal interview situations or when doing field research that requires pro-longed interaction, scholars may begin to identify with their subjects or develop a natural human connection. This kind of connection can be valuable as it may foster deeper insights into the subjects of study. However, it may also become more difficult for the researcher to evaluate her findings fairly. Kate Kaup gave us an example about field research in China: If researching how political campaigns are conducted in China's countryside, for example, the researcher may come to know one of the candidates well and find it difficult to write about his or her failures, misconceived notions, or even corrupt practices. She asserts that striking a balance between empathy and detachment is critical for presenting objective truths and advancing knowledge.

Scholarly detachment is also important in unobtrusive research such as content analysis. Danielle Vinson, our author of the content analysis chapter confided to us: "When analyzing the more subjective aspects of coverage, such as the tone or orientation of coverage, we must be careful to take what the author or speaker says at face value rather than reading our own views into the writing, and we must resist the temptation to impugn the motivations of the reporter because we disagree with what is written." When engaging in content analysis, or for that matter any other type of analysis, it is indeed important that we, as scholars, consider all possible explanations and avoid introducing our own biases—a danger and temptation that is always present.

ISSUES WITH ONE'S RESEARCH FINDINGS

We already hinted at the **ethical** dilemmas when publishing one's findings as was the case in Thalhammer's interview research on human rights activism in Chapter 5. The results may indeed carry serious implications far beyond the researcher's initial goals. This is also illustrated well by the disturbing results of a very interesting study. The researcher Keith Payne was interested in people's prejudices and their effects on perceptions.[5] In his experiment he primed the participants by showing them either a black face or a white face. Then he exposed the experimental participants to very quick randomly sequenced images of a gun or a tool—two objects that have some level of resemblance especially when one can see them only for a split second. Every time the participants saw (or believed to have seen) the gun, they were to push a button. The finding was that participants misidentified tools as guns more often when primed with a black face than with a white face.

One of us (Akan) first encountered this study in graduate school when he took a seminar in social psychology. The reaction of many classmates was interesting and telling and it was expressed in the context of a very controversial court case that Keith Payne introduces his research article with. In 1999, four New York policemen shot and killed an unarmed black immigrant from West Africa in a hail of more than 40 bullets! Yet, the policemen were acquitted on the grounds that although they made a mistake, their actions were justified at the time. The shooting was judged to be justified because at the moment that policemen ordered Diallo to stop, the victim moved, producing an object that the policemen mistook for a weapon. Later on this object turned out to be a wallet. The police defendants contended that in this ambiguous situation, they acted on the information available, sincerely believing that they were in danger.

Keith Payne's study lends support to this conclusion. Moreover, many students in the seminar concluded immediately that the results deliver a scientific basis for the existence of prejudice and racism. They had serious normative reservations about this study and the publishing of its results, as they feared it may be used to justify racial bias. Yet, the research was done objectively and it followed all ethical principles of scientific research. It is then in the researcher's discretion to evaluate the pros and cons, the benefits and the possible negative implications of publishing one's findings. Although Akan was initially shocked and had serious reservations about Keith Payne's publishing of these results, now he is in favor of such types of studies as they shed light on important fundamentals of human interactions. We need knowledge, however uncomfortable and disturbing it may be. Knowledge is a first and indispensable step toward effective measures against racism or whatever we may face.

Finally, we want to emphasize what should be obvious, namely that researchers should not introduce their own biased interpretations when presenting the results. Researchers are human beings and human beings have their own opinions and biases. While the goal of political science research is providing objective knowledge, it would be disingenuous to suggest that a researcher's own interests and sense of what matters does not affect their decision to pursue a certain research question. However, objectivity and the standards of scientific study require that the conclusions we draw once the facts have been gathered are not influenced by our own feelings or biases. As they were reflecting on their survey research from Chapter 7, Lyman Kellstedt and James Guth remarked to us: "[One] potential ethical problem was in the interpretation of results: religion involves important value issues on which people differ strongly. As researchers we are not immune to such considerations and might be tempted to interpret some data in a way that is critical of religious traditions or groups other than our own."

It is probably the case that most of us start our research program with an expectation of what we will find. Elizabeth Smith, for example, was sure that she would find that female politicians were judged more harshly than male politicians when involved in a scandal. Her expectations did not bear out. Not finding one's expectations confirmed by the research results may be disappointing at first. However, discovering that our preconceived notions are incorrect can be one of the most rewarding and interesting parts of the whole process. It is a process of learning—a process that (it is hoped) never ends and the researcher should be as open to it as she expects the readers of her research to be.

FINAL THOUGHTS

Throughout this book, you have heard firsthand from scholars using a variety of the methodological tools available in political science. These tools include the comparative case study, field research and interviews, statistical and survey research, document and content analysis, experimental research and formal modeling. We have presented these methods in neatly packaged chapters. This may have created the impression that they are distinct and mutually exclusive from one another. The astute reader probably has noticed by now, however, that these methods are not exactly distinct but, instead, overlap in fundamental ways. For example, we have a stand-alone chapter on statistical research, but you likely noticed that most methodologies including experiments, document analysis, content analysis, formal modeling, sometimes in-depth interviews and, always survey research, all rely on statistical analysis. Similarly, though presented in separate chapters, field research is not entirely distinct from interviews as it typically involves open-ended, in-depth interviews.

Additionally, researchers know that often the very best way to answer a research question is to rely on multiple methodologies. Using multiple methodologies, scholars can gain in their investigation both the depth offered by such approaches as open-ended interviews and the breadth offered, for example, by large-scale surveys. Sometimes one scholar or one research team uses multiple methodologies to address their research question. If the results obtained through one methodology are confirmed by the results that have been obtained through another methodology then we gain increasing confidence in the outcomes. The results validate each other, in other words.

Finally, research is a cumulative and sometimes messy process. Though science has the goal of finding truth, often our conclusions and findings are modified over time as we learn more and continue in the quest for truth. Sometimes we pursue false leads, as the authors of Chapter 7 did in their survey research on religion and politics. Sometimes we get frustrated in our pursuits as Kaup was by the Chinese government's limits on her access to certain groups in her field research discussed in Chapter 5. Often, we find that research can be time-consuming as it was in the comparative case study presented in Chapter 3 where the author had to assess a vast array of data about multiple countries in order to understand why nations join or do not join multilateral organizations. Occasionally, research can require considerable methodological training and skills as is apparent in the formal modeling research of Chapter 11 where survey research, content analysis, historical interpretation, and psychological theories were all employed to explain foreign policy decisions using formal models. But, if you have discovered anything from reading these chapters in the authors' own words, to a true scholar doing political science research is always, at the very least, an interesting and, at the very most, an ultimately rewarding pursuit.

Exercises and Discussion Questions:

1. Should researchers be allowed to fund their research with *monies from private organizations*?
2. Can you think of *research topics* that are "off-limits"? Why are they not (to be) pursued?
3. Why do you think that *issues of ethics* are typically only discussed in the *last chapter* of most research methodology books?
4. Which *research methodologies*, do you think, bring the least amount of *ethical challenges* with them? Why?
5. Do you think scholars can truly be *objective*? If not, what are the implications?

Recommended Resources:

U.S. Department of Health and Human Services Office for Human Research Protection (www.hhs.gov/ohrp/index.html): Learn more about Institutional Review Board guidelines and policies as set forth by the U.S.

Department of Health and Human Services Office for Human Research Protection.

National Institute of Health (www.phrp.nihtraining.com/users/login.php): Take an online training course in the ethical use of human subjects created by the National Institute of Health (this training is often required to be completed by Institutional Review Boards before approval for research is granted).

American Political Science Association (www.apsanet.org/content_9350. cfm): Download the American Political Science Association's Guide to Professional Ethics, Rights and Freedoms.

The Center for Social Media (www.centerforsocialmedia.org/fair-use/ related-materials/codes/code-best-practices-fair-use-scholarly-research-communication): See also the Code of Best Practices in Fair Use for Scholarly Research in Communication.

Notes

1 Humphreys 1970.
2 Henle and Hubbell 1938: 230.
3 English Pen 2011.
4 Zimbardo 2007.
5 Payne 2001: 81.

Glossary

Absolute law (see *law*).

American Political Science Association (APSA) the largest professional association for political scientists. Formed in 1903, this association holds annual professional conferences where scholars share their research. The APSA also publishes the premier journal in the field, the *American Political Science Review.*

American Politics a subfield in the discipline of political science devoted to understanding American politics and institutions.

Analysis of variance (ANOVA) a statistical technique that compares the means of two or more groups on some variable to see if they differ significantly.

Antecedent variable occurs in time prior to an independent variable and may act as a catalyst or a precondition for the independent variable to take effect.

Behavioral Revolution the name given to the shift in research emphasis among political science scholars beginning around the 1950s from a focus on describing political institutions to a more scientific, systematic data analysis-driven study of politics and political behavior.

Case a single event or an observation which can help researchers investigate their research questions.

Case study an in-depth investigation of a case, where the case may refer to an individual, group, phenomenon, or event.

Causal mechanism a statement that explains *why* there is a relationship between two or more variables; it is the explanation for *why* something happens.

Causality in order to establish causality three criteria must be met: first, the assumed independent variable and the dependent variable must correlate; second, the independent variable must precede the dependent variable in time; third, the relationship between the independent variable and the dependent variable must not be **spurious**.

Chi-square a statistic revealing whether a dependent variable and an independent variable are associated with one another.

Closed-ended questions questions that force respondents to pick from a set of response options.

Comparative Politics a subfield in the discipline of political science devoted to explaining politics by comparing political institutions, most often nation-states, using either the Method of Similarity or the Method of Difference.

Concepts the words that describe the phenomena under investigation.

Conceptualization the verbal definition of a concept.

Confidence interval the range of likely values of a variable in the population.

Confidence level a statistic representing how confident one is that the sample value represents the population value of the variable.

Convenience samples samples of respondents used because they are readily available.

Content analysis a method of research used to analyze communications such as speeches, news stories, etc., typically quantitatively.

Content analysis categories exhaustive and mutually exclusive measures used in content analysis to evaluate the presence or absence of variables of interest.

Content code the numeric value assigned to a variable that is of interest in a content analysis.

Control variables variables that are held constant in quantitative analysis to isolate the relationship between the variables of interest.

Controlled comparison design a method used by researchers to compare members of groups who share similar demographic characteristics in order to help alleviate the problem of selection bias in a sample.

Correlation the relative strength of a statistical relationship between two or more variables.

Cross-sectional survey when a sample is surveyed at one point in time only.

Crosstabulations (crosstabs) a statistic which shows the extent to which two variables occur together.

Data systematically collected and objective observations about the phenomenon being studied; data come in two forms: quantitative (numerical) or qualitative (textual).

Dependent variable the presumed effect in a causal relationship.

Descriptive statistics basic statistics, including frequencies and measures of central tendency (mean, median, mode), which describe the data.

Dichotomous measure a measure that can be one of two categories.

Direct observation immediate observation of the event or phenomenon of interest.

Discourse analysis interpretative analysis of communications and their underlying intent or effect.

Dummy variable a variable that equals one if it is in a particular category and zero if it is not.

Elite Interview the process of interviewing decision-makers that are under investigation.

Empirical evidence data-supported proof that a proposition is true.

Epiphenomenal *syn.* unimportant.

Episodic record secondary data that captures a particular period of time; examples include papers from a Supreme Court justice, a presidential diary, etc.

Equifinality the same outcome can be explained by different pathways or combinations of variables.

Ethical questions questions concerned with how one ought to act, morally speaking.

Experiment a method used by researchers to study causal relationships where the researcher in a controlled setting manipulates an independent variable to test its effect on a dependent variable.

External validity the degree to which methods or findings are generalizable outside of the study.

Extraneous variable a factor that could have created an "accidental" or "non-causal" relationship between the independent and dependent variables.

Field experiment a naturally occurring experiment where the researcher has no control over who is in the treatment group and who is in the control group.

Fieldwork where a researcher collects data through observation or by interviewing in a natural setting.

First differences in a logit regression, a statistic representing the likely increase or decrease in the dependent variable if each independent variable is raised from its minimum to maximum value while holding the other variables constant.

Formal model the mathematical and abstract representation of the phenomenon under investigation.

F-statistic a statistic reflecting whether or not there is any relationship between the dependent variable and the independent variables.

Game theory the mathematical modeling and study of a strategic situation in which the success of the choices of one "player" depends partially on the choices of another "player."

Generalization the process by which the findings about one event or occurrence are made applicable to all events or occurrences of the same class.

Hawthorne Effect when participants in a study act differently because they know they are the subjects of a study.

History effects a threat to internal validity in an experiment where something else (besides the manipulation) occurs between the pre-test and the post-test that is the cause of the change in the dependent variable from time one to time two.

Hypothesis an educated guess about the direction of a relationship between an independent variable and a dependent variable.

Independent variable the presumed cause in a causal relationship.

Informed consent when a participant agrees to be in a study knowing fully the risks and benefits associated with such participation.

Institutional Review Boards panels created to review the ethics of research being proposed and ensure that the participants in the study are protected.

Instrumentation effects a threat to the internal validity of an experiment caused by a change in the measuring instrument from the pre-test to the post-test.

Internal validity the extent to which the causal claims found in the study represent true cause-and-effect relationships.

International Relations a subfield in the discipline of political science devoted to investigating the relationships among various international actors, including nation-states and other political organizations.

Intervening variable an intermediate factor between the independent and dependent variables in a causal chain; it is caused by the independent variable and it causes the dependent variable.

Intervention analysis (or before-and-after analysis) a type of longitudinal analysis where researchers examine variables of interest both before and after some kind of intervention occurs.

Interview design the format used to conduct an interview; an interview can be structured with specific questions in a specific order or more semi-structured with an overall plan of questions to be asked but greater flexibility in the order in which they are asked.

Law a correlation between two variables. We distinguish between *absolute law* and *probabilistic law*. An absolute law states: "Whenever we observe x, we will observe y" or "If x, then always y." A probabilistic law states: "Whenever we observe x, we will observe y, with the probability z."

Likert scale response options to a question where the choices range from lower to higher (typically a 7 point scale).

Literature review a section of a research paper that reviews the existing scholarly findings regarding one's research question with the goal of establishing why pursuing the research question is important.

Logit regressions a statistical method that shows the impact of several independent variables on a dependent variable that is dichotomous or has only two possible values.

Longitudinal analysis analysis done on data that is collected over a significant period of time; can be one of three types —trend analysis, intervention analysis, or a panel study.

Matching a process used in a controlled comparison design where members of the groups being analyzed are chosen because they are similar on certain relevant characteristics; this allows the researcher to isolate the effect of the independent variable on the dependent variable.

Maturation effects a threat to internal validity in an experiment, where a change in the respondent over time is responsible for the change in dependent variable not the manipulation; for example, if an experimenter measures voting behavior at time one and finds that the participant did not vote, then introduces a manipulation and measures voting behavior at time two and finds that the subject did vote the researcher may assume the manipulation caused the change in voting behavior; however, between time one and time two, the respondent turned 18 and became eligible to vote, the real cause of the change in behavior.

Measurement error the extent to which an instrument fails to measure accurately what it is intended to measure; for example, when a thermometer misreads the air temperature or when a survey question is interpreted by the interviewees to be asking something different from what the researcher intended.

Method of agreement/similarity a research design by which cases are selected that all have the same outcome; at the same time, the cases must be dissimilar in regards to all but one presumed independent variable.

Method of difference a research design by which cases are selected that all have different outcomes; at the same time, the cases must be similar in regards to all but one presumed independent variable.

Mortality effects a threat to internal validity in a study caused by certain individuals dropping out of a study.

Multi-group experimental design an experiment where more than one type of intervention is manipulated in more than one group and then compared to a control group.

Multi-item index a single-scale variable created by combining several different survey items believed to measure different components of the same concept with the goal of reducing measurement error.

Multiple regression analysis a multivariate analysis statistical technique that allows a researcher to examine the unique, individual relationship between a particular independent variable and the dependent variable after taking the impact of other independent variables into account.

Multivariate analysis data analysis in which the effects of multiple independent variables on the dependent variable are examined.

N the symbol used to represent the number of people or entities in a sample.

Normative knowledge suppositions regarding how one believes things ought to be.

Normative question a question about how things ought to be in an imagined world; an example of a normative question would be: how should a country be governed?

Null hypothesis the hypothesis that there is no relationship between the independent and dependent variables.

Open-ended questions questions that allow respondents to give their own answer as opposed to being forced to choose from pre-created response options.

Operationalization turning a concept into an indicator or measure that can be analyzed; the process that lends a concept measurability.

Ordered logistic regression a statistical procedure used when the dependent variable is ordinal; it estimates the impact the independent variables have on the *likelihood* of observations being in the next highest category of the dependent variable.

Ordinal measures measures that are ordered from low to high in value (for example, from lower class to upper class), but where the increments between the values are not necessarily equivalent or definable.

Panel mortality when individuals in a panel study drop out of the study for some reason (they no longer want to participate, they move away, etc.).

Panel study a type of longitudinal analysis where the researcher measures variables of interest from the same sample over a period of time.

Participant observation the observation of any group under interest while being a "member" of the group. It allows for the development of intimate familiarity with the group.

Policy analysis a method that examines different policy alternatives to a policy problem. Policy analysis often includes a description of the problem, various policy solutions to the problem, a discussion of the costs and benefits of each alternative, and a recommendation of the best policy alternative.

Positive question a question about phenomena in the existing world. The opposite of a positive question is a **normative question**.

Positivist knowledge knowledge based on how things are; based on objective fact.

Post-test only, control group experimental design an experimental design where measurements of the dependent variable are taken only after the intervention in order to avoid testing/instrumentation effects.

Pre-test/post-test, control group experimental design the classic experimental design where participants are randomly assigned to either an experimental group or a control group; the value of a dependent variable of interest is measured in both groups before and after an intervention or manipulation is introduced on the experimental group to test the effect of the intervention on the dependent variable.

Primary data analysis research that examines data that are directly collected or observed by the researcher, such as when a researcher interviews elected officials or observes a political protest.

Probabilistic law (see *law*).

Process-tracing a method of in-depth, within-case analysis. It focuses on specifying causal mechanisms between presumed independent variables and dependent variables and it strengthens the inference of analysis through examining chains of evidence from hypothesized cause to observed effect.

Program evaluation an assessment of the outcomes produced by a public policy; often there is a focus on whether or not the program or policy is effective in meeting its stated goals.

Proposition an expression of a judgment or a declaration about the relationship of at least two concepts; it must be either true or false.

Published data data that is generally publicly available and has been collected by a government entity, private organization, or other researchers; examples include Census data, congressional roll call votes, and National Election Studies survey data.

P-value (or statistical significance) a statistic that shows how likely a value from a sample reflects the true population value.

Qualitative analysis non-numerical evaluation of data.

Qualitative methods or research research that is non-numerical; in-depth research or data collection often limited to a few cases.

Quantitative analysis numerical evaluation of data.

Quantitative methods or research statistical or numerical research that works by assigning numbers to the terms that are being studied.

Quota sampling a type of stratified sampling where researchers define categories of interest (race, gender, etc.) and then select, typically in a non-random way, a sample of respondents in each category proportional to the population of interest.

Random assignment the process in an experiment where individuals are assigned to either the experimental group or control group; assignment is completely by chance.

Random sample/selection a sample where all possible members of the population have an equal chance of being selected.

Rapport to gain a certain amount of trust from an interviewee so that s/he feels comfortable being engaged in the interview and answering the interviewer's questions.

Reactivity when a subject in a study behaves differently because they are reacting to being the subject of study.

Refereed journal a scholarly journal containing research papers which have been reviewed anonymously by other scholars before publication, to ensure quality research has been done.

Reliability the extent to which a measurement measures something the same way, time after time.

Reliability coefficient a coefficient that can range from 0 to 1, indicating the correlation between multiple variables used to create a single-scale variable or index.

Research design the plan for answering one's research question using a particular research method.

Research question a statement that identifies the phenomenon we want to study; it is generally motivated by curiosity about something that we consider important but has not been asked, addressed, and answered yet—at least not satisfactorily.

Response set when questions are worded in such a way that respondents tend to answer "agree" to every question.

Running record secondary data that is collected at regular intervals over a period of time.

Sample a subset of cases drawn from a population.

Sampling error a statistic that represents the difference between the sample value and the population value for a certain variable, calculated based on the size of the sample.

Sampling frame the list of possible participants in a study.

Scientific knowledge when objective and systematic observation of data that can be verified by others is used to explain or understand something.

Secondary data data collected by someone other than the researcher.

Secondary data analysis analysis of data that was not orig-inally collected by the researcher; this data might include autobiographies, newspaper photos, legislative records, etc.

Selection bias the bias in data that occurs when the sample is non-representative of the population under investigation.

Selective deposit a term used in document analysis to describe the bias caused by only certain information being collected (such as only a well-funded group being able to afford keeping detailed records).

Selective survival a term used in document analysis to describe the bias caused by only certain documents being preserved over time.

Semi-structured interview the interviewer has an "interview guide" of topics or issues to be covered; however, s/he is free to change the wording and order of questions and to follow topical trajectories that, if appropriate, may stray from the guide.

Snowball technique asking those interviewed to suggest names of potential interview subjects with particular characteristics, viewpoints, or opinions.

Social desirability effects a threat to the internal validity of a study whereby the respondent gives the answer they believe is the most socially accepted response.

Spurious relationship the assumed independent variable and the dependent variable are in fact not causally related, if there is, in fact, a third (hidden) **extraneous variable**.

Standard error a statistic reflecting the difference between the sample value and the population value.

Statistical analysis the use of mathematics to explain data.

Statistical inference generalizing the results from a sample to the larger population of interest.

Statistical significance (**or p-value**) a statistic that shows how likely a value from a sample reflects the true population value.

Stratified random sample a random sample where participants are chosen from certain strata, or according to some characteristic they share in common.

Structured interview consists of a list of specific, pre-set questions; the interviewer strictly adheres to the list and to the order in which the questions appear, and does not introduce any spontaneous questions or comments into the interview process.

Survey research a method used to study public opinion where a random sample of a population is asked questions which are then compiled and analyzed statistically.

Testing effects a threat to internal validity in an experiment where the measurement of the variables actually causes a change in their value rather than the manipulation itself.

Textual analysis content analysis of a written text.

Transcription transform from an oral version into typed format.

Trend analysis (**or repeated cross-sectional analysis**) a type of longitudinal analysis where relationships between the same variables in different samples are examined at different points in time.

Unit of analysis the object or the entity under study; for example, in a content analysis, the unit of analysis might be an entire news story or individual paragraphs. It may also refer to individuals or larger aggregates, such as political ethnic, religious, or any other grouping or countries.

Unstandardized coefficients coefficients in a regression equation expressing in the units of the variable itself the effect of a one unit change in the independent variable on the value of the dependent variable, controlling for any other independent variables in the model.

Unstructured interview questions are not pre-set; the interviewer elicits information (data) from the interviewee in a free-flowing conversation.

Validity the extent to which a variable is measuring what is intended; typically evaluated by looking at whether that measure is related in expected ways to other variables.

REFERENCES

Aberbach, Joel D., James D. Chesney, and Bert A. Rockman. 1975. "Exploring Elite Political Attitudes: Some Methodological Lessons." *Political Methodology* 2: 1–27.

Aberbach, Joel D. and Bert A. Rockman. 2002. "Conducting and Coding Elite Interviews." *PS: Political Science and Politics* 35(4): 673–676.

Acharya, Amitav. 2001. *Constructing a Security Community in Southeast Asia: ASEAN and the Problem of Regional Order*. London: Routledge.

Adler, Emanuel and Michael Barnett, ed. 1998. *Security Communities*. Cambridge: Cambridge University Press.

Alexander, Karl L., Doris R. Entwisle, and Susan L. Dauber. 1996. "Children in Motion: School Transfers and Elementary School Performance." *Journal of Educational Research* 90(1): 3–12.

American Heritage Dictionary. 1994. 3rd edn. New York: Dell.

Andrade, Juan. 2006. 2006 *The Almanac of Latino Politics*. 4th edition. Chicago, IL: United States Hispanic Leadership Institute.

Ansolabehere, Stephen and Shanto Iyengar. 1995. *Going Negative: How Political Advertisements Shrink and Polarize the Electorate*. New York: The Free Press.

Aron, Arthur, Elain N. Aron, and Elliot J. Coups. 2006. *Statistics for Psychology*. Pearson: New Jersey.

Asch, Solomon. 1951. "Effects of Group Pressure upon the Modification and Distortion of Judgment." In *Groups, Leadership and Men*, ed. H. Guetzkow. Pittsburgh, PA: Carnegie Press.

Bagdikian, Ben H. 1974. "Congress and the Media: Partners in Propaganda." *Columbia Journalism Review* January/February: 3–10.

Bailey, T. 1958. *A Diplomatic History of the American People*. 6th edn. New York: Appleton-Century Crofts.

Baldwin, David, ed. 1993. *Neorealism and Neoliberalism: The Contemporary Debate*. New York: Columbia University Press.

Batson, D. 1973. "From Jerusalem to Jericho." *Journal of Personality and Social Psychology* 27(1): 100–108.

Bennett, Andrew. 2004. "Case Study Methods: Design, Use, and Comparative Advantages." In *Models, Numbers, and Cases: Methods for Studying International Relations*, ed. Detlef F. Sprinz and Yael Wolinsky-Nahmias. Ann Arbor: University of Michigan Press.

Berelson, Bernard R., Paul F. Lazarsfeld, and William N. McPhee. 1954. *Voting*. Chicago: University of Chicago Press.

Berry, Jeffrey M. 2002. "Validity and Reliability Issues in Elite Interviewing." *PS: Political Science and Politics* 35(4): 679–682.

Bobo, Lawrence and Franklin D. Gilliam Jr. 1990. "Race, Socioeconomic Status, and Black Empowerment." *American Political Science Review* 84: 377–394.

Borooah, Vani K. 2002. *Logit and Probit: Ordered and Multinomial Models*. California: Sage.

Borsuk, Alan J. 2006. "Ads Take Up Cause to Lift Voucher Cap; Spot Likens Doyle to Segregationist Governors." *Milwaukee Journal Sentinel*, January 24.

Brams, S. 1994. *Theory of Moves*. New York: Cambridge University Press.

Brams, S. 2002. "Game Theory in Practice." In *Millennial Reflections on International Studies*. ed. M. Brecher and F. Harvey. Ann Arbor: University of Michigan Press.

Brysk, Alison. 1994. *The Political Impact of Argentina's Human Rights Movement: Social Movements, Transition and Democratization*. Stanford: Stanford University Press.

Bueno de Mesquita B. and R. McDermott. 2004. "Crossing No Man's Land." *Political Psychology* 25: 271–288.

Center for the American Woman and Politics. www.cawp. rutgers.edu

Clark, Brook. 2011. "Charleston would have to compete for port funding under Graham proposal." *Greenville News*, April 26.

Clarke, Peter and Susan H. Evans. 1983. *Covering Campaigns: Journalism in Congressional Elections*. Stanford: Stanford University Press.

Claude, I. 1962. *Power and International Relations*. New York: Random House.

Cole, Richard L. 1996. *Introduction to Political Science and Policy Research*. New York: St. Martin's Press.

Collier, D. and J. Mahoney. 1996. "Insights and Pitfalls: Selection Bias in Qualitative Research." *World Politics* 49 (1): 56–91.

Comfrey, A. L. and H.B. Lee. 1992. *A First Course in Factor Analysis*. Hillsdale, NJ: Lawrence Erlbaum Associates.

Congressional–Executive Commission on China. 2005. "Special Focus: China's Minorities and Government Implementation of the Regional Ethnic Autonomy Law." 2005 Annual Report. Washington, DC: Government Printing Office.

Converse, Jean M. and Stanley Presser. 1986. *Survey Questions: Handcrafting the Standardized Questionnaire*. Beverly Hills, CA: Sage.

Cook, Timothy. 1989. *Making Laws and Making News*. Washington: Brookings Institution.

Cook, Timothy. 1998. *Governing with the News*. Chicago: University of Chicago Press.

Cooper, J. 1983. *The Warrior and the Priest*. Cambridge, MA: Harvard University Press.

Cover, Albert D. and Bruce S. Brumberg. 1982. "Baby Books and Ballots: The Impact of Congressional Mail on

Constituent Opinion." *American Political Science Review* 76: 347–359.

Deal, David. 1971. "National minority policy in Southwest China, 1911–1965." Ph.D. diss., University of Washington.

Denny, Harold. 1945. "Captives confirm Reich atrocities." *New York Times*, February 17.

DeSipio, Louis. 1996. *Counting on the Latino Vote: Latinos as a New Electorate*. Charlottesville, VA.: University of Virginia Press.

Eckstein, H. 1975. "Case Study and Theory in Political Science." In *Handbook of Political Science*, vol. 7, *Strategies of Inquiry*, ed. F. Greenstein and N. Polsby. Reading, MA: Addison-Wesley.

Elman, C. M. and Elman, M. F. 2001. *Bridges and Boundaries*. Cambridge, MA: MIT Press.

Elshtain, Jean Bethke. 1996. "The Mothers of the Disappeared: An Encounter with Antigone's Daughters." In *Finding a New Feminism*, ed. Pamela Grande Jensen. New York: Roman &Littlefield, 129–148.

English Pen. 2011. (at: www.englishpen.org).

Ennet, Susan T., Nancy S. Tobler, Christopher L. Ringwalt, and Robert L. Flewelling. 1994. "How Effective Is Drug Abuse Resistance Education? A Meta-Analysis of Project DARE Outcome Evaluations." *American Journal of Public Health*, 84(9): 1394–1401.

Feijoo, Maria Del C. 1989. "The Challenge of Constructing Civilian Peace: Women in Democracy in Argentina." In *The Women's Movement in Latin America*, ed. J. Jaquette. Winchester, MA: Unwin Hyman.

Feynman, R. 1995. *Six Easy Pieces*. Reading, MA: Addison Wesley.

Fisher, Jo. 1989. *Mothers of the Disappeared*. Boston, MA: South End Press.

Fiorina, M. 1975. "Formal Models in Political Science." *Midwest Journal of Political Science* 19: 133–159.

Fiske, S., and Taylor, S. 1991. *Social Cognition*. 2nd edn. New York: McGraw-Hill.

Fleming, David J. 2009. "Parents and politics: How parenthood and education policy shape civic and political behavior." Ph.D. diss., University of Wisconsin-Madison.

Ford, Lynne. 2011. *Women and Politics: The Pursuit of Equality*. Boston, MA: Wadsworth.

Fukuyama, Francis. 1992. *The End of History and the Last Man*. New York: Free Press.

Gans, Herbert J. 1979. *Deciding What's News*. New York: Vintage.

Geertz, Clifford. 1984. "From the Native's Point of View: On the Nature of Anthropological Understanding." In *Culture Theory: Essays on Mind, Self, and Emotion*, ed. R. A. Shweder and R. LeVine, 122–136. New York: Cambridge University Press.

George, A. 1969. "The 'Operational Code'." *International Studies Quarterly* 23: 190–222.

George, Alexander. 1979. "Case Studies and Theory Development: The Method of Structured, Focused Comparison." In *Diplomacy: New Approaches in History, Theory and Policy*, ed. P. Lauren. New York: Free Press.

George, Alexander and Andrew Bennett. 2005. Case Studies and Theory Development in Social Sciences. Cambridge, MA: MIT Press.

Gerring, John and Rose McDermott. 2007. "An Experimental Template for Case Study Research." *American Journal of Political Science* 51(3): 688–701.

Geva, N., and A. Eds. Mintz. 1997. *Decisionmaking on War and Peace*. Boulder, CO: Lynn Rienner.

Gladney, Dru. 1991. Muslim Chinese: Ethnic Nationalism in the People's Republic. Cambridge, MA: Council on East Asian Studies, Harvard University.

Goldhagen, Daniel. 1996. *Hitler's Willing Executioners: Ordinary Germans and the Holocaust*. New York: Alfred A. Knopf.

Goldstein, Kenneth. 2002. "Getting in the Door: Sampling and Completing Elite Interviews." *PS: Political Science and Politics* 35(4) 669–672.

Gonzales, M. H., M. B. Kovera, J. L. Sullivan, and V. Chanley. 1995. "Private Reactions to Public Transgressions: Predictors of Evaluative Responses to Allegations of Political Misconduct." *Personality and Social Psychology Bulletin* 21: 136–148.

Green, D. and I. Shapiro. 1994. *Pathologies of Rational Choice*. New Haven, CT: Yale University Press.

Greene, Jay P., Paul E. Peterson, and Jiangtau Du. 1999. "Effectiveness of School Choice: The Milwaukee Voucher Experiment." *Education and Urban Society* 31(2): 190–213.

Grieco, Joseph. 2002. "Modern Realist Theory and the Study of International Politics in the Twenty-First Century." In *Millennial Reflections on International Studies*, ed. Michael Brecher and Frank P. Harvey, 65–78. Ann Arbor: University of Michigan Press.

Guest, Ian. 1990. *Behind the Disappearances*. Philadelphia, PA: University of Pennsylvania Press.

Gunnell, John G. 2006. "The Founding of the American Political Science Association: Discipline, Profession, Political Theory and Politics." *American Political Science Review* 100(4): 479–486.

Haass, R. 2009. *War of Necessity, War of Choice*. New York: Simon & Schuster.

Hardy-Fanta, Carol. 1993. *Latina Politics, Latino Politics: Gender, Culture, and Political Participation in Boston*. Philadelphia, PA: Temple University Press.

Harrell, Stevan (ed.). 1995. Cultural Encounters on China's Ethnic Frontiers. Washington, DC: University of Washington Press.

Heifer, Maria. 2006. "Field Sites, Research Design and Type of Findings." In *Doing Fieldwork in China* ed. Maria Heimer and Stig Thogersen. Honolulu, HI: University of Hawaii Press.

Heimer, Maria and Stig Thogersen. 2006. *Doing Fieldwork in China*. Honolulu: University of Hawaii Press.

Hemmer, Christopher and Peter Katzenstein. 2002. "Why Is

There No Nato in Asia? Collective Identity, Regionalism, and the Origins of Multilateralism." *International Organization* 56(3): 575–607.

Henle, Mary and Marian Hubbell. 1938. "Egocentricity in Adult Conversation." *Journal of Social Psychology* 9(2): 227–234.

Hess, Stephen. 1986. *The Ultimate Insiders: US Senators in the National Media*. Washington, DC: Brookings Institution.

Hinton, William (1984). *Shenfan: The Continuing Revolution in a Chinese Village*. New York: Vintage.

Hondagneu-Sotelo, Pierrette. 1994. *Gendered Transitions, Mexican Experiences of Immigration*. Los Angeles: University of California Press.

Howell, William G., Paul E. Peterson, David E. Campbell, and Patrick J. Wolf. 2006. *The Education Gap: Vouchers and Urban Schools*. Washington, DC: Brookings Institution Press.

Humphreys, Laud. 1970. *The Tearoom Trade: Impersonal Sex in Public Places*. Chicago, IL: Aldine Publishing.

Huntington, Samuel. 1993. "The Clash of Civilizations?" *Foreign Affairs* 72(3): 22–49.

Jacobson, Gary C. 2001. *The Politics of Congressional Elections*. 5th edn. New York: Longman.

Jelin, Elizabeth, ed. 1985. *Los nuevos movimientos sociales: Derechos humanos. Obreros. Barios*. Buenos Aires: Dentro editor de America Latina.

Jervis, Robert. 1978. "Cooperation under Security Dilemma." *World Politics* 30(2): 176–214.

Johnson, Janet Buttolph and H. T. Reynolds. 2005. *Political Science Research Methods*. 5th edn. Washington, DC: CQ Press.

Johnston, A. 1995a. "Thinking about Strategic Culture." *International Security* 19: 32–64.

Johnston, A. 1995b. *Cultural Realism*. Princeton: Princeton University Press.

Jones-Correa, Michael. 1998. *Between Two Nations, The Political Predicament of Latinos in New York City*. Ithaca, NY: Cornell University Press.

Kagan, R. 2003. *Of Paradise and Power*. New York: Knopf

Kaniss, Phyllis. 1991. *Making Local News*. Chicago: University of Chicago Press.

Kant, Immanuel. 1975. *To Perpetual Peace: A Philosophical Sketch*. Translated by Ted Humphrey. Indianapolis: Hacket.

Kedrowski, Karen M. 1996. *Media Entrepreneurs and the Media Enterprise in the U.S. Congress*. Cresskill, NJ: Hampton Press.

Kellstedt, Lyman A., John C. Green, James L. Guth, and Corwin E. Smidt. 1994. "Religion and the 1992 Election: It's the Culture, Stupid!" *First Things* 42: 28–33.

Kellstedt, Lyman, John Green, Corwin Smidt, and James Guth. 2007. "Faith Transformed: Religion and American Politics from Franklin D. Roosevelt to George W. Bush." In *Religion and American Politics*, ed. Mark A. Noll and Luke E. Harlow. 2nd edn. Oxford: Oxford University Press, 288–289.

Kelman, Herbert and V. Lee Hamilton. 1989. *Crimes of Obedience: Toward a Psychology of Authority and Responsibility*. New Haven, CT: Yale University Press.

Keohane, Robert and Lisa Martin. 1995. "The Promise of Institutionalist Theory." *International Security* 20(1): 39–51.

Kerbow, David, Carlos Azcoitia, and Barbara Buell. 2003. "Student Mobility and Local School Improvement in Chicago." *Journal of Negro Education* 72(1): 158–164.

King, Gary, Robert Keohane, and Sidney Verba. 1994. *Designing Social Inquiry*. Princeton: Princeton University Press.

Langbein, Laura and Claire L. Felbinger. 2006. *Practical Program Evaluation: A Statistical Guide*. Armonk, NY and London, UK: M. E. Sharpe.

Langer, Gary and Jon Cohen. 2005. "Voters and Values in the 2004 Election." *Public Opinion Quarterly* 69(5): 744–759.

Larus, J. 1964. *Comparative World Politics*. Belmont, VA: Wadsworth.

Latane, Bebe, and J.M. Darley. 1970. *The Unresponsive Bystander: Why Doesn't He Help?* New York: Appleton Century Crofts.

Lau, R. 2003. "Models of Decision Making." In *Oxford Handbook of Political Psychology*, ed. D. Sears, L. Huddy, and R. Jervis. New York: Oxford University Press.

Lawless, Jennifer L. and Richard L. Fox. 2005. *It Takes A Candidate: Why Women Don't Run for Office*. Cambridge: Cambridge University Press.

Lazarsfeld, Paul F., Bernard R. Berelson, and Helen Gaudet. 1948. *The People's Choice*. New York: Columbia University Press.

Leech, Beth L. 2002. "Interview Methods in Political Science." *PS: Political Science and Politics* 35(4) 663–664.

Leege, David C. and Lyman A. Kellstedt. 1993. *Rediscovering the Religious Factor in American Politics*. Armonk, NY: M.E. Sharpe.

Lenski, Gerhard. 1963. *The Religious Factor*. Garden City, NY: Doubleday-Anchor.

Levitt, Peggy. 2001. *The Transnational Villagers*. Los Angeles: University of California Press.

Lijphart, Arend. 1971. "Comparative Politics and the Comparative Method." *American Political Science Review* (65)3: 682–693.

Lombard, Matthew, Jennifer Snyder-Duch, and Cheryl Campanella Bracken. 2010. "Practical Resources for Assessing and Reporting Inter-coder Reliability in Content Analysis Research Projects." Last modified on June 1. http://astro.temple.edu/~lombard/reliability/#top

Long, Jay Scott and Jeremy Freese. 2006. *Regression Models for Categorical Dependent Variables Using Stata*. 2nd edn. College Station, TX: Stata Press.

Lupia, A., M. McCubbins, and S. Popkin. 2000. "Beyond Rationality." In *Elements of Reason*, ed. A. Lupia et al. Cambridge: Cambridge University Press.

"Manifesto Project Database." Accessed June 2, 2011. http://manifestoproject.wzb.eu

Manion, Melanie. 2010. "A Survey of Survey Research on Chinese Politics: What Have We Learned?" In *Contemporary Chinese Politics: New Sources, Methods, and Field Strategies*, ed. Allen Carlson et al. New York: Cambridge.

Mascaro, Lisa. 2011. "House deals symbolic blow to raising debt ceiling." LATimes.com, June 1.

McCormick, Richard. 1974. "Ethno-Cultural Interpretations of Nineteenth-Century American Voting Behavior." *Political Science Quarterly* 89: 351–377.

McDermott, Rose. 2001. *Risk-Taking in International Politics: Prospect Theory in American Foreign Policy*. Ann Arbor: University of Michigan Press.

McGraw, K. M. 1990. "Avoiding Blame: An Experimental Investigation of Political Excuses and Justifications." *British Journal of Political Science* 20: 119–142.

McGraw, K. M. 1991. "Managing Blame: An Experimental Test of the Effects of Political Accounts." *American Political Science Review* 85: 1133–1157.

McManus, John H. 1994. *Market-driven Journalism: Let the Citizen Beware?* Thousand Oaks, CA: Sage.

Mearsheimer, John. 1990. "Back to the Future: Instability in Europe after the Cold-War." *International Security* 15(1): 5–56.

Menjivar, Cecilia. 2000. *Fragmented Ties: Salvadoran Immigrant Networks in America*. Los Angeles: University of California Press.

Mignone, Emilio. 1991. *Derechos humanos y sociedad: El caso argentine*. Buenos Aires: Centro de Estudios Legales y Sociales.

Milgram, Stanley. 1974. *Obedience to Authority*. New York: Harper & Row.

Mill, John Stuart. 1862. *A System of Logic*. 5th edn. London: Parker.

Monroe, Kristen R. 1996. *The Heart of Altruism*. Princeton: Princeton University Press.

Moore, Barrington. 1966. *Social Origins of Dictatorship and Democracy: Lord and Peasant in the Making of the Modern World*. Boston, MA: Beacon Press.

Navarro, Marysa. 1989. "The Personal Is Political: Las Madres de Plaza de Mayo." In *Power and Political Protest*, ed. Susan Eckstein. Berkeley, CA: University of California Press, 247–258.

Neuendorf, Kimberly A. 2002. *The Content Analysis Guidebook*. Thousand Oaks, CA: Sage.

Niven, David. 2006. "A Field Experiment on the Effects of Negative Campaign Mail on Voter Turnout in a Municipal Election." *Political Research Quarterly* 59(2): 203–210.

Oliner, Samuel and Pearl Oliner. 1988. *The Altruistic Personality*. New York: Free Press.

Osgood, R. 1964. *Ideals and Self-interest in America's Foreign Relations*. Chicago: University of Chicago Press.

O'Sullivan, Elizabethann and Gary R. Rassel. 1999. *Research Methods for Public Administrators*. 3rd edn. New York: Longman.

Panagopoulos, Costas and Donald Green. 2008. "Field Experiments Testing the Impact of Radio Advertisements on Electoral Competition." *American Journal of Political Science* 52(1): 156–168.

Payne, Keith. 2001. "Prejudice and Perception: The Role of Automatic and Controlled

Processes in Misperceiving a Weapon." *Journal of Personality and Social Psychology* 81(2): 181–192.

Pedraza, Silvia. 1991. "Women and Migration: The Social Consequences of Gender." *Annual Review of Sociology* 17: 303–325.

"Policy Agendas Project." Accessed June 1, 2011. www.policyagendas.org

Putnam, Robert. 1993. *Making Democracy Work*. Princeton, N.J.: Princeton University Press.

Putnam, Robert D, Robert Leonardi, and Raffaella Y. Nanetti. 1994. *Making Democracy Work: Civic Traditions in Modern Italy*. Princeton: Princeton University Press.

Rapoport, A. and Guyer, M. 1966. "A Taxonomy of 2 x 2 Games." *General Systems: Yearbook for the Society of General Systems Research* 11: 203–214.

Read, Benjamen. 2010. "More than an Interview, Less than Sekaka: Studying Subtle and Hidden Politics with Site-Intensive Methods." In *Contemporary Chinese Politics: New Sources, Methods, and Field Strategies*, ed. Allen Carlson et al. New York: Cambridge.

Robinson, Michael. 1981. "Three Faces of Congressional Media." In *The New Congress*, ed. Thomas E. Mann and Norman J. Ornstein. Washington, DC: American Enterprise Institute, 55–96.

Robinson, Michael J. and Kevin R. Appel. 1979. "Network News Coverage of Congress." *Political Science Quarterly* 94: 407–18.

Rourke, John T. and Mark A. Boyer. 2010. *International Politics on the World Stage, Brief*, 8th edn. New York: Dushkin/McGraw Hill.

Rouse, Cecilia E. 1998. "Private School Vouchers and Student Achievement: An Evaluation of the Milwaukee Parental Choice Program." *Quarterly Journal of Economics* 113(2): 553–602.

Ruggie, John. 1998. "What Makes the World Hang Together? Neo-Utilitarianism and the Social Constructivist Challenge." *International Organization* 52(4): 855–885.

Rumberger, Russell W., Katherine A. Larson, Robert K. Ream, and Gregory J. Palardy. 1999. *The Educational Consequences of Mobility for California Students and Schools*. Berkeley, CA: Policy Analysis for California Education.

Schaeffer, J., N. Burch, Y. Bjornsson, A. Kishimoto, M. Muller, R. Lake, P. Lu, and S. Sutphen. 2007. "Checkers Is Solved." *Science* 317: 1518–1522.

Seltzer, Richard A., Judy Newman, and Mellissa Vorhees Leighton. 1997. *Sex as a Political Variable: Women as*

Candidates and Voters in U.S. Elections. Boulder, CO: Lynne Reiner.

Sherif, Muzafer. 1937. *The Psychology of Social Norms.* New York: Harper and Brother.

Shoemaker, Pamela J. 1991. *Gatekeeping.* Newbury Park, CA: Sage.

Sikkink. Kathryn. 2008. "From Pariah State to Human Rights Protagonist: Argentina and the Struggle for International Human Rights." *Latin American Politics and Society* 50(1) 1–29.

Singleton, Jr., Royce A., Bruce C. Straits, and Margaret Miller Straits. 1998. *Approaches to Social Research.* 2nd edn. New York: Oxford University Press.

Smidt, Corwin E., Lyman A. Kellstedt, and James L. Guth. 2009. "The Role of Religion in American Politics." In *The Oxford Handbook of Religion and American Politics*, ed. Smidt, Kellstedt, and Guth. New York and Oxford: Oxford University Press, ch. 1.

Stein, A. 1990. *Why Nations Cooperate.* Ithaca, NY: Cornell University Press.

Staub Ervin. 1984. "Steps Toward a Comprehensive Theory of Moral Conduct." In *Morality, Moral Behavior, and Moral Development*, ed. J. L. Gerwitz and W. M. Kurtines, New York: Wiley-Interscience.

Staub, Ervin. 1985. "The Psychology of Perpetrators and Bystanders." *Political Psychology* 6: 61–86.

Steensland, Brian, Jerry Park, Mark Regnerus, Lynn Robinson, W. Bradford Wilcox, and Robert Woodberry. 2000. "The Measure of American Religion." *Social Forces* 79: 291–318.

Suedfeld, P., K. Guttieri, and P. Tetlock. 2003. "Assessing Integrative Complexity at a Distance." In *The Psychological Assessment of Political Leaders*, ed. J. Post. Ann Arbor, MI: University of Michigan Press.

Sullivan, J.L., J. Piereson, and G.E. Marcus.1979. "An Alternative Conceptualization of Political Tolerance: Illusory Increases 1950s–1970s." *American Political Science Review* 73(3): 781–794.

Tidmarch, Charles M. and John J. Pitney, Jr. 1985. "Covering Congress." *Polity* 17 Spring: 463–83.

Trenholm, Christopher, Barbara Devaney, Kenneth Fortson, Melissa Clark, Lisa Quay, and Justin Wheeler. 2008. "Impacts of Abstinence Education on Teen Sexual Activity, Risk of Pregnancy, and Risk of Sexually Transmitted Diseases." *Journal of Policy Analysis and Management* 27: 255–276.

Vermeer, Jan P. 1995. "Do Challengers Even Have a Chance? Media Coverage of Congressional Elections." In *In "Media" Res: Readings in Mass Media and American Politics*, ed. Jan P. Vermeer, 86–91. New York: McGraw-Hill.

Vinson, C. Danielle. 2003. *Local Media Coverage of Congress and Its Members: Through Local Eyes.* Cresskill, NJ: Hampton Press.

Walker, S. 1995. "Psychodynamic Processes and Framing Effects in Foreign Policy Decision-making." *Political Psychology* 16: 697–719.

Walker, S. 2003. "Operational Code Analysis as a Scientific Research Program." In *Progress in International Relations Theory*, ed. C. Elman and M. Elman. Cambridge, MA: MIT Press.

Walker, S. 2011. "Foreign Policy Analysis and Behavioral International Relations." In *Rethinking Foreign Policy Analysis*, ed. S. Walker, A. Malici, and M. Schafer. New York: Routledge.

Walker, S. and M. Schafer. 2007. "Theodore Roosevelt and Woodrow Wilson as cultural icons of U.S. foreign policy." *Political Psychology* 28: 747–776.

Walker, S. and M. Schafer. 2010. "Operational Code Theory." In *The International Studies Encyclopedia*, ed. R. Denemark. Chichester, UK: Wiley-Blackwell, vol. 8.

Walker, Stephen, Akan Malici, and Mark Schafer (eds.). 2011. *Rethinking Foreign Policy Analysis: States, Leaders, and the Microfoundations of Behavioral International Relations.* New York: Routledge.

Waltz, K. 1959. Man, the State, and War. New York: Columbia.

Webster's New World Dictionary of American English. 1991. ed. Victoria Neufeld and David B. Guralnik, 3rd edn. New York: Webster's New World.

Wendt, Alexander. 1992. "Anarchy Is What States Make of It: The Social Construction of Power-Politics." *International Organization* 46 (2): 391–425.

Witte, John F. 2000. *The Market Approach to Education; An Analysis of America's First Voucher Program.* Princeton: Princeton University Press.

Witte, John F., Patrick J. Wolf, Joshua M. Cowen, David J. Fleming, and Juanita Lucas-McLean. 2008. "The MPCP Longitudinal Educational Growth Study: Baseline Report." School Choice Demonstration Project, University of Arkansas, Fayetteville, AR, SCDP Milwaukee Evaluation Report #5, February.

Wolf, Patrick J., Babette Gutmann, Michael Puma, Brian Kisida, Lou Rizzo, and Nada Eissa. 2009. *Evaluation of the D.C. Opportunity Scholarship Program: Impacts after Three Years.* Washington, DC: U.S. Department of Education.

Woliver, Laura R. 2002. "Ethical Dilemmas in Personal Interviewing." *PS: Political Science and Politics* 35(4): 677–678.

Zimbardo, Philip. 2007. *The Lucifer Effect: Understanding How Good People Turn Evil.* New York: Random House.

Zimbardo, Philip G. 1971. *The Power and Pathology of Imprisonment.* Congressional Record. (Serial No. 15: 10–25). Hearings before Subcommittee No. 3, of the Committee on the Judiciary, House of Representatives, Ninety-Second Congress, First Session on Corrections, Part II, Prisons, Prison Reform and Prisoners' Rights: California. Washington, DC: U.S. Government Printing Office. 2010. "Rep. Weiner Gored by Goat in Washington," myFOXphoenix.com, June 11.

INDEX

Note: 'N' after a page number indicates a note.